'One of the many things I love about l... advice, tips and tricks that you can ea... immediately. This woman is all heart an... ...ing down with her book feels like you are sitting down with one of your long-time besties.'

Melissa Ambrosini, author, speaker and podcast host

'Now more than ever we need voices like Lorraine's to lift women up and continue the conversation about what it's going to take for us all to get ahead, together. I'm excited that Lorraine has helped amplify this conversation and excited to see what comes of her insights. Bravo!'

Olivia Ruello, CEO, Business Chicks Australia

'Lorraine's award-winning experience in business makes her the go-to expert on how to get organised, productive and ultimately achieve more from life. This is the book I wish I had when I started my businesses alongside my family, but one that will help me now achieve further growth and satisfaction.'

Angela Priestley, owner and editor in chief, *Women's Agenda*

'This is the generous and practical guidebook I'd happily recommend to parents and parents-to-be, not just those running businesses. Lorraine admits to not having all the answers but she certainly helps readers by writing so honestly about what has and hasn't worked for her.'

Georgina Dent, author, commentator, *Women's Agenda* editor

'Lorraine helped me to find pragmatic ways to honour the two important roles in my life as mum and a business owner, without any sacrifice or suffering, and to prioritise the potent in both my home life and business.'

Dr Kristy Goodwin, digital wellbeing and productivity expert

'Lorraine consistently saves me from overwhelm and returns me to clarity and confidence. Lorraine offers practical, power-packed nuggets of wisdom that bring you back to centre, so you can once again lead the way for those who rely on you to do so.'

Helen Jacobs, author and mentor

'As an entrepreneur, a mum and a wife I felt like I was doing a lot of things but not a lot of things well. Lorraine gave me instant clarity on not only how to calm the chaos but how to thrive.'

Laura Macleod, founder, Macleod Education

'Lorraine has helped me to shift and grow my mindset to one that is not daunted by the challenges I have set myself but is filled with confidence to tackle them, and has given me a skill set so I actually can.'

Claire Behrmann, owner, Jellystone Designs

'Working with Lorraine, every day I get to see first-hand how cleverly she blends her roles as mother, wife, friend and kickass business woman. Not afraid to show her vulnerability, Lorraine's willingness to share the warts-and-all of her experiences brings great comfort to those who know her.'

Michelle Broadbent, business manager

'Lorraine has been there with kind and encouraging words as we've journeyed together as friends, business owners and passionate mums. She deeply understands the tension of trying to grow both a business and a full life as a parent. I hope her words and our experiences give you an insight into what's possible.'

Richenda Vermeulen, founder and CEO, ntegrity

Praise for *Remarkability*

'one of Australia's leading up-and-coming entrepreneurs'

Jack Delosa, founder and CEO of The Entourage

'If you're looking for real business insights from the trenches of a busy start-up, then look no further than this book.'

Emma Isaacs, global CEO of Business Chicks

Praise for *Get Remarkably Organised*

'I literally could not put Lorraine's book down. I began to make changes and implemented so many of her suggestions – they were easy to put into practice, with a huge, immediate payoff.'

Sally Obermeder, television presenter, radio host, author, and co-founder and creative director of SWIISH

'Lorraine is in a class of her own as a thought leader, and her wise, down-to-earth words have helped this previously disorganised journalist actually manage to get her act together.'

Libby-Jane Charleston, journalist (previously associate editor, HuffPost)

Baby, You're REMARKABLE!

The no-BS guide to business with a new family

LORRAINE MURPHY

hachette
AUSTRALIA

hachette
AUSTRALIA

Published in Australia and New Zealand in 2019
by Hachette Australia
(an imprint of Hachette Australia Pty Limited)
Level 17, 207 Kent Street, Sydney NSW 2000
www.hachette.com.au

10 9 8 7 6 5 4 3 2 1

 A catalogue record for this book is available from the National Library of Australia

ISBN: 978 0 7336 4176 3 (paperback)

Cover design by Grace West
Cover photographs courtesy of Shutterstock and Lorraine Murphy
Author photograph by David Rouse
Text design by Kirby Jones
Typeset in Sabon LT Std by Kirby Jones
Printed and bound in Great Britain by Clays Ltd, Elcograf S.p.A.

 The paper this book is printed on is certified against the Forest Stewardship Council® Standards. McPherson's Printing Group holds FSC® chain of custody certification SA-COC-005379. FSC® promotes environmentally responsible, socially beneficial and economically viable management of the world's forests.

For Wade, Lexi and our shooting star.
Thank you for making me a mother.

'there's no escaping the fear. ... The fear that I can't be both the best mother and the best tennis player in the world. I guess my only choice is to live, and find out.'

Serena Williams, *Being Serena*

Contents

About this book

Welcome to my book! *Beckons you over imaginary doormat into my imaginary book house*

I am fizzing with excitement to be writing this book and to set off on this adventure together.

My first book *Remarkability* was published in 2016, and it's the story of starting my first business – and all the trials, lessons, ideas, 'aha' moments and adventures that entailed.

Book 2 came into the world in 2018 and was an extension of the chapter on organisation in *Remarkability*. It is called *Get Remarkably Organised* and it covers the whole gamut of what's required to get your shit together – from routines to weekly planning time, from nixing procrastination to overcoming distractions.

I wrote *Get Remarkably Organised* partly when I was very pregnant, and mostly with a tiny human sleeping in her bassinet next to me. The story of becoming a new mother was interwoven in the background of the chapters as I wrote them. And here I am, with Book 3.

When I was an aspiring author manifesting the crap out of getting a book deal, the 'trilogy' of my first three books was always going to be that – first entrepreneurship, next organisation, then the motherhood/business mash-up.

So it feels distinctly surreal to be tapping out the opening lines of my third book – especially when I think of the enormity of everything that needed to happen in order for me to be doing this particular book. To put it mildly, it's been epic.

I'd like to start our adventure together by very clearly stating what this book is NOT.

It is NOT a how-to manual to having a career and family. There is no step-by-step as every family, every business, every child and every parent is different – so one-size-fits-all is pretty much guaranteed to fit no-one here!

It is NOT an expert's guide. Lord knows I've still very much got my training wheels on with this new gig. However, what worked with *Remarkability* was me sharing my start-up experience when those days were still a recent memory – so I hope this book will do the same.

It is NOT a monthly breakdown of pregnancy and beyond. There are many (actually qualified) people who do that job very well.

It is NOT a manifesto on how you should be living your life. You're entering a judgement-free zone, folks.

It is NOT a discourse on flexible working, paid parental leave or government policy on childcare subsidies. As a business owner, I've kind of operated outside the matrix when it comes to leave and childcare.

Ok, now that's out of the way …

What this book IS is an honest account of my personal journey in running a business and having a baby. It's our family's story, plus as many other experiences/perspectives as I can squeeze in from other parents. That simple.

Of course, I have downloads, lists and a reading treasure trail – like all my books do. You can download the suggested reading on my website. However, that cool stuff takes a backseat to the personal stories and experiences in this book. Because I believe the biggest personal growth originates from trading stories.

Becoming a mother was transformational for me – I think you'd struggle to find any parent who wouldn't say that, right?

Lexi's birth led to my own rebirth as a woman, a businessperson, a wife, a daughter, a spiritual student, friend, every 'hat' I wear in life. Life is unrecognisable now when I compare it to my life before 13 minutes past midnight on Tuesday 13 June 2017.

From day dot of having my own business – and indeed a factor in deciding whether or not to start a business – was how a family would integrate into that business. Having gone out on my own, that question loomed constantly, like a balloon permanently tethered to me. Not quite in sight, but always present, bobbing along behind me.

Now I'm doing it, I want to share the behind-the-scenes story on how that blend manifests itself IRL (In Real Life) – beyond the glossy, filtered version of life presented in little squares on Instagram.

This is the book I needed to read when I was starting my business, and the book I desperately wanted over the last few years on the journey I've been on to get to the point I'm at now.

And really, I thought that's who this book was for – women in the same boat as me. They've either got a business or a career (or even both) and starting a family is imminent, or they may already have kids in the picture. They're trying to figure out how they can do both and are like homing devices to any woman they see already combining biz/career with a family – like I was, and still am.

This week, I realised that I had been getting that wrong, quite wrong, in fact.

Wade (my husband – don't worry, I'll brief you on who's who in the zoo very soon) asked me to speak to a group for his business, which takes university students to developing countries to create businesses on the ground there that help the local communities.

So last Monday I dropped Lexi off for her first day at daycare (tears: Lorraine 1, Lexi 0) and drove an hour north of Sydney to present to the group. I spoke for two hours and covered a pretty broad scope of content: entrepreneurship, overcoming fear, leadership, organisation, sales approaches, marketing and personal brand.

At the end, a group (mostly of women) gathered around me with questions. Two women in particular couldn't get their words out quick enough, their urgency was so intense.

They wanted to know how I ran a business with a family.

I was shocked.

These women were 20 years old. Twenty! And they were already stressing about how they might one day have kids and still pursue the career they wanted.

You guys, they weren't even in the workforce yet!

And it wasn't just these two women – the other young women in the group also said that they, too, were worrying about this. This blew my mind. Chances are, these women wouldn't be looking at having a family for another, what, ten years?

So were they going to stress about this for that entire time, and would the stress compound as the clock started to tick closer to their most fertile window? This concept scares the absolute bejaysus out of me.

Sheryl Sandberg shared a story in *Lean In* about how a young colleague came to her and asked how she managed a family with her career at Google. After some conversation, Sheryl discovered that the woman had no plans to have kids for quite a while – in fact, she didn't even have a partner yet!

I didn't believe that this level of worry amongst young women was a 'thing' – as to be quite honest, it never even crossed my mind when I was their age. Maybe this next wave of women are a lot more forward-thinking than I was in the early 2000s …

The conversation with those women lit an epic rocket under my ass. You see, I *thought* this book was for women like me, but it's not *just* for us. It's for the women coming up behind us in the ranks, too.

We cannot be what we cannot see – and that applies to all of us, whether we're a 70-year-old pensioner or a seven-year-old school girl. What we women need most urgently is models. Models who prove to us that something we want to do is possible: be that completing three marathons, getting to the C-suite, or having a kid and a career.

My wish for you is that you see this book as an opportunity to hold in your hands a living, breathing case study of women who are blending their careers/businesses with their families – and absorb their stories. We're not doing it perfectly – as perfection is, after all, an illusion.

But we ARE doing it.

And it IS possible.

If I know one thing about women, it's that we're fucking resourceful. So my second wish for you with this book is that you find between these pages an arsenal of resources to help you on your own adventure into babies and business – whatever that looks like to you.

The first half of the book is my personal experience of wanting, trying for and having a baby, and the broader ripple effect of that pretty momentous event. The second half is my reflections on motherhood and how that interacts with business, relationships and me as a woman.

We all have that friend who whips out her phone constantly to share the great new naturopath she's seeing, the podcast she's obsessed with, the Insta person she finds so inspiring, the movie she loved. I call them 'Notepad Friends'.

As you read this book, I'd love for you to feel like you've sat down with your Notepad Friend and had that kind of honest, share-y chat. And from that, you have an action plan.

My greatest wish for you is this:

I wish – more than anything – for you to feel courage, pride and confidence in the life choices you're making (or want to make one day) for yourself, your career and your family. Because it's your life and you get to live it however the hell you want to.

Right, let's get this show on the road ...

Lorraine Murphy,
Sydney, September 2018

PART ONE

OUR STORY ... SO FAR

CHAPTER 1

Me

Before we get stuck into the business/baby stuff, I thought it would be instructive and also display basic manners to introduce myself.

I know quite a few of you will have read my first two books (thank you!) and therefore have the download on my story to date – however, many of you won't. So this mini-chapter is just for you.

In case my name didn't give it away, I'm originally from Ireland – Dublin, to be precise. A small town called Rathcoole just west of Dublin, to be even more precise. I was raised in a very big, very close family – my mum is one of nine and my dad is one of seven. I have a younger sister Jenny and a brand spanking new niece Fiadh, but our extended family is so close that we pretty much feel that our 25+ cousins are brothers and sisters too.

I had a clutch of part-time jobs throughout high school and university as well as a side hustle of tutoring school kids. I chased accounts receivable for a printing company, managed reception for a GP practice and had a retail job in a fashion store.

I graduated with a degree in Communication Studies in 2003 and after applying (and failing) to get a job at every PR agency in Dublin, I decided I should get a more specific qualification. I enrolled in a full-time Postgraduate Diploma in PR & Event Management and from that course landed an internship, which then turned into my first PR role.

In 2005, I decided to stretch my wings beyond Ireland and took 34 kilos of luggage to start my new life in London. There, I pretty much got retrained in a larger agency and stayed in London for three years.

My British boyfriend at the time and I decided to try out the famed Aussie lifestyle and in January 2009 we set off for Sydney via a seven-week trip through Brazil and Argentina. I got a job in a boutique PR agency and was given a team of ten to manage. Between the brand new country, a very hands-off MD and my total lack of confidence in my own leadership abilities ('cos I had none!), the role was a struggle. The relationship didn't work out either and we broke up four months after we arrived.

I moved into a single bed in my friend Nikki's bedroom until we found a house together. I was excited to be single – my plan was to fly solo for 18 months, then at the age of 28 I'd find myself a husband. Simple!

The Universe had other plans, however, and I met Wade on a doorstep in Newtown on 8 November 2009, the week after my 27th birthday. At our first date the next night, it was immediately clear that he was The One.

Wade had studied finance at university, and then decided to enter the Australian Army as an infantry officer. When I met him, he had left the army and just returned from a year of travelling and was training for the Special Forces selection process.

Becoming an army wife wasn't part of my plan, so I accepted that we'd probably have a couple of months together before he'd set off on this next chapter of his military career. But an injury prevented him from this route (yay for me, not so yay for his hip) and he instead moved into investment banking.

When the account director I'd been covering for at work came back from maternity leave, I was shocked to be made redundant two weeks later. I took the redundancy incredibly personally and it shook me to the core. I was panicking about being kicked out of the country as my visa was attached to my job, and having just met and fallen deeply in love with Wade, that would have been heartbreaking.

I managed to find a new role at a much bigger agency and spent two years working with the brightest people I'd ever worked with, and in a culture I had never experienced before. It was a lesson for me that the Universe has a much better handle on what events we need to help us reach our highest potential!

During that time, I began to take notice of the rising power of bloggers and began to immerse myself in the fledgling Aussie blogosphere – I could see how their audiences were growing while TV and print numbers were dropping, and I wanted to be a part of this brave new world.

Based on the relationships I built with bloggers and the great results from the tentative early work I did with them on behalf of my clients, I decided to start the first talent agency for bloggers in Australia. I had some savings, a big idea and an endless drive to make it a reality. I handed in my notice and threw open the doors of the business on 16 May 2012. The bedroom doors, to be precise, as I started the business in our spare bedroom.

For the first six months of the business, it was bona fide pushing shit uphill. Once I realised that I needed to educate the market on the latent power of bloggers, things began to change. In October that year, I hired my first employee, secured Woolworths as a client and doubled the number of bloggers we represented.

Wade and I got married in November, in a tiny ceremony on the same doorstep we had met on. Only my sister and his best friend knew it was happening, and we told our parents the night before.

By now Wade had joined a start-up financial advice firm, so both of us were fully immersed in the Sydney start-up scene and made lots of brilliant friends in the space.

My business went on to be something of a surprise success (most especially to me). It won a shelf-full of awards, including Emerging Agency of the Year, Entrepreneur of the Year and Start-up of the Year. We grew to representing 26 digital influencers and I had a team I adored. Over the years we diversified our model with innovative and freaking exciting new offshoots to the brand. Annual revenue was in the multi-millions.

I began to be asked to speak at events, sharing my story. I was terrified of public speaking, and thus ensued a commitment to getting out of my own way by working on that fear.

I wrote my first book *Remarkability*, which was published in 2016, and shared my adventures in early-stage entrepreneurship. The day after it hit the shelves, I flew to Necker Island with Business Chicks and spent five days with leading businesswomen and Sir Richard Branson.

That same year Wade started his own business with some co-founders, and we were back into start-up mode again.

Our daughter (writing that still takes my breath away – I have a *daughter!*) Alexis was born in June 2017 – and life overnight became infinitely more magical.

I wrote most of my second book *Get Remarkably Organised* while she was a tiny newborn and it was published in 2018.

As I'm writing this chapter, Lexi is 15 months old. She's enjoying her third day of daycare and was too busy climbing onto a ladybird toy to kiss me goodbye this morning. I pushed the empty pram back to our house, and settled in for a day of writing these words to you.

So that gets you up to speed if this is the first time we've spent together!

CHAPTER 2

Deciding to try

As I prepared to write this chapter, I had to timeline out the various events that got us to this point – and it was a pretty hectic timeline! It's also almost exactly four years since the journey started, so it's a long timeline.

That journey started with a conversation at an industry conference in Queensland, with Shelley, a woman I respect enormously.

It was August 2014 and I was flying high two years into the business. I had a kickass team that I loved working with and my drive for what we did was at an all-time high. I had just taken the team on our first retreat, to the Hunter Valley. We had just come off the back of our most successful revenue quarter to date and were looking at even more ambitious targets and global expansion. One of my best friends Sarah had joined the business earlier that year and was the senior safe pair of hands I'd dreamed of. Wade and I had been married for three years, and his career was upwardly spiralling as well. It's pretty safe to say that it was a golden era.

Shelley and I had connected immediately when we met three years earlier, and we were both lovers of deep conversations. Small talk was instantly ticked off, and we'd dive right into the juicy stuff when we got the opportunity to catch up at industry events. She was in her mid-40s and had been trying for a baby with her partner. She'd previously told me that she hadn't planned for a family earlier in her life, she'd been happily focused on her career and simply hadn't met the right man. Then when she met him, it appeared that it was too late for them to start a family the 'traditional' way.

We discussed her options: egg donation, surrogacy, IVF, adoption ... In the end, Shelley looked me straight in the eyes and said: 'Lorraine, don't end up in the situation I'm in now.'

Simple words, but words that were like a huge inflatable hammer whacking me over the head. The only way I can describe the impact of them was an epic wake-up call.

Wade and I had agreed early on that we'd both like a family, and even though we had been married three years and most of our friends had already jumped into family life, the prospect of having a baby still felt like some distant step on our path. It *certainly* wasn't something we were considering in the following 12 months. We each had our fair share of activity on the career front and that was where the vast majority of our focus, time and energy was going.

At the time, I was approaching my 33rd birthday. Sitting where I am now, I'm fascinated at how – for someone who wanted to have kids – actually getting started on that was just not even on my radar. At all!

Don't get me wrong: I had regularly wondered how I'd manage the business if/when we did have a family, although there was zero urgency or imminence to that pondering.

After that conversation with Shelley at the conference, I knew it was time to 'start trying', and with that realisation came a cocktail of emotions: huge excitement, total terror and a sense of stepping into the complete unknown.

Of course, first Wade needed to be filled in on this plan.

I got back to Sydney on Sunday evening and decided to hold off having The Conversation with him until we went away together the following weekend. I cannot hold a secret to save myself, so I'm still proud of the self-control I exerted in not dumping the contents of my brain on him the second I arrived back from the conference.

We had booked a cottage in the Blue Mountains and, as well as all the usual hiking, eating and cosying up in front of the fireplace, Wade and I wanted to spend some time talking about our five-year plan together. Of course, now I knew exactly what that plan was ... I can still see him sitting there on the sofa, looking at me expectantly with this spiral-bound A4 notebook and pen, ready to brainstorm our plan together.

'Well,' I said, 'I've been thinking about this plan ... And I think we should start trying for a baby.'

His eyes almost popped out of his head – that was definitely *not* what he was expecting! First global office for my business, yes. But a baby? No chance.

I told him about the conversation I'd had the weekend before and the Wake-Up Lorraine feeling it created in me, then tentatively floated the idea that maybe there wouldn't be the 'perfect' time to try. We just had to decide to start trying. After all, I had Sarah as a safe pair of hands and the business was in a great place financially.

Wade got onboard with the plan surprisingly quickly, and the decision was made. We each explored and shared our fears about having a family – which then became a wish list of the kind of parents we wanted to be.

I said that I'd need to dial down my ambitions for the business, for example pushing back the timing of taking the brand global. At this point he got impassioned.

'Babe, we need to make our kids the reason and not the excuse,' he said – meaning our (potential) future family should be the motivator for us to reach higher and further in our individual lives, and not the crutch we lean on to talk ourselves out of making big moves.

This resonated deeply with me – as he was bang on. I had recently read a Carl Jung quote: 'The greatest burden a child must bear is the unlived life of its parents.' Ouch!

We didn't want to play smaller because we had a family. We wanted to play bigger and better than ever. Firstly, so that we had maximum fulfilment from the commitments in our lives and felt that we were striking out in pursuit of our highest abilities. And secondly, so that we could be living breathing examples to our (again potential) future children that that's how life should be lived.

That wish list has been buried in several house moves over the 4.5 years since it was written, but I tracked it down in a dusty box when editing this chapter. It was like a time capsule of a moment as we began to set our sights on the family we might one day create.

There were 13 points in total, including:

- We have 'puppy-trained' kids that people love being around, kids that don't dominate the situation.
- Decisions are made based on the question of whether this will be an inspiration for our kids, anything less is not good enough.
- We travel with our kids, and every trip is doable.

We drove back to Sydney the next day excitedly anticipating what was to come.

Project Make Baby

Of course, I treated getting pregnant as if it were another business project.

I had a clear set of objectives I wanted to achieve before we got pregnant, and I flung myself into Fertility 101. I just stopped short of working up a pretty colour-coded Excel project timeline (it was very seriously considered).

I devoured books on everything related to the topic, from pre-conception foods, to ovulation tracking, to pregnancy. My favourite book was *The Impatient Woman's Guide to Getting Pregnant* – how apt.

I started taking supplements, booked in a 'last hurrah' big night out with my friends, ordered a thermometer and ovulation testing strips online, and boosted our diets with super-charged food. I invested in some eye-wateringly expensive fermented cod liver oil capsules, reasoning that I'd only need them for a couple of months.

Wade and I had booked a very belated honeymoon to Africa in January, so the plan was that we'd get the conception bus rolling then. Given how much both of us were travelling separately with our work, being together for a full month was a pretty exceptional opportunity – and I was absolutely convinced that we'd get pregnant immediately. After all, I was an efficient person and surely that would extend to the creation of new life – right?

Our plan got thwarted on a visit to get our vaccinations. As we'd need to take anti-malarials while we were in Africa, no baby-making could take place. I was gutted as my perfect picture of our (admittedly three years later) honeymoon baby wouldn't materialise and I very seriously proposed to Wade that we not take the medication.

He argued that it wasn't worth contracting malaria and potentially dying for the sake of waiting a month or two to start trying. Which was fair enough, I supposed ... so Project Make Baby was delayed until after our trip.

When we got back from Africa and had popped the last anti-malarial tablets out of their blister pack, We Were On. I had been tracking my cycle and taking my temperature for the previous four months, so I had a solid base of data to draw on – surely this would spell instant success for my latest project!

It makes me LOL to myself writing this now that I was *shocked* when we didn't get pregnant that first month. *Shocked!*

But I picked myself up and off we went for another month, and another month. And then another month, and even more ...

Women far wiser and smarter than me had told me that becoming a mother requires surrender. 'Yep, I can surrender, no probs,' I told them – while again fashioning yet another contingency plan if I got pregnant the following month. I did the opposite of surrendering and felt I needed an iron-clad grip of control on this baby situation. It was completely flummoxing me that we weren't conceiving.

At this time, the business team had grown and developed to a point where I didn't have sole responsibility for sales and most team members had their own budget target to hit each quarter. However, the senior-level client relationships still sat with me, and I felt that as a heavy responsibility. We had 25 influencers who we represented exclusively, and for most of them the income we brought in on their behalf was the income they depended on – and a lot of them had families. Add my team in there and the buck essentially stopped with me to feed 50+ people each month – not to mention myself and Wade's cat. How my getting pregnant would affect them was a significant source of worry to me, and it occupied a lot of real estate in my mind both before the decision to start trying for a baby and when the call had been made.

For much of this time, I felt a sense of inertia with my leadership of the business. I was itching to get my 'Lorraine's pregnant' plan into place – namely working with Sarah so she could step up and cover my absence while I went and did the baby thing for a few months. I felt I couldn't move forward with any plans until I knew when this much-discussed baby would be arriving.

As soon as Wade and I had started trying, I'd also started to step back somewhat from my relationships with the talent we represented, as I didn't want them to feel there was a void where I had been when (if?) I did get pregnant. Of course, they had no idea what was going on behind the scenes, and me pulling back certainly had an impact on the business.

There was one instance where I left it to Sarah to manage a situation with a couple of our talent, telling myself I was empowering her and it would be good practice for when I was on maternity leave. This was without the hint of a baby coming, so I was most certainly being over-prepared on this front!

I should have been the one to manage the situation. It pre-dated Sarah's joining the business and in retrospect it was something that meant a huge amount to the influencer involved. A month after me thinking the situation was resolved, that influencer left us – the crux of it being due to how that situation was managed (namely my hands-off approach).

This ramped up my already high stress levels about how the business would operate while I was off having a baby. Which wasn't happening right now, anyway. I rarely lost an opportunity to angst over either or both of these things. At the end of 2015 and after ten months of trying to conceive, I had become intensely frustrated.

I remember driving back to Sydney from a weekend in Canberra with Wade, the two of us discussing where we were at. 'Worst case,' I said, 'Sarah and I are both pregnant at the same time.' Wade looked at me, taken aback from the driver's seat. 'Worst case, babe? Would that really be such a bad thing?'

Even through the intense frustration I was feeling at that point, I could see what he was saying. For Sarah and I both to be expecting babies really couldn't be described as a worst case scenario. My true north was way off course.

The problem with starting your own business is that it's all consuming – and by that point I had been consumed for three years. Nothing seemed as important as having the business succeed. Really, a pregnancy and the hopefully resulting baby was something that needed to be mitigated, planned and worked around – not only celebrated.

It goes without saying that I was investing heavily in trying to get pregnant. Psychics were consulted, much acupuncture was had, naturopaths were sought out and the exxy AF cod liver oil supplements were still being ordered.

Of course – as happens in these instances – it felt like everyone and their sister was getting pregnant. Initially I was super-happy when someone announced their pregnancy, inwardly giddy that next time it would be me.

Then a close friend called me to say she was pregnant – and I just felt angry. Completely irrationally, I was angry that they had been married for a lot less time than us – as if us being married for four years gave us some kind of headstart on getting pregnant!

My high levels of stress around a) getting pregnant and b) how I'd manage the business if we got to that point was stressing Wade out bigtime.

He constantly told me to relax (Worst thing to say! But he was right!) and that everything would work out, but I was in such a state of fear and frustration that I really don't believe I was thinking straight. The whole topic felt extremely negatively emotionally charged and it was like a heavy black cloud constantly in my peripheral vision.

Of course, having a wife who had made getting pregnant her primary goal did not exactly make for a spontaneous sex life. Sex stopped being a fun and exciting activity and instead became something that needed to be ticked off multiple times on the days marked with a cute little egg on my fertility tracking app.

Starting the New Year marked a full year that we had been trying, and I suggested to Wade that we get some specialist input. He was furious when I raised it, and I totally understand why.

I think I had come to terms with the fact that we would need some help a couple of months earlier, so for me this was the obvious next step. I had had some basic checks done via my GP and Wade had also had his sperm tested. Both avenues came back saying we should be ok to conceive.

Wade hadn't been giving this topic anywhere near the mental airtime I'd been giving it, so it came as a shock to him that we may in fact need some medical assistance. He was also frustrated that we hadn't gotten pregnant by now, particularly as health had been a big focus for both of us for several years. But he hadn't spent day and night thinking about it.

I got the name of a fertility specialist who our friends had seen and made an appointment for us. Sitting in an IVF clinic was a surreal experience. I felt very sad that the hopeful, optimistic frame of mind we'd had heading into this adventure a year ago had turned into something so fraught with stress, tension and pressure.

The doctor stepped us through the process on how he worked. Given that Wade had already been tested, the investigations would be focused on me. This would start with a test to check that there were no blockages in my system. I booked the procedure for the following week.

Lying there with my legs in stirrups waiting for this decidedly un-fun experience, I felt absolutely fucking infuriated that all men had to do was wank into a cup to get their all clear.

As it turned out, the doctor performing the procedure couldn't go through with it. She explained that there was scar tissue over my cervix, which meant she couldn't get the tube where it needed to go. Later when I was dressed, she explained to Wade and me that the laser procedure I had to remove pre-cancerous cells when I was 23 may have resulted in residual scar tissue, which was preventing me from getting pregnant. She referred us back to our fertility specialist.

Sitting in his office a few days later, the next steps were being laid out for us. We could go straight to IVF now, or I could have an operation to try to resolve the scar tissue and investigate if anything else was going on.

We decided we'd go for the operation, then give it till Christmas to see if we might have some success ourselves before embarking on IVF. Three months later, I went in for the operation and, thankfully, it all went smoothly. I recovered quickly and had my period at the forecast time the week after. It seemed Project Make Baby was back on – this time with a clean bill of health.

So what did I learn about trying?

Let's take a little breather here for a teaching break. What did this whole experience teach me?

I don't generally hold onto regrets, however if I was to have a do-over of those 18 months of trying to get pregnant, these are the things that I would do differently:

I wouldn't have stepped back from the business

I was so eager to set the business up for me to do the baby thing that I mentally ejected myself from it way earlier than necessary. I'm talking almost two years too early!

We were still successful in that time and there were certainly big highs during those two years, but I do wonder how much higher we could have reached if I was 100 per cent in the business – mentally, emotionally and spiritually – and not having one leg almost in the next life season before that season had even arrived.

I know for sure that my enjoyment and flow of the business would have been so much greater had I not been constantly analysing, questioning and changing cast-in-stone plans each month that the pink line didn't materialise on the pregnancy test.

If I was back in that position again, I would absolutely keep trying to get pregnant. However, I would keep my focus trained mostly on the business and not centre my strategy on when I might get pregnant.

I would have practised surrender and trust

Those wise women were definitely wise when they talked about the concept of surrender.

If I was to have that time again, I would still try everything I did that would help us to get pregnant (though possibly not spend so much on cod liver oil), but I would simultaneously try to trust that a little gem of brilliance would settle into my uterus at the time that suited them – not me and my business.

Of course I needed to go on that journey myself to fully take that lesson onboard – and as it turns out, I needed to learn it several times! Everything unfolded precisely as it was supposed to, and I don't feel that there's some alternate reality that I *should* be in where we have a three-year-old child – the path I trod was exactly the one I was supposed to walk to learn the lessons that were meant for me.

CHAPTER 3

Pregnancy

By August 2016, it had been two years since Wade and I had the 'Let's Start Trying' conversation. I had been thinking a lot on the future of the business, and how I would steer the ship forward – particularly as the influencer marketing space was unrecognisable from when I had started the business in my spare bedroom nearly three years before.

From being just one of two operators in the space, we were now in a pretty saturated market. At a conservative guess, there were 30 other businesses helping brands in some way work with digital influencers. Brands were a lot more savvy with the space, which was great – however, given the breadth of options available to them, they were also extremely confused.

I felt hamstrung talking to my brand clients as I wanted to provide them with over-arching strategic guidance, but of course I had a major conflict of interest given that our first obligation was to the talent we represented.

To add to this complexity, any emerging industry will attract not-so-ethical parties and our space was not immune to that. I was increasingly finding that potential clients had been burned by shifty or incompetent operators, which made it more challenging to, firstly, get them onboard as clients with us and, secondly, to guide them to take more (calculated) risks with the work they ultimately did with us.

I felt fiercely protective of our fledgling industry and the businesses that had the best interests of brands and influencers at heart, and itched to create something that could set more of a broader-reaching benchmark for the industry.

Earlier that year, I had started to workshop a new business that would sit parallel to what we were doing on the influencer representation space – essentially an independent model that would provide advice to major brands. I could see the idea had legs, but I decided that I couldn't go ahead with it in all consciousness. As much as I could attempt to keep both companies separate, I was still at the end of the day the owner of both – so I didn't feel I could go out to market with integrity claiming that the strategic model was 100 per cent objective and unbiased. I mentally parked the concept to come back to the following year.

We had begun to branch out from straight influencer representation, launching Australia's first talent search for influencers, and even launching the first talent agency for pet influencers. It was all tremendous fun and taking these concepts from the seed of an idea to living, breathing, public entities lit up my entrepreneurial flame.

My own 'personal brand' (hate that term but you know what I'm talking about) had also begun to take off. The publication of my first book *Remarkability* had gone surprisingly well and even hit bestseller status in its category. I was weekly receiving handwritten notes, emails and social media messages from people thanking me for how the book had helped them.

I was also increasingly being asked to speak at business events. I loved chatting to other business women and hearing their challenges – some had even read my book, and this gave me an insight into the impact I could potentially have outside of the ad industry bubble that I had been a part of for so many years.

But with the highs come the lows and I was about to lose my Most Valuable Player. Sarah was leaving the business, for reasons I fully understood and supported, but I must admit that at the time I simply couldn't imagine the business without her. She had taken incredible care of our talent, and as a result I could focus on growing the business knowing that they were in excellent hands. Losing Sarah was *huge*. I was in a tailspin on what I'd do about the business in light of that change.

I was speaking at a Business Chicks event in Melbourne two weeks later, and Wade was coming down to spend the weekend with me. I decided to spend the week beforehand in Melbourne as well, seeing both current and potential clients.

I knew that I would be ovulating early in that week I would be in Melbourne. This was frustrating, as Wade and me being in different states at that point wouldn't exactly be conducive to the baby situation …

Each day I tested for ovulation and no sign of the little smiley face. I passed my usual ovulation day and still no happy face. As Friday (and Wade's arrival) rolled around, I started to think that we may not get a crack that month after all.

We had a brilliant weekend together, and Wade pitched in to help at my stand at the event on Saturday. On Sunday, flinging toiletries into my bag while getting ready to check out, I realised that I hadn't tested that day. I quickly did the test … and – finally – there was the little smiley face on the digital screen of the stick. I was ovulating! Perfect timing! We headed back to Sydney, my heart full after having such an on-purpose weekend at the expo and having Wade alongside me as well.

Over the following weekend I did a pregnancy test and it was negative. When I reported this to Wade, he looked really disappointed – the first time he'd had that reaction. I guess he thought that the operation would have worked its magic and our little baby would be on their way by now.

That Sunday I met my friend Melissa Ambrosini at her favourite café in Bondi. We were only supposed to be having a tea, but I was ravenous and devoured a hearty fish pie during our chat. The following afternoon, it occurred to me that I should do another test just to rule out a pregnancy 100 per cent. I peed on the stick, but because I felt the test was just a formality, I brought the stick in to our bedroom and put it face down without looking at it.

A few minutes later, I turned it over – and there was a very definite pink line! My heart immediately started racing, my hands were shaking and I was in tears. All I could think was 'You're here! *You're finally here!*'

I did a second test to confirm, and it seemed I was in fact pregnant. Wade had said he was going to catch up on emails and he'd be home a bit later. I tried to call him, but he didn't answer his phone, so I sent him a text instead asking him to come home sooner.

I was climbing the walls of the bedroom having this big news and not being able to tell anyone, so I called my sister. She's a teacher and was in class, so she didn't answer.

So I called my mum. 'I'm pregnant', I said bluntly – and it felt like the oddest thing in the entire world to vocalise those words. She was shocked, excited, afraid to get excited so early on – all the feels.

I thought Wade would never, *ever* get home. When he finally came in (in fairness it was only an hour later – an hour in which my entire world axis had shifted) I managed to contain myself until we were both sitting on the sofa. Then I told him that under the cushion was a surprise. He found a note:

Dear Daddy,
I can't wait to meet you.
Love,
Baby
x

He stared at me speechless, as if he was wordlessly asking me if this was for reals – then he burst into tears and gave me the biggest hug. We were both crying, both laughing, and both spinning out fully at what was happening.

And then it was like we just snapped back into everyday life – we cooked dinner and ate it, all the while marvelling that we'd just gotten this massive life-changing news, yet on the outside everything was exactly the same.

•

So I'm pregnant. Now what?

The next few weeks in the business were full-on. I had another trip to Melbourne – during which I filmed an interview with some of our talent, Show + Tell. One of the questions they asked was about future family plans, and it took every ounce of my poker-face efforts not to joyfully yell out: 'WELL ACTUALLY, I'M SIX WEEKS PREGNANT!'

Meanwhile, I was also thinking deep and hard on how I would fill Sarah's role. I was very aware that it was an intense and demanding position, and I knew that not many people would be as above-and-beyond loyal as Sarah had been.

I was also shit-scared about how I'd manage the business without her. It sounds selfish, I know, but I'd relied on the idea that she would lead the business while I went and did the baby thing. Now that she was on her way out the door, I didn't know how I'd keep the whole thing afloat without her.

Another concern was money, something I would imagine most prospective parents feel. Wade was just ten months into his new business and his income – as you would expect – wasn't where we would ideally like it to be with a baby on the way.

Aside from a couple of diabolical quarters, my business had grown substantially year-on-year. However, that growth had slowed in recent months, largely due to the saturated industry and client overwhelm when it came to our space. A handful of our core talent had also resigned from the group, which rattled me somewhat. If more of them decided to go, we wouldn't be in a good position at all.

And given that our influencers were so attached to Sarah, some relationships could be on rocky ground when I announced that she was leaving – never mind when I backed that up with the news that I was pregnant.

Above all, I was growing a small human! Given that it was such early days, I was afraid to get excited in case it didn't work out for us this time. Of course, to be able to get pregnant was huge progress, but given the stats, I knew that fact alone didn't mean happily ever after.

I found myself constantly going down mental rabbit holes of fear: *What if I lose the baby? What if I can't find anyone to replace Sarah? What if revenue continues to drop? What if I get bad morning sickness? What if sickness means I can't get out and hustle like I need to? What if there's a problem with the baby?* … and probably 67 variations on these.

One day a set of affirmations came to me, which I would lean on heavily in those uncertainty-laden times. Whenever I found myself hurtling down into a rabbit hole, I'd repeat these four sentences to myself:

- Our baby is happy, safe and well.
- I am safe and well.
- The right people will come into the business at the right time.
- We have an abundance of everything we need.

It was such a simple thing, yet it saved me from countless hours of angsting. I can see now that in the face of so much uncertainty, these basic affirmations put the brakes on any catastrophising I might do and kept my mindset in a much more positive space.

Very early on in the pregnancy, I made a conscious decision to reduce the impact of the stress of the business on me. This tiny being (who was probably only 1 cm long at the time!) had a heart and soul all of its own, and would feel every single emotion that I did. This made me incredibly aware of how I was feeling day-to-day and I would very intentionally choose to not take on the stress like I used to.

I was insanely lucky not to have any morning sickness. My heart goes out to women who get sick when they're pregnant, and most especially to those women who don't have any option but to push through – whether that's pushing through work, driving, taking care of kids or cooking meals when feeling as sick as a dog.

The fact that I felt well was a huge gift as I knew I needed to devote a lot of energy to the business to get it sorted before Baby made their appearance.

I started to tap back into my idea earlier in the year to create a strategic business to complement what we were doing on the representation side of things. Client confusion had worsened even in the five months since I'd last been considering the concept, and – to confirm my concerns – there was the falling revenue.

I was extremely worried about how I'd navigate our talent relationships when it came time to step back from the business. I had a great team, of course, but ultimately I was the business owner and any of them could get a better offer elsewhere at any point. The responsibility of the business was mine alone, I was the one who wasn't going anywhere ...

But now I was. All going well, in seven months time I'd be headed into Baby Land, and a whole new human would need me to be their world for quite a while.

I went around and around in mental circles trying to figure out how to move forward. I had coffees with a broad spectrum of potential Sarah replacements and it took a lot of self-control not to fully freak out about the quandary I was in.

This was *precisely* the situation I had been afraid of. It's funny how the Universe forces us to confront our deepest fears. Well, maybe not *funny*, but certainly interesting!

However, that Monday I'd been dreading – the first without Sarah – arrived, and we survived.

Then one morning when I was about eight weeks pregnant I was at home getting ready to go to the office when I had a moment of pure clarity on what I should do: *Completely pivot the business. Resign all our talent. Focus instead on providing objective strategy to brands.*

This was a fucking crazy plan, on multiple levels.

First off, it was a massive financial gamble. Representing influencers had brought in $2 million in the previous year – so I would essentially be kissing goodbye to a shit tonne of money. I also had very little certainty that a strategic model would work; no-one had attempted it before.

It would also be hugely disruptive to our talent. For 4.5 years they had been the centre of my world and I felt I owed it to them to keep the representation model going.

It was also perilous to our team – what if it didn't work out and I couldn't afford to pay them any more? Or pay myself, and I had to close the business down altogether?

Regardless of all these very valid cons, it felt like the right thing to do on a cellular level.

Wade had cooked us breakfast and I calmly sat down opposite him at the kitchen table and announced over poached eggs that I was going to resign all our talent.

And so it was.

I had a call with our accountant that afternoon, who confirmed my basic projections that we could keep the business going for a few months while we established the new model.

And then came the shitty bit: telling our talent.

I hung up from the accountant, and walked back to my desk to immediately send emails to each of them asking for a meeting.

Over the next week, I travelled from Sydney to Adelaide to Melbourne, then Brisbane, the Gold Coast and back to Sydney. I met with each of our influencers and explained the situation – in short, that we were now embarking on a strategy model and couldn't represent both brands and talents with full focus and integrity, and so we were resigning all our talent.

It was hands-down the toughest thing I've ever had to do in business – and I had gotten pretty comfortable with difficult conversations over the previous years.

It is to their enormous credit that the talent were without exception consummate professionals about the news. We agreed to represent them until the end of the year, however if they found alternative options before that we would release them from their contract sooner.

Next up was announcing our pivot to clients and the industry, and I was heartened by the support we received. The following weeks were about transitioning our talent on to new management and keeping the ship steady with the team. I started to pitch our new concept and almost immediately clients were signing up. My relief was epic!

On our fifth wedding anniversary, we got to see our baby at our 12-week scan. What a way to celebrate! The next day I spoke to a group of 300 people at Google, and I was convinced I had a bump (I didn't).

While the business changed course and the new model was established, I was courting a few different people to replace Sarah. However, because I didn't really know how the revamped business would look while I was doing the baby thing, I didn't have a clear plan. I was hoping that would emerge at some point in our conversations, and the 'right person' would bring it.

In Melbourne again in November, I met Natt. She had just finished up as an MD at a social agency that we did quite a bit of work with, and was taking some time-out to hit the reset button and decide what she wanted to do next. We agreed to stay in touch.

Wade and I went on our babymoon over New Year to Vanuatu and spent probably some of the most intensive vision/goal setting time we've had together as a couple. Our conversations ranged from the family-friendly house we'd need (a child's bedroom, how exciting!), to how I'd like to structure the business around our new family (also exciting, but in a different way).

I decided that the time was right to bring on a partner to the business. Of course, I needed someone senior in the business so I could focus on Baby, but I also felt it was time to bring some fresh thinking into it. I'd been at the helm for almost five years at that point and broader expertise would be good for me, the team, our clients and our model.

I wrote four names in my notebook, in order of preference. Natt was number one. On my first day back after the holiday, I contacted her and, Natt being equally keen, we planned to have lunch the following week when I would be in Melbourne.

In preparation for our meeting, I wrote a one-page document listing all the things I hoped for – my vision for the business, my day-to-day life and how it would work around Baby's arrival, the relationship I'd like to have with a business partner and what the deal might look like.

This was probably the most valuable planning I did, as it articulated very clearly in black and white what *I* wanted. Here's what my list looked like:

- I wanted to work in the business three days a week and have the rest of the week to devote to my Remarkability work – my second business that housed my mentoring, speaking and writing work.
- I wanted to step back from the business for four months – a month before the baby was due and three months after they were born.

- I wanted to take the business global, so I planned on spending some time in the UK, after a family visit to Ireland, to scope out how our model would work there.
- I wanted the partner to buy into the business, because I wanted them to be as motivated as me to grow it.

I encourage any woman expecting a baby (business owner or not) to think carefully about what their Baby Boundaries are – what time they want to have off, what time they want to be in the business/at work when they go back after Baby.

Life has a daunting way of creating our plans for us unless we act first and clearly articulate what *we* want first. I didn't realise it at the time, but what I was doing at this point was placing some boundaries around how I wanted this new gig to work for me, for our family and for my business.

I've used this one-pager I created as the basis for a Baby Biz Vision worksheet that will help you map out your own personal plan. You can download it for free on my website.

Back to my meeting with Natt. I have a track record of getting excited once I start talking to people, and this was too important to fluff, so I very unapologetically laid out my ideal plan to Natt when we met. And guess what? She'd done her own pre-thinking and planning as well. We were on the same page! Ultimately, she came onboard as an equity partner in February, three months before I was due.

I had always said I'd work right up until Baby arrived, but when it came down to it I realised that I wouldn't get this time again – and resolved to wrap up work at 37 weeks.

Natt and I worked hard to get her up to speed in the business. We were also still very much establishing the new model, so I was hands-on with pitching to clients and working on strategies. She came up almost weekly from Melbourne to have as much face time with me, the team and our clients as possible. Our clients were universally supportive and encouraging of my pregnancy, and I think having a co-owner onboard gave them a lot of reassurance that all would sail smoothly while I stepped back for a few months.

In the background, I had been chipping away slowly at my second book, but the business needed my focus, so that wasn't progressing very quickly. I decided that the few weeks before my due date would be the perfect time to get as much of the book done as possible. It was winter, so I envisioned cosy days in my study sipping tea and eating cake while I powered through chapters and patted The Bump.

I was full pelt in the business until around the 35-week mark, when things started to feel a little overwhelming. Catching the train to the office felt stressful – too many people and too many bodies around me. So I started catching Ubers or walking home. Client and team dramas felt more intense than usual, and I was extremely grateful for Natt's solid, reassuring presence in the business.

I learned that when a woman is pregnant, all our energetic channels are wide open – meaning that we are dramatically more sensitive to energy than we normally might be. This explained why train stations felt hellish, as there was so many different people's energy packed into a small space.

We hosted a group of close clients and media in a hotel private dining room in my last week of the business to celebrate its fifth birthday. This was my last hurrah, as such, and I finished up at work the next day, with a surprise baby shower thrown by the team.

My first day of maternity leave was hectic. I was up for an Industry Leader of the Year award and the presentation to the judges was landing when I would be 40 weeks pregnant. In case Baby arrived before then, I filmed a piece to camera that could be played by Natt in my absence for the judges.

In the following weeks, I did some work on the business and had my weekly catch-up with Natt. I tried desperately to write the book, but it simply wasn't flowing, and as my due date approached it became more difficult to focus on it. I did hours of yoga and had a massage each week to stay on top of any pregnancy-related aches. I also became a regular visitor at the local cake shop (maybe even daily!).

My tips for a healthy, happy, positive pregnancy

I enjoyed a very healthy, very happy pregnancy. I actually felt better pregnant than not, with all the gorgeous hormones flushing through my system, the relaxin easing my usually cramped neck and shoulders ... not to mention the dramatically enhanced cleavage situation!

Here are some things that really helped me to stay calm, happy and focused while running a business during my pregnancy:

Affirmations

Affirmations are very effective at heading off any negative, fear-driven thoughts and I would strongly suggest that you craft some affirmations of your own when you are pregnant. Your fears may be related to anything from health to money to career/business – just like mine were. To help, I've created a worksheet that will guide you through this process. You can find it on my website.

Magnesium

Pregnancy can bring with it all kind of crazy-ass aches and cramps, and magnesium is a great reliever of those aches. It's better absorbed via the skin in spray-on form. I also read some research in *Beautiful Babies* by Kristen Michaelis that claims magnesium deficiency is a contributing factor to morning sickness.

Yoga

My yoga practice really came into its own during my pregnancy. It became my calming, safe space, and also a time when I felt most connected to the growing baby in my belly. The breathing practice and diving deep into uncomfortable poses were excellent preparation for birth. It also gives you a solid dose of self-care each week – which is even more important if you already have kids to take care of!

Massage

One thing that drove me up the wall while I was pregnant was how overly risk-averse massage therapists were given my 'condition'. If you can, find a massage therapist who will actually give you a decent massage, and see them as often as you can. View it as an investment in your comfortable pregnancy and post-birth recovery rather than a pampering treat.

Acupuncture

Acupuncture can be a great support during pregnancy as it boosts your energy levels and helps you chill the hell out when life is feeling too much on the hectic side. The treatments can also ease aches and pains, or other symptoms such as indigestion.

Other people's stories

Ah, Other People's Stories – OPS.

I feel that a pregnant woman is like a homing device for others to share their own stories – whether that's with pregnancy, birth or beyond.

I noticed early on that my bump acted as an invitation to other people to tell me what I should expect – purely as it was something they themselves had experienced, or their sister's best friend's auntie had experienced.

Given that we're already dealing with all the uncertainty that a baby on the way entails, this is unhelpful to say the least. It planted seeds of doubt and worry in my mind, and I found myself automatically assuming that just because X person had had that experience, I would be the very same.

One of my friends was a few weeks ahead of me in her pregnancy, and would give me a download on the symptoms she was experiencing at a particular time. I would immediately take all of this on and start to be hyper-aware of any sign of those same symptoms myself when I reached the same point.

For example, she told me at one stage that she was starting to feel very dizzy, especially at night when she woke up to go to the bathroom. *Of course* I decided that this would be my experience too.

Wade was in Europe for three weeks early in my second trimester and our bedroom was up a rickety, uneven staircase from the bathroom. I'd wake to pee in an empty house and be terrified I would have a dizzy spell and pitch headfirst down the stairs. In fact, I had no dizziness/light-headedness whatsoever during my pregnancy!

I decided that I couldn't continue this worrying-about-everything for my entire pregnancy, and made a conscious decision to not take on Other People's Stories anymore.

I employed my energetic forcefield when someone told me how their pregnancies had been or what I was going to experience. I would silently say to myself in my head as they were speaking: 'Just because that's their story doesn't mean it will be mine. We'll create our own story.'

Funnily enough, the decision I made seemed to somehow actually dramatically reduce the amount of Other People's Stories I had coming my way – almost as if the Universe backed me up! Magic!

People can say the most thoughtless, stupid and even cruel things to pregnant women and their partners.

One of my mentees Abbie White – a stonkingly successful businesswoman and expecting mama – was told (*by another woman people!*) while she was pregnant that 'she would definitely get postnatal depression' when she attempted to have her baby and run her business.

When Abbie told me this over a coffee when she was 35 weeks pregnant, I experienced stabs of white-hot rage that someone would feel it was ok to say something like that to someone who is vulnerable and also preparing for such an exciting life event.

People like this need to fuck right off.

However, we also need to proactively protect ourselves (and our babies) from Other People's Stories – using the forcefield practice or an affirmation like I did, or any other way that moves you into a more empowered, positive state.

Of course, I include my stories and the stories of other women in this book you're reading. That's all they are – our stories. You, your baby, your partner and your family will write your own story.

How to create a forcefield

When we're pregnant, our energy field and that of our unborn baby are essentially the same – meaning that anything we take on energetically (our partner's stress, an unhappy client, a narky Uber driver), our baby automatically takes on too.

This fact made me hyper-aware of the energy I was taking on. If I felt I was in the presence of negative, aggressive or fearful energy, I would visualise an imaginary forcefield descending around me and my bump – shielding us from the heavy stuff that otherwise would be coming our way.

This is an especially helpful tool if we're operating in high-stress situations in our jobs, as it gives us a constructive way to deal with that stress – and no-one needs to know that you're forcefielding them!

Nine months is a long time

If I could only go back and tell Past Lorraine one thing, I would tell her that pregnancy is actually quite long – almost a year! – and that when I did (hopefully) get pregnant, there would be enough time to put the plans I needed in place during that time. And that she should just chill the hell out – surrender the planning.

When I think about the amount of energy and time I lost to manufacturing endless plans and contingency plans while I was trying to get pregnant, it makes me sad. For those two years between us having the Let's Start Trying conversation and us actually finding out we were pregnant, I devoted so much effort into going round in circles with plans that were never required – ultimately, they were dead ends.

As it was, when I finally got pregnant, the path became clear of its own accord. I managed to navigate Sarah's departure, pivot the entire business, find a kickass business partner, onboard that partner, move offices, get four major corporates for our new model, secure sponsors for round two of our talent search concept, write 20 per cent of my second book – oh, and move house.

If you're a good operator (which I have no doubt you are, if you're drawn to a book like this) you can get a hell of a lot done in those nine months. We women are nothing – *nothing* – if not resourceful and terrifyingly capable. Just ask any man!

CHAPTER 4

Getting ready for Baby

As you might have deduced from our time together in this book so far, I quite like to be organised. So getting ready for our baby's arrival presented another project to get organised for.

My pregnancy was quite action-packed with business activity, and we really did precious little to prepare for our bundle of joy (or tsunami in a blanket?) until the point that I went on maternity leave when I was 37 weeks pregnant.

Thankfully Baby didn't arrive earlier than that, as all they would have had ready for them was a pack of newborn nappies that Wade's cousin Kate had gifted him as a joke for Christmas and a bassinet that friends had recently given us.

So when I 'officially' clocked off in the business, it was time to get our shit together for this tiny human. First, though, I had to get the business sorted.

The principle of your Future Self

Those of you who've also read my second book *Get Remarkably Organised* will already be familiar with my concept of the Future Self. For those of you who are reading this thinking 'My future what?', here's a quick debrief.

When we have created an especially tricky problem that we ourselves will ultimately need to deal with, it's become a popular joke to say, 'That's Future Me's problem.'

For example, I leave the dirty baking trays, pots and dishes from a big Sunday roast stacked around the kitchen as I've had one too many glasses of red and the CBF (Can't Be Fucked) Index is high. That'll be Future Lorraine's problem.

The next morning (Monday, and I've got a big week at work), I stumble into the kitchen with a woolly head and parched mouth to a disaster zone of crusted-on mashed potato, congealed chicken fat and lipsticked wineglasses. Future Lorraine is not a fan of Past Lorraine!

Or I procrastinate on sending my accountant responses to her month-end queries. Two months later, my BAS (Business Activity Statement) is due, and Future Lorraine has to spend most of her day working through spreadsheets, Xero reports and emails – all the while screaming 'WTF' in her head at Past Lorraine.

If we flip this joke on its head and use it to our advantage, the results can be staggering. Rather than deferring tasks to our Future Selves, if we can instead *take care of* our Future Selves by doing something for them and making their lives that little bit easier, life overall starts to flow more smoothly.

I have built this concept into every area of my life.

So all the 'stuff' I do to stay organised – the meal planning, the structured to-do lists, the task batching, the habit layering – all of it, without exception, is geared at helping my Future Self.

Conversely, in the times I'm feeling stressed, overwhelmed, behind schedule or under pressure, it's because in some way I didn't watch out for my Future Self.

Here are some things I do for Future Lorraine:

- I do a big Saturday cook-up so that we have plenty of already-prepared food to fuel us through full days in our businesses and family life.

- I proactively address a worrying business situation so that Future Lorraine doesn't need to worry about it next week.
- I write my to-do list and leave my desk clear and tidy at the end of my work day so that Future Lorraine can sit down and start work straightaway the next morning (and not give herself an excuse to procrastinate).

All of these things ladder up to a general sense of calm – the more I embed the principle of the Future Self into my life, the calmer life gets. And judging from the feedback I've received, it's not just me who has embraced it. Many people who read my second book are also looking after their Future Selves and have reported that it's made their lives calmer and happier in the process.

This chapter will help your Future Self when Baby arrives, and I'll be sharing all the preparations I made for Future Lorraine in the run-up to birth.

I, of course, had a clear idea of how *I wanted* our birth to go, and had clearly briefed the Universe on the kind of child I'd like (good sleeper, non-fussy eater, friendly with other people). However, the fact is I had no idea how birth would be, or – all going well – what kind of baby we'd be getting. I had no idea how much energy I'd have, how the baby would sleep, if I'd have any health complications post-birth.

It was all 100 per cent uncertain.

I decided to do as much as I could for Future Lorraine in the time before our due date, to make her life as easy and happy as possible – which in turn would make Wade and our newborn's life infinitely easier and happy as well.

I wanted to work pretty soon after Baby arrived – both writing my book and also on the business. We had a major event happening a few weeks after my due date and I was also hoping to attend the awards that I was a finalist for. I figured that anything I could do to help Future Lorraine would dramatically increase the odds of me having both the time and mental bandwidth to focus on work with a newborn.

Getting the business ready

In the previous chapter, I talked about the specific business changes I had to make to be in a position to step out of work while I sailed into Baby Land. Here, I'd like to share my general experience of being a business owner and pregnant (or intending on being pregnant soon, as I was for two years after Wade and I had the Let's Start Trying conversation).

I've realised that my preparation essentially boiled down to four key phases:

1. Preparation
2. Skeleton
3. Transition back in
4. Business as usual

1. Preparation – from the beginning of your pregnancy to the date you want to step back/step out of business

This is all about laying the foundations for you being able to step out for whatever time you have decided on – be that a week or a year.

Boxes to tick in this phase would be:

Team recruitment and development

You are essentially building the infrastructure within the business that will enable you to step back to whatever degree you want to. One of my friends Pamela Jabbour has run her business – Total Image Group – for 14 years and has been focused in recent years on building a management team who would enable her to lead more on a top level as the visionary and ensure if she stepped away for a little while the business would continue to function. She says: 'The arrival of baby Lucas pushed this plan forward by forcing me to hand over any bits of the day-to-day I was still holding on to and pushed my management team to step up and take control because I wasn't always around to help.'

It may be that you don't have a team, like some of the entrepreneurs I'll talk about in this book. One of my mentees, Janine Wade, has a mortgage broking business and had a couple of part-time admin support people. As her due date approached, she contacted another broker and set up a deal where she could refer her leads to them for the time she was due and when her baby was tiny.

Establishing clear systems and processes

Anything that needs to be done on the regular in the business should be clearly systemised. You want to deal with as many questions and instances of human error as possible in time for Baby's arrival. One of my friends Meredith Cranmer runs a wildly successful brand experience agency, and one of the steps she put in place was a governance document, which clearly broke down the decisions she didn't need to be involved in when she stepped back to have her babies, as well as which ones she absolutely needed to be consulted on.

Communicating with stakeholders

Keeping key players in your business across what's happening when you do the baby thing and beyond is a critical part of preparing to step out/back from the business.

So time should be booked in, ideally face-to-face, to reassure clients and anyone else you rely on for your business's success. This gives you a chance to help them feel valued, for you to communicate your plans post-pregnancy, and for them to ask any questions they might have.

Clearing out whatever isn't working

Right now is the time to deal with anything that might rear its ugly head further down the track. Products or services that aren't performing, team members who are disengaged or who aren't living up to their job descriptions, that horrible customer who everyone dreads dealing with – anything that's festering needs to be proactively dealt with.

The last thing you want is for the shit to hit the fan when you've been up half the night with a cluster-feeding baby and are prone to tears. My friend Richenda Vermeulen has a flourishing digital agency in Melbourne and planned to step fully out of her business for six months after their daughter arrived. She says she has never been so ruthless in her entire life as she was in the run-up to her due date, and describes it as 'Lean In on crack'.

Setting up post-birth communication structures

If you do have a team, then it's a good idea to speak to them now about how they and you would like communication to run once Baby arrives. For myself and Natt, we kept up our weekly management call until the week I went into labour and picked them back up when Lexi was two weeks old. That's what worked for us, each of you will have your own preferred communication rhythm.

Meredith's 2IC would come to her house for monthly WIP meetings from when her babies were a month old, and they would have a call halfway through the month.

Decide what is the best use of your time in the business

I borrowed this one from my friend Jack Delosa, who told me years ago that the secret to growing a business is that the owner devotes as much time as possible to the key tasks that they and only they can do.

The reason we want to know this now is so that you can a) get maximum return for the time you put into the business before Baby comes, and b) you know where to put the reduced time (and it will be reduced) once Baby arrives so you can be assured that you're using your time as wisely as possible.

For me in my businesses, these key tasks have always been planning the future strategies, nurturing high level client relationships and leading the profile building of the business.

You'll have your own core skillset in your business that it's likely you're the best-placed person to manage.

2. Skeleton – from the beginning of your maternity leave to the date you think you'll go back into the business

This phase sees you doing the closest to the bare minimum that you need to in order to keep your business alive – so that you can focus as much as possible on keeping this new human alive!

For Tara, a woman I recently mentored, this was her weekly WIP call with her team. She figured that the 90 minutes would keep them motivated and she could get a handle on where they were at, even if she wasn't doing her usual 30-hour work week while she settled in her third baby at home.

I would strongly suggest you switch on your Out of Office. You may be planning on checking your emails every day (I'm pretty sure I did), however it buys you some delayed response time if you don't get to your inbox as regularly as you planned.

For me, this skeleton period lasted for three months. In that time, I had calls and email exchanges with Natt about key developments in the business – for example, she chose to exit a team member in that time, so we were in close contact as she worked through that process.

I also acted as a sense-checker and troubleshooter on challenges the team experienced – and it surprised me how effective I could be in that role. I was physically removed from the day-to-day of the issue, and I could have a wider perspective than I might have if I'd been in the thick of it with the rest of the team.

On the Remarkability side of things, I maintained my program of a monthly call with my Mastermind group of mentees – and of course I was writing my second book.

3. Transition back in

This phase sees you begin to re-enter the business, without putting the pressure on yourself to fully get back into the swing of it. (Which, if you've looked after your Future Self, will be much easier and more enjoyable.)

For me, my transition back into the business was a London study tour and working from home for a couple of days a week for a fortnight after we got back – including team gatherings and having a strategy session at our kitchen table with Natt.

My friend Pamela spent her first month back in the business focusing only on internal meetings, then made herself available to clients and external stakeholders after that.

I would suggest quite firmly that, if at all possible, you do ease yourself in gradually. Returning to work – even if it's only two days a week – will bring with it a unique set of logistics, and also probably emotions, and I believe that is a lot easier if you don't have to switch into full-on mode straightaway.

4. Business as usual

This is whatever your new normal looks like – and hopefully it aligns with the Baby Biz Vision that you articulated! My watch-outs as you enter this phase would be:

Go gently

Even if you had a super smooth transition phase, a lot has changed since you were last in BAU mode. Make sure you're balancing the additional work hours with time to fill your tank (more on that in Chapter 11). Justine Flynn, co-founder of Thankyou, shared with me that she really struggled with this stage:

I found I returned to work after maternity leave with a similar workload to before, but with even more demands from different directions, and with less time. This caused me to fall into a season where I was frantically trying to meet all those expectations and run at a pace that was too unhealthy and unsustainable. I was in back-to-back meetings with no breaks and having to do emails/my own work tasks at night after Jed was down. This was unfortunately one of the catalysts (along with a few other health issues) that caused me to have to take 12 months off last year to allow my body to heal and restore. During this time I have learned to breath, to embrace rest and play, to find a pace of grace and walk with a stride in my step that is productive rather than frantic.

Draft in extra support at home if you can

A lot of couples might reduce the amount of help they have at home while one of them is on parental leave. Going back into whatever your version of BAU is is a good time to up the ante on help. If possible, having a cleaner to do a full clean each month, or signing up for a meal delivery service, during times that will be more full-on, will help.

Take the time to reconnect with your team/customers/clients

They will have missed you for whatever period of time you stepped back, and prioritising a coffee or lunch meeting with those who are key in your business will make them feel loved and valued.

Getting ready for Baby

Of course this baby will need kit!

The first home Wade and I had together was a tiny 1.5 bedroom cottage – the spare bedroom of which I started my business in. We had chatted casually about whether it would be a good house for a baby, and Wade was firmly of the opinion that it was.

'Babies are *tiny*,' he said. 'They take up hardly any space at all.'

I started to list all the equipment that this tiny human would require. 'Where would we park the pram? And where would the cot go? And the high chair, and the change table, and their toys?'

He looked at me like I was losing my mind. '*Surely* they don't need all that stuff?'

Ha!

And now, here we were at the rite of passage for new parents – getting Baby Stuff. Which meant a Sunday morning excursion to Baby Kingdom, which we swiftly realised was Baby Hell. Our jaws were scraping the floor at the sheer scope of shit that you could buy, and the insane price tags on much of said shit.

However, I had my list and we decided to divide and conquer (even at that we weren't very successful). We also decided to press pause on investing in random stuff we encountered until we had time to decide if we really actually needed it or not. Baby stores are filled to the gills with bright shiny baby things that all seem critically necessary! Once our Baby Hell-induced heads had stopped spinning, we got ourselves organised pretty easily.

Get as much secondhand stuff as you can

We had a budget to get baby-ready, but my Irish genes baulk at spending cash on stuff that will a) get wrecked and b) only be used for a short amount of time ... or both! There is a thriving pre-loved market out there, between friends, family and online sites. Getting secondhand also benefits the business-owner-parent-to-be because, apart from saving money, you'll save time (and angst) with endless shopping around. It's better for the environment, too, and I must admit I just enjoy buying pre-loved stuff.

Only buy as you need it

Our plan was to co-sleep when Baby arrived and have them in the bassinet during the day, so we didn't buy a cot for months. Not having chunky items like that around until we actually needed them made a big difference – not to mention helping cash flow. When we're expecting a baby (particularly if it's our first), we feel we need *all of the things* ready to go. This is no doubt helped along by our consumerist society. At times, I *completely forgot* that shops would still be open after Baby arrived – and that we could actually pick things up ad hoc if we needed them.

Ask for recommendations from friends

Every parent will have their stuff-they-couldn't-live-without and recommendations were super-helpful to us. With everything Wade and I had going on in our businesses, we just didn't have time for endless comparisons and multiple shopping trips. Selecting a pram, for example, can be quite the exercise in overwhelm. So ask your new-parent friends, who have no doubt already asked their friends before they made their purchases. Tap into the power of recommendation to save many hours and a lot of cash.

See if you actually need some things before investing

Beyond the core things like clothes, nappies and a sleep vessel of your choosing, a lot of the things we buy are optional. I suggest you see how you go without item X before buying it. These turned out to be optional for us and I'm glad we didn't buy them: nappy bin, baby monitor, nursing chair. This is not to say that these items are not essentials for other parents, but for our lifestyle and what we needed, they would have been surplus to our requirements. My point is that it's better to wait and see what you actively need before giving over time, money and space in your home to baby kit that may not get used.

Tell family what you'd like

You'll likely have some friends and family who want to give you a gift for Baby. It's a good idea to actually tell them what you'd like – it means they're confident they're getting something you actually want/need, and you know you're getting something you'll really love and use. Our parents contributed towards our pram, which was the biggest ticket item we bought, so that was a great help and it's something that we'll use for years to come.

Getting ready for you

Now that business is on track and Baby is prepared for, it's time to get you organised!

Food

One of the biggest things I did to make Future Lorraine with a Newborn's life easier was to prepare tonnes of nourishing, tasty food. I wanted her to be as taken care of as possible, and to spend her time gazing at her newborn or doing some productive work rather than spending endless hours in the kitchen.

We bought a small secondhand freezer that we set up in the garage, and I got into the habit of making double meals when I was cooking in the final few weeks of my pregnancy.

I stocked up on glass baking/storage containers that come with plastic lids, which were brilliant as we could take them out of the freezer to defrost, take the lid off and whack them straight in the oven to reheat. I also got a combo of different sized plastic containers to freeze soups, broth and other dishes.

Cooking in those last weeks was a really beneficial activity for me. I find cooking to be a moving meditation, and it kept me focused on something other than how the business was doing or my book was going. It was the ultimate nesting for a food-obsessive like me!

The magic of bone broth

I prepared a *lot* of bone broth. This is the perfect food to have post-birth as it replenishes so many of our minerals.

There are few things that soothe my soul as much as a warm mug of broth, and it's a godsend on days when you're surviving on less sleep or Baby is on the crotchety side.

It takes a while to cook – it's definitely not fast food – and there's a bit of clean-up, although once a big batch is made you can forget about it for a couple of weeks. A slowcooker is definitely the way to go as you can set and forget it once it's loaded up.

Side note: if you haven't got a slowcooker yet, it'll be one of the best investments you make – I guarantee you!

You can buy broth readymade in the fridge at butchers and whole/health food stores, and you can also buy powdered versions. I have never found one that tastes as good as homemade, however you'll still get health benefits from the shop-bought ones. I've included my recipes for chicken and beef bone broth in the Recipes section at the back of this book.

Load up the freezer

You want to stack your freezer with meals that you're excited by – that you'll look forward to for dinner at the end of a full-on day as you adjust to life as a new parent and keep the business moving forward as well.

You also want food that's super-nourishing and comforting, and likely food that's heavier than you'd normally want, with all that post-birth recovery, milk production (if you breastfeed) and baby-tending you'll be doing! Personally, I wanted a lot of red meat, milk, cheese, bread and pulses. Oh and sweet treats – but that's pretty standard for me …

My knock-it-out-of-the-park offerings from our overflow freezer were:

- Chicken and beef bone broths
- Beef chilli and homemade corn bread
- Fish pies
- Vegetable and lentil soup
- Chicken and mushroom pies
- Chocolate and macadamia brownies

- Easy-to-cook single/double portions of protein – think chicken thighs, salmon fillets, sausages, veggie burger patties – anything that you can grill/fry/BBQ quickly and have with a simple salad

Establish your Baby Boundaries

As your due date approaches, it's a good time to think about what kind of boundaries you want to put in place for when Baby makes their grand entrance. This can be a tricky one, as it can be difficult to predict who you'll want around and when – particularly if this is your first baby.

Each of us will have a different landscape of family, friends and colleagues who will want to meet Baby or stay in contact with you for whatever reason after Baby arrives.

When I had passed the 12-week 'safe' point, my mum booked flights to come from Ireland to stay with us for three weeks. Her arrival date was ten days post my due date, so we figured that Baby would be here by then and we'd probably have a few days as a threesome establishing our little family before she landed. Wade's parents live a five-hour drive away, so there was a loose plan that they'd travel down once Baby was earthside.

My team at The Remarkables Group was prepared for me to be out of contact for a couple of weeks post-birth, but there was no hard and fast plan in place around when I would/wouldn't be contactable. This set-up worked for us, however it may be that you'd rather set more solid boundaries in place.

These boundaries will vary depending on the nature of your business and the nature of your team. A great place to start would be to clearly articulate the level/frequency of contact you would like to have once Baby arrives, then consult team members, suppliers and customers on what kind of support they envisage needing from you. After that, you can work out an arrangement that will ideally suit everyone.

Ultimately, it all worked out fine for me. I suggest that you and your partner give some dedicated thought to how you want this all to play out, particularly in the key couple of weeks post Baby's arrival.

Manage visitors

I've had friends who we've visited at home when their baby was a few days old and we've been treated to sumptuous cheese platters, and friends who we haven't seen until Baby is a month old as they chose to bunker down as a new family and not have any pressure to see anyone. Either scenario – or somewhere in between – is perfectly fine as long as it suits you.

Some suggestions I would have for managing visitors in those early days are:

Try not to have people staying with you if possible

In the final furlong of pregnancy, there's a lot going on both physically and emotionally. And in the days immediately post-birth, there is even more going on! Unless they'll be helping in a big way (like my mum did), try to avoid having house guests around that pivotal time.

Put visitors to work

Dr Oscar Serrallach, an Australian GP who specialises in Postnatal Depletion, advises that there's no such thing as visitors when you've just had a baby, only staff. While his view is extreme, it makes sense. A new mum (and their partner) has already got a lot going on without being 'on' for excited visitors. Giving your visitors tasks – such as dealing with the laundry, assembling the baby kit or going to the shop to get some fridge replenishments – means they can help out and feel useful, plus it lessens the intensity on you to host.

Keep visiting times short

Having visitors stay for hours can be incredibly stressful for new parents, not to mention the baby. It's a great idea when you're still pregnant to clearly state to future visitors that you'd like them to only stay an hour (or what you feel comfortable with – I suggest you keep it lower rather than higher, just in case!). That way when Baby arrives, you don't have to have the awkward conversation – or worse, sit through endless baby viewings.

A newly minted mother is in a slipstream of probably the most intense emotions of her life, not to mention the physical recovery she's going through after the marathon that is birth – regardless of how that birth went. She has a tiny human who is solely dependent on her and who she wants to bond with. She needs her mental, physical and energetic space protected in order to do all of this life-changing work. And that means that other people will need to cope with some temporary boundaries.

The best advice I've received, and that I would pass on to other new parents is this: Just do you. Trust yourself, your intuition, your baby, your strength. Even if it may not always feel like it, you *have* got this.

CHAPTER 5

Birth

Ooh I've been looking forward to writing this! I've devoted an entire chapter to birth as it's a topic I feel cellularly passionate about. I don't believe that birth gets enough airtime in our society (at least, not enough positive airtime) and this is my book so I get to devote a whole juicy chapter to talk about it. Boom!

Before I start, I want to say …

- I first shared our story on my blog, and I've decided to share it again as part of this book. I deliberated a lot about sharing our birth story as it's deeply personal and private – not just to me, but to Lexi, Wade, and all the people who were part of our birth story. However, I got so much from reading other women's birth stories, and I felt it was right to pay the privilege I had from reading theirs forward by sharing my own.
- The decisions we made were the ones we felt were right for us. I have zero – and I mean zero – judgement on how any other families choose to plan or end up having their births.
- If you're reading this and you're pregnant, please please remember that this is our story – not yours. Remember the OPS (Other People's Stories)! You will create your own special

story with your baby, and just because we had X experience, doesn't mean that you will too. Remember that no two births are the same, and that each one is as unique as a fingerprint.

My fears

I had significant fear around the experience of giving birth – I decided to not even go there mentally until the third trimester.

My three greatest fears were:

1. The pain – I had heard countless times how painful childbirth is. Marina Go, a woman I respect enormously, even wrote in her book *Breakthrough*, 'Never let anyone tell you that birth is anything other than hell.' **gulp**
2. The 'grossness' of it – I am relatively prudish with Wade. The thought of being there in all the glorious gore of birth with him was seriously weighing on my mind.
3. That I'd have a long labour – When I shared this fear with Wade, he suggested I just see labour and birth as a marathon, to which I replied, 'Do I look like a fucking marathon runner?!' I would *definitely not* describe myself as physically resilient on any level so being in labour for anything beyond 12 hours freaked me out no end as I didn't believe I would have the strength and/or endurance to see it through without medical help.

Why we wanted a homebirth

If you're able to make choices about the way you give birth, there are so many options out there for you and Baby. It is an incredibly personal choice to make, and my own preference was for a homebirth. I'm so grateful that I was both healthy enough and lucky enough to have the resources that made this feasible.

When we embarked on our journey to educate ourselves on birth, we found that 110 years ago, just 5 per cent of births took place in hospital. Fast forward to the present day, and only 3 per cent of babies in Australia are born at home. It seemed to me that us women had become disempowered when it came to bringing the babies that our amazing bodies had created into the world – even though our bodies are ingeniously designed to do exactly that.

From watching the documentary *The Business of Being Born*, reading Ina May's *Guide to Childbirth* and having a lengthy discussion with our doula Nadine Fragosa, we decided that welcoming our baby at home was the right choice for us and our soon-to-be family. Happily, we managed to get private midwife Jo Hunter to say yes to us at the relatively last minute of 29 weeks (thanks to some sweet talking from Nadine, as I found out later!).

The luxury of having a private midwife is that all the appointments took place in our own home, so max convenience and comfort.

Jo saw me monthly for the first couple of months, then we went weekly from 34 weeks. Rather than the 15-minute check-ups I was used to, our sessions ran for at least an hour each time, which meant we could build rapport and a whole lot of trust over those weeks we spent together.

Jo was also on the other end of a text message whenever I had any questions or concerns, as was Nadine. She saw us the day after Lexi arrived, and every couple of days until she was a week old.

Being able to build those relationships, and have that dedicated support, was an unbelievable privilege, and one I know isn't available to everyone.

The preparations

Wade and I had each heard wonderful things about Calm Birth, so we booked in for a weekend workshop when we were 26 weeks pregnant. As it happened, we moved house the day before the course, so we were slightly scattered throughout it.

Calm Birth is a birthing philosophy that works with the natural process and hormones that a woman's body experiences during birth, and shares simple tools that women and their birthing partners can use to have a comfortable, even peaceful, birth.

What we learned from our teacher Lauren at the workshop opened our eyes to how powerful women can be in birth, and how perfectly designed our bodies are throughout the entire process – from the delicate dance of hormones, to the muscles that come into play, to the ability our minds and breath have to control our bodies.

The biggest take-out for us was the idea of Fear>Tension>Pain – meaning that when a woman is afraid, she gets tense and the result of that is her experiencing pain during labour. The opposite to this (and the Calm Birth approach) advocates that when a woman is relaxed during birth, her body is also relaxed and instead of pain she experiences pressure. This seemed too simple to be true, and I must say I was doubtful that it would actually hold up once we got to the pointy end of the pregnancy. But, as it turned out, the breathing and presence I learned in those classes – and the meditation techniques and information booklet we were provided with – helped me no end during labour and birth.

So in preparation I did my Calm Birth meditations, tonnes of yoga and pre-natal classes. I read Ina May's book at least four times and also read *The Down to Earth Birth Book* by Jenny Blyth. Nadine sent us a batch of birthing videos, which Wade and I watched together as part of our 'birth homework'.

Preparing our birth room was so much fun. We took over the future baby's room and decked it out with crystals, salt lamps, essential oil diffusers, an exercise ball and special mementos like a framed photo of my late Nana – who had birthed nine children, only having pethadine for one!

I had a shelf on which I arranged everything I wanted to hand for the birth, and that could be thrown into a bag if we needed to move to hospital for whatever reason.

I also engaged my trusty laminator to laminate ten affirmations and beautiful images of Nature, that I stuck around the walls in our bathroom, bedroom and birth room. I didn't make a conscious practice around saying the affirmations, but it was amazing how many of them came back to me at the perfect time during labour.

The affirmations I used were:

- I am not afraid of change, that's where I discover the most about myself.
- I am calm.
- I am filled with trust that I am bringing our baby into the world safely and confidently.
- I am grateful for every wave. Every one is bringing our baby closer to us.
- I am safe, I am loved, I am protected.
- I am healthy, strong and filled with energy.
- I didn't come this far, to only come this far.
- Kind heart, strong mind, brave spirit.
- I trust my body completely. It knows exactly what to do.
- This is not scary, it's just new.
- This power and intensity cannot be stronger than me, because it is me.
- We get to meet our baby soon!!!

Going into labour

I fully expected to go early, or at least the week of my due date. After all, I see myself as an efficient and organised person!

That was not to be and so it became a very challenging time, mentally and emotionally. Not having any control over when this baby would choose to arrive was extraordinarily difficult for a Type A over-planner like myself. Physically, I felt great so I comforted myself with that fact.

At one week past my due date, I took myself off social media, as seeing all the women who were due at the same time as me with their precious little arrivals wasn't helping my morale – and neither were the messages asking if the baby had arrived yet.

(I found it fascinating that people would message me asking 'Has the baby arrived yet?' Never those in my inner circle of trust, or even those on the outer edges of the circle – but clients I hadn't seen in years, and even someone I'd had one coffee meeting with when I was pregnant!)

At 42 weeks, Jo's protocol advised us to have an ultrasound (all was fine) and to have a consultation with an obstetrician. As such we were booked in for the following Tuesday when I would have been 42 weeks and three days – during which time we all prayed I would go into labour naturally.

Day 1 – Friday

On the Friday that I ticked over to 42 weeks Mam and I went for a walk in Bondi. After lunch, I felt an odd sensation and sat down quickly on a nearby wall.

At dinner that night, I started to get some contractions. It wasn't a big 'oh my God I'm in labour!!!' moment like I expected it to be – and like I'd seen in movies.

I had tried to imagine so many times what contractions would feel like – and here they were. For me, it felt like period cramps that got more intense as time went on.

Wade and I went to bed, and promised to wake up my mum if things got going.

I need to make a short aside on the pain thing right here. It turns out that the smart people at Calm Birth were exactly right. The more I relaxed into a contraction, the less it hurt. Thankfully I learned this early on, so the majority of my labour was not painful. I chose to see contractions as waves moving through my body and went into a place of deep, deep focus during each one. Coupled with breathing and my TENS (transcutaneous electrical nerve stimulation) machine, I was surprised at how I was able to cope with them.

Day 2 – Saturday

As the sun came up, the contractions started to space out and we accepted that things had slowed down. I spent most of the Saturday in our bedroom and had a couple of meals. I was having contractions anything from five to 20 minutes apart throughout the day. That night, the contractions picked up again and were a lot more intense.

Day 3 – Sunday

Yet again, as the sun came up the contractions spaced out to about every 20 minutes and my heart sank.

We spoke to Jo and she recommended we go to the hospital that afternoon to have the baby monitored and check that they were doing ok after all the activity they'd been experiencing over the last two days.

At the hospital Jo, Wade and I were taken to a delivery suite and I was hooked up to the monitor. The baby was perfectly fine, which was extremely reassuring.

As we had come to expect, the contractions again picked up on Sunday night.

Wade called Nadine at around 4 a.m. as we thought we were getting close. She arrived at 4.45 a.m. and was in our bedroom with the three of us, but between contractions I was wondering why she hadn't called Jo to come yet. She obviously didn't think it was going to happen that night, and – gah! – the contractions started to space out again once the sun came up.

Day 4 – Monday

Nadine told me she was going to leave at around 9 a.m. and said she'd come back later.

By this point, I was feeling very, very over it all. I was coping ok physically, although I was very tired from not sleeping for three nights. The more it went on, the more I became afraid that I would need some kind of assistance to finally birth our baby.

Jo arrived at around 5 p.m. and examined me. I was 6 cm dilated – I hugged her on hearing that news. I was so *so* glad that all the hard work was showing a result.

Jo suggested I try to eat and drink to get my blood sugar up, and hopefully that would kick the labour off some more. I had some orange segments and coconut water, and as dusk came – like clockwork – the contractions picked up.

I was downstairs in the living room talking between contractions to Wade, Jo and my mum and all of a sudden Jo was going out to her car to get her kit. I had visualised this happening so many times, and now – holy shit – it was happening!! As I looked at her oxygen tank, weighing scales and other equipment in the hallway, I realised that the baby must be finally about to come.

Right around then, Jo and I realised that the baby had done their first poo (the meconium) inside me. Jo said the words I really didn't want to hear: 'We're going to need to go to the hospital, love.' There was a chance that the baby might inhale the meconium and that it would block their airway.

My heart sank. After all the preparation and three days of labour – and I was going to end up in the hospital anyway?! I was gutted.

Plan B

When people asked throughout my pregnancy where we were having our baby, I had always said: 'At home.'

For some reason around the 34-week mark, I instead started to respond with '*Plan A* is to have the baby at home'.

So in that hot, horrible, scary moment with Jo that night, my brain just clicked over to Plan B – and that meant the hospital.

It was decided that Jo would drive me with Mam, and Wade would pack up some birth stuff and join us at the hospital. Jo called Nadine, who said she'd meet us there.

Arriving at the hospital

It was now around 9 p.m. Seeing the little baby trolley/cot all set up with a fresh blanket was another – holy shit, we're having a baby! – moment. Nadine and our birth photographer Bel met us at the hospital.

Wade arrived just after us. I had put some essentials on a shelf in the birth room just in case we needed to go to hospital –PJs, underwear, pads for me and nappies, vests and blankets for the baby.

Not only had he brought that stuff, he had also packed up everything portable in the birth room into two plastic tubs – the speaker, oil diffuser, essential oils, photos, salt lamp, my birth clothes, crystals. He even packed all my birth snacks into a cooler bag and remembered my Nana's necklace, as he knew I wanted to wear it.

I have no idea how he did it so quickly and so thoughtfully, and I think it's probably the most romantic thing he's ever done for me.

In the bathroom, Jo told me that she thought I was fully dilated – and that if I wanted to, I could probably touch the baby's head. After some initial trepidation, I reached down and sure enough – I could feel the soft crown of Baby's head!!! This was such a great morale boost as I realised we were not far off meeting them, and it made them feel more real somehow to me as well.

I spent most of this time on the floor leaning over an exercise ball. Frankincense was diffusing, the very long playlist was on, and I was also inhaling clary sage on a tissue – it was so calming. The TENS machine was still going strong, and I took sips of water every now and then.

I upped the ante on my focus on the contractions, and tried to stay in the moment and screen out any activity going on around me.

It was only a few weeks ago that I realised not once had pain relief crossed my mind. I checked with our midwife Jo and she told me that there would have been plenty of time to have an epidural if I had wanted one, however it didn't even enter my head. A big surprise for me!

Push time

I had read about 'the urge to push' and was on high alert for any sensation that might feel like that. When it came, there was absolutely no mistaking it. It was like my body just took over and knew precisely what it needed to do. I was amazed at how natural it felt to bear down.

I continued pushing on the birthing stool. Wade was at my left shoulder with Nadine, my mum on my right and Jo was directly in front of me and never once dropped eye contact with me when I needed it.

I didn't find out till later on that night that after Nadine had met us at the hospital she had been called to another client's house, travelled to the hospital with them, and caught their baby in the back of the car – before making it back to me in time for me pushing! The first time in her nine years as a doula that two babies have arrived on the same day.

The grand entrance

I moved onto the floor against a bean bag later, and the atmosphere in the room changed quite quickly. The trace on the baby's head was showing that their heart rate wasn't coming up as quickly between contractions – so the pressure was on for me to get him or her out. I pushed with every ounce of effort I had, and more.

There were a couple of paediatricians on standby to check the baby when they arrived, and the room started to feel a little full.

Thankfully the numbers were behind me so I couldn't see them, however at one point I asked Jo 'Is this ok?' She replied: 'We really need to get the baby out now.' That frightened me and I doubled down even more on the pushes.

Then finally, the top of the head was showing! I realised that we were very close when one of the midwives asked a doctor to move out of the way so she could see the clock to know the time of birth.

However the heart rate was slowing more and there was a definite air of panic. I agreed to an episiotomy and pretty much instantly, the baby was here.

Time of birth: 00.13 on 13 June 2017.

One of the hospital midwives swung the baby quickly onto the table and the paediatricians worked to clear their airways. As the baby was being lifted up, my mum said: 'It's a girl!' I was shocked. I had so wanted just one daughter, and now *she* was here. I could hear a tiny cry, our baby's cry!

I had the injection in my thigh and delivered the placenta a couple of minutes later. Jo had already said to me that even at home I would need to have a managed third stage of labour given how long I had been in labour. It felt like the easiest thing – a tiny push and it was out.

I was moved up onto the bed and Wade was with me, but I asked him to go to the baby and comfort her. I so desperately wanted to hold her and it's still a sadness to me that she didn't get the soft, warm welcome on my chest that I wanted her to have.

Bel took a photo of her and brought it over to me – so the first time I saw her face was on a camera. I couldn't believe how huge her eyes were!

Meeting our baby

After about ten minutes – although it felt like forever – Wade carried her to me. As he walked towards me with this tiny, naked, beautiful (and surprisingly chubby!) human, I realised for the first time that *I was a mother*.

I took her in my arms and I will never, ever forget how soft her skin felt next to mine. She gazed up at me and we locked eyes. It felt like a moment of recognition for both of us. Just writing these words takes me back to that state of pure elation, and deep, deep pride in both of us for completing her journey into the world together.

Once she was with me, the hospital staff seemed to evaporate and all of a sudden it was just me, her, Wade, my mum, Jo, Nadine, Bel and Sharon, our hospital midwife. The room felt so peaceful. I remember Emma Isaacs telling me that a birth brings a special energy to a space, and I knew then exactly what she meant.

Lexi

Mam asked what the baby's name was, and I asked Wade if he was still happy with the name we had picked for a girl. He nodded. 'It's Alexis,' I said, 'Lexi for short.' We had chosen the name while we were on a bushwalk in the Blue Mountains before we were married, when babies were still a very long way off for us.

We called my sister, my dad and Wade's parents. I smashed a large bar of Irish Dairy Milk and was devastated that my toast didn't come with any butter, as I would happily have eaten an entire loaf of bread, if not three. I couldn't believe that after so much waiting, and those long days of labour, we were out the other side of it – and we had this bundle of absolute perfection as a result.

My mum, Nadine and Bel left and Wade had skin-to-skin bonding time with Lexi while I had stitches. The doctor was an absolute sweetheart and managed to keep me chatting and laughing throughout. I had been offered gas and air for the stitches, but I said I'd see how I went – and it was fine. Clearly the post-birth endorphins were sky high!

Jo helped me shower – the sweetest shower – and I got into

my new much-anticipated post-birth PJs. She finished writing up her notes and said goodbye.

Our family

Then it was just the three of us. Our little family. Wade and I marvelled at Lexi. By now she was asleep and he took her for a quick check-up in the nursery. He was like a proud peacock pushing her out in her little trolley thing and coming back.

Activity kicked off in the suites around us, so we had about three hours of just gazing at her and talking through the events of the night. I just couldn't believe that she was here, that I HAD DONE IT!

At 6 a.m., we went to our room. Wade fell asleep immediately on the foam mattress on the floor, and Lexi was peacefully sleeping in her trolley next to me. I wanted to take her into bed with me, but I was nervous in the little single bed. I fell asleep on top of the world.

I woke first at 9 a.m. and it took me a couple of seconds to realise that the night before had actually taken place. I shifted over in bed to look at Lexi – still fast asleep – and realised that my entire body ached. Like, every single muscle. I was also ravenous. I ate Wade's breakfast and my own.

We completed the hospital checks and paperwork, and discharged ourselves at 2 p.m. As Lexi had had meconium, the medical team wanted us to stay in until midnight (so 24 hours after birth). We were keen to get home and settle her in, and the thoughts of getting home after midnight did not appeal at all. We also reassured the hospital that Jo was coming over in a couple of hours to check her again. And so Lexi, Wade and I left the hospital to begin our new life.

Post-birth reflections

Afterwards, I felt quite sad at times that we hadn't had the homebirth we wanted. I was especially upset that I hadn't been able to take Lexi in my arms as soon as she was born and even now – she's 16 months as I write this – I still wonder about how she felt in those first minutes earthside. Was she scared? But then I tell myself that she is perfectly fine, and I don't for a minute think it affected our bond.

I was also grateful for the hospital facilities, and that we still got to have Jo and Nadine in the room with us that night. As it turns out, Jo had all of the equipment required to clear Lexi's airways, but I'm glad we made the decision to go to the hospital as we didn't know how it was going to play out – and that's a call we could never change if it didn't work out.

Giving birth was the most profoundly empowering, intense and magical experience of my life. Even though it didn't go to plan, I wouldn't change any of it. Every part of the birth taught me something and was an element of the journey that we all needed to go on.

I am inordinately proud of myself and my body and what it did over those three days. Every minute of preparation was worth it, and I would happily go and do it all again right now. I'd probably eat a few burgers to keep me fuelled up first …

And out of it all, we got Lexi. Our chilled little rockstar.

CHAPTER 6

Newborn days

Lexi, Wade and I arrived home that afternoon, and our new life as a family kicked off. We didn't know what this 3.4 kg bundle had in store for us – and we realised that we were fully in her tiny, wrinkled little hands.

I had no idea how the following days and weeks would unfold, and for such an over-planner like me, this was quite the adjustment. I had heard horror stories of parents walking around like extras from *The Walking Dead* for months after their little person arrived, and – as someone who *does not cope at all* on no sleep – I was worried about that.

Wade's previous life as an infantry officer in the Australian Army had given him plenty of practice in sleep deprivation – even doing a week-long exercise where he was dumped in the bush and not allowed to eat or sleep for seven days. Seven days! I'd be a blubbering mess!

I will say right here that we were spared the intense sleep deprivation – for which we will be forever grateful to Lexi. Somehow, we landed a sleeper. My heart goes out to parents (and children) who don't have as smooth a ride as we did on that front.

Lexi and I were obviously up every night, but I found the night feeds to be a beautiful time for us and we both dropped back off to sleep easily after them. That's not to say that we haven't had some big baby rave nights over the 16 months of her life, oh we've had our share of those ...

What amazed me was how much I could do, even on broken sleep and even after completing my equivalent of a three-day marathon during our labour and birth together. I think we 'modern' women forget that our bodies have been growing, birthing and nurturing babies since the beginning of time – and they've become incredibly adept at doing that.

I quite honestly feel completely fine after a big night on the baby party bus – something I would never have believed if you'd told me that before having Lexi.

I was up pretty much all night with her screaming when she was ten months old. When she finally went to sleep at around 4 a.m., I couldn't sleep as I was so stressed about the fact that I had a four-hour gathering with my Mastermind mentoring group the next morning, then a three-hour corporate training workshop that afternoon. Both went incredibly well – go figure.

Our bodies are so uniquely and powerfully wired to deal with lack of sleep, and we have a magical cocktail of hormones and other physiological helpers propping us up throughout those night feeds and when tending to sick babies.

For all Wade's military training, I coped much better in the very early days after Lexi's arrival. He was *wiped* after four nights of little to no sleep, and in the photos of the week after the birth he looks like a ghost. I, on the other hand, with my super-charged adrenalin, endorphins and oxytocin, look like I'm lit from within (which I guess, I was!).

In fact, one of the tips I give to all soon-to-be parents is that the partners bank up on their sleep as well, as their bodies won't give them the extra oomph that the baby mama will get.

For the purposes of this section, I'll refer to dads – however, these little gems will hopefully help anyone supporting a new mum.

I really do feel for new dads. There is an over-supply of advice out there for new mums, from their relatives and girlfriends, from books, online forums and the oracles that are Instagram and Facebook groups. Some women have the support of pre-natal yoga classes, and even one or two friends who are pregnant at the same time as them.

Soon-to-be dads get two-fifths of none of this advice, support and connectivity. So I've taken it upon myself to share the biggest insights Wade and I had in those newborn times, in the interest of saving you the arguments we had!

Give her gold stars ... loads of them

By nature, I crave recognition when I've done something well, and running a successful business got me that in spades. From a happy team member, to an award win or landing that new client, I had oodles of external 'proof' that I was doing a good job.

Keeping a small human alive doesn't attract anywhere near the levels of recognition that I was used to, and after getting cranky at Wade a few times for not celebrating me for the hero I thought I was, I laid it out for him. 'Look,' I said, 'I need you to give me gold stars. Loads of gold stars.'

What I meant was not for him to literally go create a sticker chart and whack it on the fridge (though to be honest I'd quite like that), but to verbally acknowledge all the tiny, routine things I was doing every day to keep Lexi fed, clean, comforted, rested and warm. Whether that was a (virtual) gold star for clearing the laundry basket, having dinner in the oven when he got home or hitting my target word count on my book that day, I needed him to a) acknowledge it and b) celebrate me for it.

We still have this running in our relationship and home today. When I get up to settle Lexi during the night, he whispers 'thank you' when I crawl back into bed. It's small stuff, but it's bloody big to a woman who has just birthed a baby and is trying to find her way in the world of motherhood.

Make yourself useful

I know that a lot of dads feel powerless/useless when they think they aren't able to 'do' anything while their partner soothes their screaming bundle of joy or is cluster-feeding a growth-spurting baby around the clock. 'I just feel I can't *do* anything,' Wade would say. This is likely intensified when Dad goes back to work post-birth.

The reality is that there's a shitload for new dads to do. Starting with the laundry.

Then there's teeing up dinner for that evening, holding the baby so Mama can have a shower, changing nappies, filling Mama's water bottle, vacuuming, clearing the baby detritus from the dining table so you can both sit down and eat without feeling you're drowning in bibs and wet wipes …

A lot of dads, I think, wait to be given instructions on how they can be of use, when in reality the actual issuing of those instructions can be the straw that breaks the emotional camel's back for an exhausted new mum. More on *this* in Chapter 12 on the Mental Load.

My advice to new dads is to switch on your eyes.

'Switch on my eyes?' you say. Yes, switch on your eyes.

Many men have a wonderful ability to simply *not see* dirty laundry, dishes that need to be put away or the fact the hallway is a deathtrap of abandoned Lego. Switch on your eyes – try to see the house like she sees it and try to clear some of the mess/laundry/tasks before she has to get to them.

Be the calm in her storm

Above all, the new dad's role is to be the calm in the new mum's storm, to help the storm pass more quickly for them.

In the days up to, during and post-birth, a new mama's hormones are all over the shop – she's up, she's down, she's full of energy, she's totally exhausted. It's a crazy-making roller-coaster for her, never mind her partner and support crew.

As much as our newborn days weren't the immensely stressful time I had been primed for, there were still moments of exhaustion and overwhelm – when I needed Wade to just hold the space and not engage in lengthy solution-driven conversations with me.

Having a partner who can see that moment for what it is, and not check themselves into Hotel Everything is Fucked alongside the new mother, provides that balance to her storm. Which will pass.

Settling into Baby Land

New mums often get told to 'nap when Baby naps', which is, of course, excellent advice.

I would add to that to 'nap *without your phone* when Baby naps'.

When Baby has just been born, There. Is. So. Much. Correspondence. Instagram comments and DMs, Facebook comments and Messenger messages, WhatsApp messages from family overseas, BFFs texting to see how you are, your partner texting for photos of Baby ... It's epic!

And on top of all that, there's a good chance that as a business owner, even if you're 'offline' or have stepped back from the business, there will be non-baby correspondence to attend to. Possibly a lot of it.

I'd get into bed when Lexi went down for a sleep, and find myself still responding to messages when she woke up two hours later – and of course I was gleefully posting cute photos of her on Instagram and scrolling through photos of her while she slept next to me.

My mum suggested one day that she keep Lexi and my phone downstairs, so that I could actually get some sleep. It worked brilliantly! She brought Lexi up to me when she had been awake for a while and was now ready for her visit to the Milk Café. My phone stayed downstairs and I got a solid three-hour block of sleep. I had the luxury of my mum for those first ten days. I know a lot of women won't have family nearby, but we can hopefully still turn off our phones and rest when Baby rests.

Wade went back to work the day after Lexi was born, as my mum was at home and we figured he'd be needed more after she left. My mum was a godsend – powering through the incessant laundry and doing personal shopping missions for me: breast pads, maternity bras, she bought the lot! Again, I was lucky to have Mam but it also comes down to what I mentioned earlier – if anyone offers to help, ask for what you need.

I was back online with the business fairly quickly, as I'd said I would be available on an ad hoc basis if needed. Our team member Ashleigh sent me a text when Lexi was two days old to see if she could potentially ask me a few questions about the talent search project she was working on. I proposed a time that suited me (and Lexi) and then Ashley and I chatted for about 20 minutes on the phone. I remember marvelling at the fact that my brain was still functioning after the baby epicness of the previous week.

However, reality soon hit. Ten days after Lexi was born we were hosting the finalist party of the talent search. We had strategically chosen the party's venue to be as close as possible to our house – for which Future Lorraine was very thankful. I was keen to see the team and catch up with our clients, but I admit I did wonder if we should go. We decided to make it a short visit, leaving the proud grandmother with Lexi.

It was fun to be out and see the results of all the team's hard work, I spoke to as many clients and finalists as possible and did my little spiel on stage, although I felt a little like I was having an out-of-body experience. It felt like my identity had shifted and I had this teeny-tiny baby who was my world, and here I was doing the welcome in front of a crowd of 50 people.

After an hour at the party, Mam messaged to say that Lexi was unsettled, and we were jumping into an Uber approximately four minutes later. I could hear her crying as we pulled up outside the house and scrambled up the steps to our front door.

The next day, Mam, Lexi and I walked up to a nearby hotel (again chosen strategically by the team) to say hello to everyone at the educational event we had arranged for the finalists.

Mam headed for home that weekend, and then it was just the three of us. Once she left, it felt like we entered into our new life as a little family. Lexi and I found a daily rhythm together. I can honestly tell you that I loved every single minute of those days – it was not stressful and it was not overwhelming.

I fully appreciate that this is not every woman's experience, however I need to be honest about how it was for me. I believe that we get fed a lot of horror stories as a society, and that it's important for the scales to be balanced (so to speak) with positive stories, too.

Much of the ease of those days came from the fact that Lexi was such a laidback human. She really did make it an incredibly easy adjustment for us to have her in the home that, until a few weeks before, had consisted of two very busy and very selfish people. The prep that we had done beforehand made an enormous difference as well, and eased the demands on my energy and time in those early days.

Looking back, I can also see that I didn't have any expectations of how those days would be – so each day that passed gracefully felt like a huge bonus.

I think back often and fondly to our little daily routines in those first six weeks. There wasn't much 'me time' and mostly I didn't care, though I (and Wade) realised how crucial it was one morning when I lost it. Lexi slept in our bed, so when she started to stir in the morning I would wake and hotfoot it to the bathroom before she woke fully. That ten-minute hot shower was *life* in those early weeks, especially when my body was still aching and in full recovery mode post-birth. One morning Wade came into the bathroom while I was in the shower and asked me about something to do with his business. I eyeballed him and with some choice words – in full psycho-bitch mode – sent the tough ex-soldier backing out of the bathroom.

When you have this tiny human to care for, they are likely attached to you in some way for 60–80 per cent of their day – so small windows of 'me time' become incredibly important. I urge you to protect your 'me time', too.

After my shower I would feed Lexi and then – another important lesson I learned in the first months – feed myself. Properly. For me, it was a slice of my favourite sourdough bread smothered in butter and cut into soldiers with two soft-boiled eggs. Then a pot of fancy green tea and a second slice of toast with homemade marmalade (the tea and marmalade came in a 'care package' gift from Wade's team and felt like total treat-y indulgence).

This might seem like a tiny, irrelevant thing but I can tell you that this delicious (and no fuss) breakfast added 900 per cent more contentment to my day when it was just Lexi and me.

Babies need a shitload of love and care, and I can see how the days could feel overwhelming and monotonous. Little self-care moments like my ten-minute shower and New Mama Breakfast were – in their own humble way – transformational for me as I adjusted to this new role.

Another benefit of these little daily rituals during the newborn days is that they create pockets of certainty. As human beings, we crave in equal parts certainty and uncertainty. That's why we start to get antsy when our jobs are too predictable, or – on the other end of the spectrum – feel anxious when we don't know anything about what next week is going to look like.

Newborn babies should come with a label saying: 'Caution: high uncertainty'. We, as the hapless parents, don't know when they'll feed, if they'll feed, when they'll sleep, if they'll sleep, when they'll puke, when their nappy will explode, when they'll cling to you all day, when they'll happily lie on the floor by themselves. Having small easily executable daily rituals like a shower or proper breakfast essentially create pockets of certainty – meaning we are more easily able to roll with the uncertainty of parenthood.

After breakfast, I was ready to face the laundry (it blew my mind how much a baby generates!) and generally get our house in order, including grabbing a dinner from the freezer (thoughtfully organised by Past Lorraine) to defrost over the day.

Lexi slept in her bassinet during the day so I could park it next to my desk while I worked. I restarted writing my book when she was about ten days old, and there was always correspondence from the business to deal with. I would feed her in the armchair in my office when she woke up. In the late afternoon we'd get out of the house to catch the last glimpses of daylight.

Wade would get home for dinner with us, then the three of us would cosy up on the sofa until – like clockwork – Lexi started to scream for her feed at our bedtime of around 10 p.m. She would usually fall asleep feeding, and only had one night feed in those days, so Wade and I were fortunate to get some sleep. However, we do believe that having our little routines helped tremendously in the first months of Life with The Tiny One.

The importance of household systems

I wrote in *Get Remarkably Organised* about the power of household systems. We talk a lot in business about systemising as much as we can; essentially building in tiny things that we practise observantly every day so that we make the Future Self of everyone in the business happier.

For example, we have template email responses written to speed up the time it takes to clear the info@ email address. We have a checklist to tick through before the office closes for a long weekend or the Christmas holidays (phone divert – tick, Out of Offices on – tick, all computers off – tick).

Wade and I had a few household systems in place before Lexi arrived – we would do the dishes from dinner and leave the kitchen clean before going to bed, we made the bed every morning before we left for work, I had a big cook-up on Saturday to fill the freezer for the week, and so on.

We tried as best we could to look after our Future Selves by maintaining these basic household systems. But these systems needed a radical upgrade when Lexi arrived!

Some systems that helped us were:

Tidying up before bedtime
This became critically important once our home was awash with nappies, wipes, nipple cream, blankets, baby kit, a seemingly endless flow of laundry and hell knows what else we leaned on in those early days.

We maintained our habit of cleaning up fully after dinner but tried our best to also clear the living room before we went to bed. The sofa was pretty much Family HQ on those nights, and it was much nicer for me the next day to come downstairs with Lexi and not have to clear plates, glasses, blankets etc. from the night before.

Staying on top of laundry
This can escalate at a terrifying speed when you're recovering post-birth and you have a newly arrived tiny person. You and Baby will likely be stain-creating machines and I'm pretty sure

our washing machine quadrupled its pre-baby output. It can be an overflowing laundry pile that's the final overwhelming straw, so staying on top of it is a massive help.

We had a bucket constantly filled with laundry soaker and water, and would chuck all the stained clothes straight in there as soon as they came off us. We also put on a wash daily, flinging the contents of the bucket straight into the machine. If you can, get a clothes dryer – it's a big help in winter or on those hectic business days.

Having a takaway budget

We didn't have one of these, however next time (if there is a next time) I would allow X amount of dollars to get food delivered. We obviously had a freezer full of food ready to roll, but on some evenings we didn't feel like having the same food again and would order in. I can still remember how good the hamburgers tasted one night when Lexi was only a few days old! Having a budget for this means you know it's there and don't need to feel guilty about treating yourselves every now and then.

Creating stations

Revie Jane, a successful businesswoman and mum of two, shared a stellar tip recently on Instagram. With a two-year-old and very recently a newborn baby, she created stations around her house with the key essentials her two daughters and she herself would need multiple times during the day. So, for example, there'd be a station of maternity pads, both sizes of nappies, wipes, etc. in the bedroom, living room and bathroom.

I swear I transported my nipple balm and feeding cushion from upstairs to downstairs – and back again – at least 100 times in the first fortnight, before I wised up and invested in a second pillow and second tube of lanolin.

I also had a mini changing station in my home office in those newborn days, and a cushion and cloth for feeding.

These are the things that made those early newborn days more comfortable, more contented and more healthy for all three of us. I hope they help you if you're expecting a baby soon, or if you're stumped on what to gift a new mama. I can guarantee that if you rock up to her house with one of these things, you'll be her BFF 4EVA!

Essentials
- Laundry soaker and bucket – for obvious reasons!
- Maternity pads – hint: you'll need more than you think. My favourite were the TOM Organic pads.
- Lanolin – this is a secret weapon in protecting your precious nipples and a tube lasts forever.
- Baby carrier – helps calm an unsettled baby and leaves both hands free to cook/work/look after other little ones. We have an Ergo.
- Comfortable PJs – a couple of pairs that you feel good in, and ideally ones that open easily at the front.
- Washable breast pads – these work out to be so much more cost effective than disposable ones, and are much more comfortable in my opinion. I used the Avent breast pads.
- Your favourite tea – Pukka does a special tea just for breastfeeding mums.
- Treat-y breakfast foods – whatever floats your boat: a slightly fancy muesli or nice bread.
- Pampering shower products – something that smells delicious and will make you feel special.

Extras
- Salt lamp – for calm night feeds that don't wake you and Baby up fully.

- Qiara probiotics – these saved me from further boob issues (see page 79).
- Breastfeeding cookies – if you have supply issues, it would be worth trying some cookies to see if they help. I love the Franjo's brand.
- Baby nest – this made it easy to move Lexi from A to B when she was small without waking her. Ours was a Bubnest.
- Baby swing – a lifesaver to keep Baby happy for a spell while you work, cook or have a shower.

Transitioning back into the business

Right in the midst of my transition phase when Lexi was two weeks old, we went to the Mumbrella Awards, where I was up for the Industry Leader of the Year Award. Beyond the two events I had popped into the week before, this was the first major business event that I was attending after having Lexi – and I was staying for the full thing.

In order for Wade and me to go to this night, a military-level logistics plan had been devised. Natt and her husband Ryan were coming from Melbourne for the awards, so they booked into a hotel room at The Star, where the awards ceremony was being held. Ashleigh, on our team, was Lexi's inaugural babysitter (other than my mum) and cosied up with room service and a newborn for the evening. I fed Lexi while I was having my hair and make-up done at the kitchen table, and again when we got to the hotel room.

Wade and I walked into the lobby where the awards were being held – and it was *the weirdest thing ever* to be there. I had gone to dozens of these industry nights over the previous few years as a businesswoman, but to be there now as a mother – well, I just couldn't reconcile those two parts of myself.

Lorraine pre-mamahood was in her element at these things – working the room, catching up with industry acquaintances, comparing notes on moving and shaking in that world.

Lorraine as a mama was spending her days tending to a very small baby – changing her breast pads, tackling poo explosions and feeling softer and more open that she had ever felt before in her life.

It's almost like Past Lorraine was a tough nut and super on the ball, and Now Lorraine was this squidgy, lovesick being with her boobs filling up fast with milk.

We sat at a table with Natt and Ryan, and my bestie Richenda (who was up for the same award) and her husband Kyle. I didn't think I would win, but in the unlikely event that I did, I was wondering how I'd go with getting up on stage in front of more than a thousand people in my heels and LBD to accept the award. To go from my small, insular, milk-drunk cocoon to this big, bright, flashy casino function room was quite the culture and energy shock!

Ashleigh was under instructions to text me as soon as Lexi woke up – which she did, just after we'd finished our first course. I buttered a bread roll lavishly (#breastfeeding), wrapped it in a napkin and speed-walked through the casino to the hotel and up the elevator to Lexi. Once she was fed and settled, I sped back down again, just in time to eat my rapidly cooling main course. (Wade had thankfully saved mine from the clearing waitstaff, preventing an extreme hanger episode by doing so.)

I didn't win the award, but it was brilliant to know that with the team and Wade's support it was still possible for me to attend a big industry night like that. Though I will also say that the next day was *extremely* low key, and it took a couple of days to get my energy back after all the excitement.

Over the following two weeks, I doubled down on my writing and tried to be as productive as possible with that. I was in regular touch with the team, and Natt and I picked up our Tuesday management call again. I interviewed a potential candidate by phone and helped the team with the next steps on the talent search.

While I was getting back on board with work, I had a health scare that really shook me up. When Lexi was nine days old, I developed a painful lump in my right boob. I had it checked by Jo, who told me to keep an eye on it and advised me to massage it under a hot shower. Which, of course, I did. The lump didn't go away, nor did it get any bigger, and mostly it didn't cause me any pain so it wasn't a huge concern. But two weeks later, it was still hanging in there, and I started to get worried about it.

I saw a lactation consultant, who tried to break it up using an ultrasound machine – but it only got worse. It was definitely getting bigger, and the pain was becoming unbearable.

I got an SOS appointment with a local GP one Monday morning when Lexi was four weeks old and left her with Wade while I walked the couple of blocks to the medical centre. I assumed the GP would refer me for an ultrasound and maybe give me some painkillers, so I panicked when she said I would need to go straight to hospital – the lump was measuring 9 cm wide and she was very concerned about it.

I walked home in tears and did a Lorraine-quality freakout to Wade when I got in the door. He packed water and a few snacks for us and we piled into the car.

At the hospital, I was diagnosed with a breast abscess, which was drained. Lexi and I had to stay overnight so I could be treated with antibiotics. We were back on the same floor we had been on when she was born – it was surreal waking up in the hospital four weeks to the day after I'd woken up with a newborn next to me.

Taking care of my poor hardworking boob and getting myself well became my first priority after that. I secured an extension on my book deadline from the publisher and told the team I wouldn't be working for a week. I slept as much as possible and spent the afternoons watching TV with Lexi sleeping on my chest.

I can see now that I definitely pushed myself too hard in those four weeks after birth. I believe that the breast abscess was my body's way of communicating that to me – which took me two weeks to finally acknowledge (sorry body).

What I would do differently next time

If I was to go back and do the newborn days again, I probably wouldn't attend the talent search events, and I would also have given myself a lot more buffer with the book deadline. I think that I was feeling so well – way better than I thought I would – that I gripped that shit up and over-committed myself (and by default, Lexi). I must stress right now that this was 100 per cent my doing – the team had no expectations of me, my publisher was utterly understanding, and I didn't *need* to go to the awards night.

It makes me sad sometimes that I didn't spend more hours snuggled up on the sofa with Lexi, just soaking her up and embracing the fact that I had an A1 excuse to sit in my PJs and fling cake and tea into my mouth all day.

If we are lucky enough to have another baby, I know that the experience with Round 2 will be very different to Round 1, as I won't have the veritable luxury of being able to be completely in the newborn zone.

I heard a woman say somewhere that first-time mums should really enjoy their time breastfeeding their first baby, as that feeding time is a very different proposition when an active toddler is trying their damnedest to pull the house apart around you while you're nursing your newborn.

If I was to go back to Past Lorraine during her pregnancy, as she was planning commitments once Baby arrived, and whisper some words of advice in her ear, I would have told her to dramatically under-commit with business and writing commitments – and if I felt like doing a couple of hours on them any day, to see that as a bonus rather than a necessity.

I would also tell her that The Outside World could tootle along very happily without her for a few short weeks, and to soak up those precious ickle-Lexi days as much as possible.

I would tell her to see rest as a long-term game, and not chase after short-term achievement-focused gains.

I would tell her that her system was still overflowing with all kinds of magic-making hormones, and that even though she *felt* like Superwoman, her body, mind and soul were doing some deep recovery work she wasn't even consciously aware of – and that all levels of her needed to rest.

When Lexi turned six weeks old, we went on an eight-week trip to Europe. As the three of us set off for the airport, I realised that the little newborn bubble we had been in was at an end.

CHAPTER 7

Back in the business

Wade and I had planned an eight-week trip to Europe, taking in my sister's wedding in Ireland and time with family and friends there, a week-long holiday in Italy and two weeks in London to explore business opportunities.

My family in Ireland was in raptures at the new half-Irish half-Aussie addition to the clan and Lexi slept through the entire wedding ceremony and the afternoon drinks reception.

The week in Italy was heavenly – just us three in a farmhouse next to a cute-as little village in Sorrento. Travelling with Lexi was easy. Many people had said we were brave to do it, but we knew that this was likely to be the easiest time to travel with her. She slept *so much* and all she needed was my boobs, clean nappies and cuddles.

Sitting on the rooftop of the farmhouse, I mapped out the new life that we'd have when we went back to Australia. I sketched out the days I would spend in The Remarkables Group and also the time I wanted to commit to my second business, Remarkability. I visioned up a live-in nanny and plenty of time with Lexi and Wade.

My grand plan with The Remarkables Group was always to take the model global – and the UK seemed like the obvious first port of call for that. The market was quite similar to the Australian one, and the fact that London was a short hop back to Ireland made it appealing now that the first grandchild was on the scene.

Wade's business was growing quickly in Australia, and a key stepping stone to his team's vision was operating in the Northern Hemisphere as well. Before Lexi arrived – and in line with our 'our family is the reason not the excuse' mantra – we had decided to move to London the following February, when she would be eight months old.

The plan was that I'd start the London office of my business, and Wade would spearhead the UK expansion for his team. I had shared this ambition with Natt before she joined the business, and the plan was that she would lead the Australian operation while I focused on our global mission. We saw the three months of my 'baby leave' as something of a dummy run for that – when I stepped back in after the UK trip, Natt would continue holding the reins of the operational side of the business to facilitate a seamless transition when I moved to the other side of the world.

Wade and I were both filled with excitement about researching our new London life – where we'd live, where our offices would be, the friends we'd make, the travel we'd do. We rented a flat, did a big stock-up at the supermarket and flung ourselves into meetings. Of course, I had a ten-week-old sidekick, who travelled everywhere with me, zipping around on the Tube, in Ubers and cabs. She loved the adventure.

As Lexi was so tiny and was still sleeping so much, I had no qualms about taking her to meetings. I had obviously never had a baby before, so I was figuring this shit out as I went along.

My biggest objective with the meetings I was having was to run a listening exercise on the UK market. I wanted to do my best sponge impression and soak up any insights anyone could offer on what the state of play was, and I especially wanted to understand if we could simply transplant our Australian model north, or if we would need to create something more bespoke for the UK market.

I reached out to all my UK contacts, and also did a shout-out on LinkedIn and Instagram. Pretty soon my (and Lexi's) dance card was full.

One of our clients in Australia had recommended an account lead at their creative agency who had moved to the UK. We had met in Sydney once before, and I had rated her and liked her. So I got in touch, she was keen to meet again and we arranged to have lunch the following Thursday. She said she would choose a venue and, as I had done with every other meeting, I flagged that I would have Lexi with me.

'*Perfect!*' I wrote. '*NB I'll have our little girl in tow so somewhere with a bit of parking space for the pram would be awesome.*'

The next morning I was checking my emails and saw that she had replied. My entire body got a chill when I read what she had written. That chill instantly turned to white-hot anger.

'Oh my God!' I exclaimed with such shock that Wade stopped what he was doing and came over. 'I think someone has emailed me by mistake,' I said, and showed him the email.

Clearly meaning to email her assistant, the contact had instead emailed me direct.

She wrote: '*Just found out she's bringing a pram and her kid (wtf) so would you see if we can get a table with room to park it.*'

I was *furious!* For so many reasons – the complete lack of understanding that I was travelling overseas and therefore I had no option but to have Lexi with me. For the inaccurate assumption that somehow Lexi would be highly disruptive. But – most of all – that this sentiment was coming from *another woman!*

After calming down, two hours later I replied:

Hi X,

I'm assuming this wasn't meant for me.

Just to explain, my daughter is ten weeks old and I'm only in London for two weeks. No-one else I've met this week has had any issue whatsoever with me bringing her along to meetings and she has been a little rockstar at every single one.

I find it difficult to envisage a future where women can successfully blend their careers and families if this is the kind of response it elicits in fellow women.

I'd rather not meet.

Thanks and have a good weekend,

Lorraine

I posted the email exchange (covering her name, of course) on my social platforms and it sparked a much-needed conversation about, firstly, bringing children to business meetings and, more broadly, the challenges that come with blending a family and career – especially when it's your own business.

The person replied the next day and was naturally completely mortified about what had happened. She was still keen to meet, but I could think of nothing more awkward.

As it happened, Kat Thomas – founder of PR agency One Green Bean – commented on my LinkedIn post and graciously offered to fill the lunch gap that Lexi and I had found ourselves with.

This Meeting-gate episode was picked up by a few online media titles, including *The Huffington Post* and *Women's Agenda*.

For the record, I found that 99 per cent of people were perfectly fine with Lexi accompanying me to meetings and events in that window of time. I do not bring her to meetings now – there's a big difference between a fourth-trimester sleepyhead and a terrifyingly active 16-month-old!

Still in London, I took Lexi to an evening Social Media Week event. She snoozed in the baby carrier for most of it, and when she woke up to feed I moved to the back of the room and fed her quietly so I could stay for the event.

One of my friends Uldouz Van Eenoo wanted to attend a business seminar and emailed the organisers to ask if she could bring her two-week-old baby as she was still breastfeeding – they replied, saying no. This spurred her on to create her own event business, Mother's Den, which hosts inspirational speakers at a mid-morning time slot – and with onsite childcare!

I've had women bring their babies to my events and I welcome them with open arms. Everyone else at the event is thrilled to have a cute little human joining them, and – as a bonus – I get to steal cuddles while the group is working on an exercise.

There are going to be instances where kids need to attend meetings or come to work. For example, during school holidays I see a big upswing in the number of kids at the co-working space I work from occasionally.

I've also had a senior client at a very large corporate have his daughter sit in on my sales pitch as she wasn't feeling well that morning and keeping her with him was the only option he and his wife had that day. She was attentive, and I found her presence to soften the energy of that meeting – plus, seeing her super-important dad fawning over her gave me a whole new perspective on him!

Just last week, I ran a four-hour workshop in Canberra and a woman brought her ten-year-old son with her. He was having a hard time at school and sat at the side of the room, reading, doing math problems she had pre-prepared and watching shows on an iPad with headphones.

I have zero issue with any of this, and I have yet to see a kid being disruptive or distracting in these environments. I believe it's for the individual parent to make the call on whether or not their offspring's behaviour/life stage makes it acceptable to bring them to a business commitment. If they're disruptive or require a lot of attention, then that's just disrespectful to the person you're meeting with and their time. But if the child has no effect on the meeting, then there's no reason why they can't be there.

The Grand Plan vs The Real Plan

We arrived back in Australia when Lexi was three months old. I couldn't wait to see the team, and it was a super-special reunion with Lexi and me over a long lunch in Sydney.

That afternoon, Natt and I talked business strategy at the kitchen table in our house. She had done an exceptional job at leading the business over the previous four months – no small achievement when she'd only had three months of the founder being fully in the business before I stepped back!

As Natt had been solely overseeing all aspects of the business, our sales pipeline was not looking very solid, so we decided that I would get into full-on hustle mode to secure new clients. I would also take responsibility for our business profile, focusing on growing the profile of our business within the wider industry.

We decided that this approach would make sense with the imminent UK expansion, as I could drum up new business and amplify our profile as a business, and Natt would continue running the show. Once I had the new clients onboard and our industry profile humming, I could step out stage left to London five months later.

Natt also pushed me for what my weekly commitment to the business would be. We hadn't discussed what this would look like when I stepped back in, and it was completely fair that she would want to know where I was at – especially as I had my second business as well. It didn't matter to her if I did one day or five days a week in the business, as long as she had the certainty of knowing what I was doing and that it would remain consistent.

While it was necessary and a relief to have this open conversation with Natt, on a personal level it rattled me, and I immediately began to question the fairytale life I had cooked up on that Italian rooftop – the harsh realities of actual life didn't quite marry up with the expansive (and expensive) picture I had painted.

I knew I needed to commit to X amount of time with The Remarkables Group, but I didn't want to stop the mentoring that I was doing in my second business as it was so fulfilling.

Wade and I had no childcare in place yet, and our income was certainly not going to accommodate the full-time live-in support I had dreamily envisaged. Besides, Lexi was still so young and I felt that full-time work would be too much for her and me.

By the next morning, I was in full panic mode. Wade realised how overwhelmed I was and delayed his departure for the office to do a whiteboard session with me in my office at home. Just working through it made me feel a whole lot better, and we went into proactive mode.

After speaking with Natt, I committed to working in The Remarkables Group on Tuesday, Wednesday and Thursday each week. I would work from home on Mondays in Remarkability (which suited me because at that stage the work was mostly calls with my Mastermind group) and Fridays would be my day off or time to wrap up loose business ends if needed.

Months earlier Wade had mentioned in passing that he would like to have some regular time with Lexi, but I was staggered when he suggested an entire day. His business was incredibly demanding at that time, and the fact that he would prioritise our little family meant the world. I also felt a lot better knowing that Lexi would be with one of us for most of her week. Looking at what best suited him, Wade chose Wednesdays, which meant we only needed a nanny on Tuesdays and Thursdays.

I hit up my friend Julie, who I knew had a small army of nannies saved in her phone contacts. By absolute luck, Iva, a nanny who Julie knew well, was just finishing up with another family and would have a couple of days a week available.

I then had a short phone chat with Iva and we planned for her to come over for an interview the next evening. She emailed her references in the meantime, but to be honest I didn't even look at them – Iva had looked after Julie's daughter since she was the same age as Lexi, and I trust Julie's opinion implicitly.

Iva arrived and was just lovely. She sat at the kitchen table, expectantly waiting for Wade and me to start asking interview questions – but we didn't know what the hell to ask! So we just had a chat and we told her about Lexi, who was asleep in her pram the whole time (so not a great help on the HR front).

Fortunately for us, Iva agreed to start the following week, so our first go at our new family/working routine had the green light.

Interview questions for nannies and babysitters

Thankfully I have gotten better at knowing what questions to ask a potential nanny. I thought it would be helpful to share some suggestions in case they help other nanny-interview rookies like we were.

- How long have you been a nanny for?
- What do you love about it?
- Tell me about the experience you have with children aged X (whatever age your child/children are).
- What activities do you do with children that age?
- Do you have first-aid training?
- What stresses you out?
- How would the families you've worked with before describe you?
- Are you still in touch with your past families?
- Are you happy to take on other responsibilities while the child sleeps? (E.g. Iva was happy to do some food prep, but not ironing, while Lexi had her naps.)

The Bottle Challenge

I just had one pretty important problem ...

I was feeding Lexi myself and our attempts at getting her to take the bottle had been failing dismally since we started trying it a month earlier.

When we first introduced her to the bottle during our visit to Ireland, she would scream hysterically. I waited till she was hungry, Wade tried, my sister tried, my mum tried, and no – Lexi was quite certain she didn't want the bottle, thanks anyway. By the time I was going back to work proper, she would just about tolerate the bottle teat in her mouth, but she had zero notions of actually sucking on it.

We had accumulated something of a bottle graveyard, with the teats and bottles that Lexi had rejected – even the ones that other parents had sworn was The One that finally got their baby taking the bottle. I threw more of my own milk down the plughole than I can bear to think about, and I was starting to feel very stressed about how we'd manage when I was away from her for three days a week.

Many people – including lactation consultants, midwives and seasoned parents – told me that some babies just wouldn't take the bottle. That potential reality couldn't sit with me. After all, babies' brains develop at lightning speed – surely a new skill like drinking from a bottle was something they could learn? And how could I do what I wanted to do in the business if I had a milk date every four hours?!

Iva's first morning with us rolled around the following Tuesday. I didn't have any expectation of how I'd feel, mainly as there was so much going on with both businesses and generally adjusting to life back in Sydney.

Getting ready to leave the house, I felt very tightly coiled, a lot of which was to do with simply getting *myself* organised to get out the door to an office for the first time in months – and now with the added breast pump kit and baby logistics to coordinate at home.

Lexi would need a feed mid-morning and we still hadn't had any progress with the bottle. In the spirit of wild optimism, I left a bottle of expressed milk in the fridge. If Lexi didn't want the bottle (which – let's be realistic – was 99 per cent likely), then Iva would drive her to me at the office. She had a baby capsule in her car, which meant that they could be fully mobile.

I wasn't worried about leaving Lexi with Iva at all – I had full trust in Iva and knew how adaptable and self-assured Lexi was. I was very upset getting into the car, though – mostly as it was the end point of our newborn days.

I was going back to work now properly, in an office, back with my team, and that narrow window we had to hang out together all week long was closed. In reality, it had closed before we left for Europe, but for me it felt like that morning was the milestone.

Once I was at the office, I had great fun. The team had moved to a new co-working space while I was away, and I fell in love with the office. I also met a lot of people I knew there, which made me feel more connected with Pre-Mama Lorraine. I set up my new desk, had a meeting with the team … and then I got the text from Iva: 'We didn't want the bottle, we're on our way to you now.'

Thankfully, the office had a feeding room so Lexi had a feed and a snuggle, then Iva took her home for her nap. That afternoon I left in time to be back for Lexi's afternoon feed.

And that's how we rolled for the next three weeks – Iva or Wade would bring Lexi to me at the office, so I got bonus baby hangs on those days.

Wade revelled in his Wednesday Dad Day. He would work at home while Lexi napped in the morning, then come to me in the office – where he had made a couple of ping pong buddies. He'd play ping pong while Lexi had her feed, and they'd set off on their adventures again.

The business required a lot of my energy and after the initial week of honeymoon 'Wow, I'm back in the business!' time, I was hustling hard. We designed a new sales strategy, and I pushed that forward.

I got to spend time with clients, which was wonderful after not seeing them for a few months, but Natt and I were conscious that I didn't plug myself in there too much – given the upcoming UK plans.

One Friday (my usual day off), a meeting was booked in with a key client. The purpose of the session was to present the results of a major sponsorship package they had done with us over the previous year, and it would be very beneficial if I could be there as Natt was still based in Melbourne and wouldn't be in town.

Iva could look after Lexi, but we still had the feeding challenge. The meeting would be at 1 p.m. and the drive could take up to an hour each way – meaning that if the meeting finished at 2.30 p.m., I would be back late for Lexi's afternoon feed. This was precisely the reason I had been worried about the 'No To The Bottle!' campaign that Lexi was so passionately engaged in.

After much figuring out, it was decided that Iva would drive myself and Ashleigh to the meeting with Lexi in the car, then I could feed her as soon as I came out of the meeting, then we'd drive back home.

It worked out well on that occasion but I realised that this bottle situation needed to be resolved. Two hours in the car on a summer's day, plus an hour walking around Chatswood Shopping Centre with Iva, was not the best way for a four-month-old baby to be spending her time.

I redoubled my efforts at Lexi's bottle training program. This highly sophisticated curriculum involved me dancing/singing/waving books around while – as calmly as possible – I tried to get her to ingest a few drops of precious pumped milk. I would talk her through step-by-step what was happening, tell her why it was important for us, thank her in advance for taking the bottle and generally make her feel like a baby rockstar.

Around this time, my friend Peta gave me a golden insight. She suggested that maybe Lexi was fine with me going back to work, but her not taking the bottle was her way of ensuring we weren't apart for too long during the day. I think she was 100 per cent right.

Four weeks into this baby milk shuttle arrangement, and Lexi finally – FINALLY – took a bottle. I was so proud of her, and so glad that I had kept the faith. A new world opened now, where we could have stretches of time apart that could span longer than four hours.

Reflections on this time

As I'm writing these words, I'm one year on from this period in the business – adjusting to working and mama-ing – and I find it fascinating that I really can't remember a whole lot of detail about those few months.

Life was intense; not just due to the new dual-role I was figuring out but also because of some heavy family stuff that was going on, and both Wade's and my business going through challenging periods.

Sarah once said to me that the six months after she returned to work after having her first child Cara were a total blur – she said she feels she must have been sleepwalking for that time. I told her she was a pretty good sleepwalker in that case as that was during the time when she started working at my business!

CHAPTER 8

Selling the business

And I was back. Lorraine in Her Element. It was thrilling to be working with the business again, we were getting momentum on the new sales strategy, Natt was flying, the office space was just so vibe-y. With the Bottle Challenge overcome, I felt I'd struck the perfect balance between business and babyhood. For the next couple of months I flung myself into reconnecting with clients, finetuning our business strategy with Natt and creating content for the business.

In October I bought a ticket to an industry conference – given that I was Chief Officer of the New Clients Hustle, I thought it would be good to meet some new faces. The conference was being held at a Sydney CBD hotel. For some reason, I hadn't been able to leave milk for Lexi so Iva and I had arranged to do a bottle drop mid-morning.

Thirty minutes before I was expecting Iva, I tried to get comfortable in the disabled toilet and pumped a bottle for Lexi – and for the first time I felt really sad that I was pumping and not holding her close.

Iva sent me a text when she was leaving, so I told her where I'd be and stood on the side of Elizabeth Street with my little bottle of milk in one hand and my phone in the other.

She slowed down as she approached, but there was traffic behind her so she rolled down the passenger window and only stopped for a second – enough time for me to lob the bottle into the front seat and grab the briefest of glimpses through the back window of Lexi's tiny feet sticking out of the capsule.

I dragged my sad ass back to the conference and tried to muster the energy and motivation to go say hello to new people.

I just couldn't be fucked.

My heart felt heavy.

I missed my baby.

I wanted to be holding her close, not sitting in an anonymous conference in sessions that I didn't care about. I sat on my own for lunch – I'd never done that before at one of these things – and at 2 p.m. I'd had enough and decided to leave.

Lexi and Iva were out for a walk when I arrived at the house, and it felt like they'd never get home. When Iva handed Lexi to me, I squeezed her probably 30 per cent harder than might be recommended.

The only way I can describe it was that I inhaled her. I felt my heart would burst with the amount of love I had for her, and I feel teary even writing this a year later at how intense that feeling was. I snapped a quick selfie of the two of us to capture the moment (the photo you see on the cover of this book). As soon as I was done cuddling her, I put her into the Ergo carrier so I could keep her as close as possible to me.

That was the first day that I really, *really* missed her – and I realised the reason was that there was absolutely no ROI (return on investment) for me being at that conference. And that it was absolutely not worth being away from my baby for.

The truth was, the business felt different.

It felt different because *I* felt different.

That day planted something of a seed in me, and I started to closely observe how I was truly feeling about working in The Remarkables Group. My days in that business were Tuesdays,

Wednesdays and Thursdays – and on Mondays I worked in my second business, Remarkability. The only 'product', so to speak, of that business was my Mastermind mentorship group.

Ever the itchy entrepreneur, I opened up for spots for ad hoc mentoring that would allow me to help people on a shorter-term, high-impact model. I called it Turbo Mentoring.

I put the word out on Instagram and figured that maybe one person might be interested in working with me ... the spots were booked within a couple of days, and I found myself with a waitlist.

These sessions filled my soul right up to the brim. In the four hours that I sat next to each of those four people, I lost all track of time and space – and (no offence, Lexi) I didn't miss my baby.

I met with one mentee on a Saturday while Wade looked after Lexi, and while the mentee (actually Uldouz – she of Mother's Den success) worked on exercises, I daydreamed about the life I could live if I removed all the commitments and expectations I currently had of myself. The list read:

- No team to be responsible for/accountable to
- One support person who I work closely with
- Flexibility to work wherever and whenever I want
- To do work that fills my heart and soul
- To help people more by sharing my gifts (writing, speaking, mentoring)
- To be an example of living an inspired life
- To make more money than I even dreamed of
- To bring Lexi on cool adventures
- To know I'm living to my full potential
- To have the bandwidth to support/enjoy Wade
- To live in a beautiful home that I'm happy to wake up in
- To have time to meditate/pray/think
- To be in Nature every day
- To know I'm making every year a golden year

- To be glowing with health and totally vibrant
- To be excited about every day I get to have
- To have a tribe of people around me who love me and inspire me
- To invest in other businesses
- To know our financial situation is solid and on track for financial freedom
- To be planning a long trip or spiritual journey

I had loved leading a team for the previous five years, but something in me was ready to step out of that role – at least for a while.

Perhaps it was the dramatically increased sense of responsibility from becoming a mother and I just didn't have the capacity to care for anyone beyond Lexi. Perhaps I had just burnt out. Or maybe I just didn't want to be responsible for a team anymore.

I filed the list in the back of my journal that evening and doubled down on my key objectives within The Remarkables Group.

One Friday morning in November, Lexi and I went for breakfast with a group of entrepreneurial friends and I shared with them how conflicted I was feeling. Simply articulating my feelings to them started to put some order and sense to my emotions about the business, and what my potential options were.

Walking back to my car, I chatted to one of the group – she was the founder and CEO of an incredibly successful business, and in the midst of starting and growing that enterprise, had had three children in four years. At one stage she had three little people under the age of three while leading the business. I know, superhuman!

With my current situation in mind, I asked her how she coped with everything she had on her plate. She leaned into me, put her hand on my arm and looked me dead straight in the eyes. 'Honestly,' she said, 'I wake up during the night at least three times a week on the verge of a nervous breakdown.' Her words hit home with me.

The influencer marketing space had provided me with a pioneering business idea and a whole world of opportunity within which to create and discover the entrepreneur within me. However, I wasn't passionate enough about it anymore to offset the inevitable stresses that growing the business would bring with it.

My big gameplan for the business was always to work my ass off, take it global, sell it, work through my earn-out, then I'd be able to write, speak, mentor and train full-time. That's my 'soul on fire' stuff. I feel fully present when I'm helping people through those channels, like I'm in exactly the right place, with the right person, doing exactly what I'm meant to be doing. But in that plan it was at least 2025 before that would be a reality.

By the time December 2017 rolled around, Lexi was already six months old, and I realised just how quickly those eight years would go by. I wondered if there was a possibility that I could cut to the endstate I so desired and just write, speak, mentor and train … now?

One of my fears before having a baby was that I would somehow, in the process of giving birth, lose my drive for my business. And here it was – that fear materialising! It made me question my sense of identity, wondering where that hard-hustling Lorraine was hiding.

I know I'm not alone in this. At the time of writing, Pamela Jabbour's little boy Lucas is five months old and she reflects: 'I have really changed since becoming a mum and I am still trying to work out what that all means. When I am at work, I'm passionate and get absorbed in what I am doing and definitely feel driven, but then on days at home with Lucas I can completely forget about work and not want to leave my bubble with him. Work and home were always the same for me – I took work everywhere with me, to the shower, on walks, in the garden. I was eating, breathing and sleeping the business. So, the fact that I am not breathing work all the time makes me wonder sometimes if I have lost my drive. But then I am also so grateful to be living in the moment, something I could never do!'

Now that I've had time to reflect, I can see that rather than melting away like warm gelato, my drive was instead transforming into a different flavour.

Rather than the drive (let's call it espresso flavour) that was tied to awards, revenue, head count and fast growth, this new fledgling drive (maybe pistachio?) was less about ego and more about seeking out my unique purpose for being put on this earth in this body, and aligning myself to that as much as possible.

That's not to say that you *can't* have an award-winning, highly profitable business that is taking flight with a rapidly growing team *and* a happy family – that just wasn't what my soul calling was anymore.

Listening to a podcast interview with Oprah, she said: 'Everyone knows that there's a time that comes in your life that where you are is not where you're supposed to be.'

This was that time for me.

But there was a lot of shit to figure out. And I was scared.

Firstly, I had made a commitment to Natt to grow this business with her. How could I let her down just three months after coming back in?

Secondly, what would life look like without The Remarkables Group? It was my firstborn; my identity and its identity were tightly intertwined. Who would I be without it?

Thirdly, what would I do next? I had done mentoring and speaking as a side hustle for a couple of years, but making that my main gig was a very different proposition.

The first thing I needed to do was speak to Natt. With pages of talking points prepared, my hands shook as I picked up the phone to call her.

In classic Natt style, she took it in her stride and by the end of the one-hour conversation, we had hatched a plan. She would buy me out of the business, and I would stay on as an adviser for the duration of 2018.

Much admin (so much admin) later, the deal was done. I signed my resignation letter and officially handed the business over to Natt.

Moving on

I got two main questions when we started to share the big news:

1. How do you feel?

I felt so damn grateful. To Natt, for being so understanding and excited to take the business to the next level. To have had the idea to start it. To have had the opportunities that idea gave me. To have the relationships I have as a result. To have had a big, beautiful sandpit full of opportunity to explore.

I felt proud of the brand The Remarkables Group had become – and the brand I knew it would continue to be.

I felt free. Not in a sense of having off-loaded something, but in a sense that I didn't feel I had anything to prove anymore. I built a great business. I entered the awards, wrote the opinion pieces, connected with the right people, all to move that business forward. And – right then – it was just me. Lorraine. Weirdly, that was a strange place to be but I was keen to feel my way around it.

I felt excited. I knew for sure what set my soul on fire and to have the opportunity to pursue that full-time felt like the most outrageous luxury. That's not to say I knew what that pursuit would look like – having been in full Getting Stuff Done mode in the weeks since the decision to sell was made, sitting down and mapping out my new business model didn't happen.

2. Is this so you can have more time with Lexi?

I got this question *a lot* – many people made the immediate assumption that the main reason for me selling the business was that I wanted more time with Lexi.

This hadn't even crossed my mind.

Now that the year anniversary of the business sale is approaching, I can see how easy my role at The Remarkables Group was in terms of blending it with Lexi.

I had a business partner who was happy for me to work three days per week, and I went into an office and sat with my team for those three days. I would be in the office for 9 a.m. and home by 5 p.m., I didn't work nights or weekends and I didn't need to travel.

My role was focused on three things: 1) bring in new revenue 2) build the business's profile and 3) grow the business globally. All the other things, including the (you know, necessary) thing of actually delivering our product of strategy and implementation of influencer programs, were managed by the team.

Life as a business owner is always uncertain, but I was – to some extent – quite comfortable. I had great relationships with long-term clients and was considered an industry expert in what we did. I had an easy rapport and bond with my team and had reached that beautiful point where they just 'get' you and you don't need to over-communicate anymore.

Now six months properly into my second business Remarkability and I'm in start-up mode again – wearing most of the hats in the business with the support of a business manager and outsourced team of creatives.

I've created, or am in the process of creating, eight different concepts. Some of my work – such as events or group coaching calls – needs to be done at night or at weekends. I quite honestly feel I'm working more than I've ever worked in the past, now with Lexi to factor in, too.

So the answer to the question needs to be answered in two parts:

1. I didn't sell my first business to be with Lexi more, as I actually have less time with her now – and the intensity of this still-early-days second business means that it requires much more of my mental bandwidth.
2. *However,* the time I am with her feels infinitely more potent as I know that time I'm away from her is committed to what I believe is my life's purpose, and that is what I want her to know when she's older.

Babies, business and ROI

Just one element of my rebirth that Lexi's birth set in motion is learning that my work must bring a whole new level of significance, and that in order to continue to be fulfilled in my career I should aim – as much as possible – for the highest possible ROI that I can from my work.

And just to be *crystal clear,* that ROI is not linked to how much we get paid, whether we get a designated parking space or get to work from home one day a month, but to how filled-up our soul is when we're engaged with whatever that work is.

I fully appreciate that not everyone will have the flexibility to radically change their work like I did. However, it's still an excellent motivator to generate that ROI while still in the same business/role – whether that's by upskilling ourselves, finally addressing a challenging relationship with a colleague, or asking our boss for a one-on-one to map out our career progression beyond the role we're currently in. It's up to us – as much as we can – to make sure the time we spend away from our children is worth it.

CHAPTER 9

A year of challenges

I signed my resignation letter to The Remarkables Group the day we closed for the Christmas break and the next focus was to pack up our family of three plus cat to drive to Port Macquarie to spend Christmas with Wade's family.

I kept waiting for the 'OMG I sold my business!' feeling to drop, however it all still felt incredibly surreal, like I was just taking the usual festive break from the business. It was Lexi's first Christmas, so excitement was high and the family activity kept me distracted from the momentous event that had just taken place.

Wade, Lexi and I stayed in a house on the Gold Coast hinterland over the New Year. We enjoyed extra-long days (or so it felt with the 4 a.m. Queensland sunrise) of simple family time and catching up with friends who were also holidaying in the area that week.

I had started floating the idea of a Gold Coast move to Wade in late 2016, and here we were a year later getting a taste of that dream – revelling in the glory of Nature, with the GC's abundance of organic food, incredible cafés and healthy-living options, falling asleep to the sound of cicadas and waking in the morning to a chorus of native birds ... I was in heaven.

Given that I was no longer a part of The Remarkables Group, there was a lot more potential for me to base myself outside of Sydney and I started to very seriously consider a Queensland move. I also began lobbying Wade to take a flight of fancy with me on what that lifestyle would look like.

I imagined the slower pace of life. The proximity to Nature. The idea of Lexi roaming barefoot through her childhood days. The whole sunbleached dream.

It probably couldn't get more opposite to the life we were leading in Sydney at that point: renting smack-bang in the middle of Surry Hills, with roadwork or renovations going on all around us, most of our life within the radius of a few blocks walking distance, constant noise, traffic and general city hum.

Sure, we had the best gelato on our doorstep, and any number of quick-bite food options within yelling distance of our house, but to get a Nature kick we needed to get in the car and drive to either Centennial Park or the beach and Lexi's daily walks were on busy Surry Hills streets.

One morning during our holiday, Wade was out for a run and met a local woman, who he chatted with. She told him about a house that was for sale in the area, which had been on the market for quite a while.

Later that day, we went to check it out – and it ticked all the boxes. Space, light, bright. Walking distance to the local swimming pool and café. Set amongst Nature. And even our own small permaculture farm with 80 different types of vegetables, fruit and herbs planted on the property.

In the space of a few weeks, Wade got in touch with the owner, an offer was made, an offer was accepted, we managed to get a mortgage (no small feat, we discovered, when both of you are self-employed) … and we were on our way to become homeowners.

And then the figuring-out-how-the-hell-we-do-this began.

The plan was that Wade would commute down to Sydney on Tuesday mornings and come back to us on the Gold Coast on Friday evenings, renting a room in Sydney mid-week. With the house being only 18 minutes to the airport and the flight to Sydney only taking an hour, this seemed very achievable.

Longer term, Wade would lead the business's expansion into Queensland, with a view to relocating himself permanently within a year.

As we had the space in the house, we'd hire a live-in nanny to care for Lexi – this would also mean I'd have the flexibility to travel for my own business when I needed to. I'd work remotely and build my new business around that. I'd find a tribe of friends easily and quickly, and would travel back to Sydney to catch up with friends regularly. And that, pretty much, was The Plan.

Parallel to all of the house back-and-forth going on, my second book *Get Remarkably Organised* was published in mid-January 2018 (Lexi was seven months old) so I was fully consumed with organising the book launches and doing media interviews. I also had a tonne of demand for my Turbo Mentoring sessions, and clocked up 16 four-hour sessions over four weeks.

My book launch was a little surreal – it was another time where Old Lorraine met New Lorraine. Rather than a bigger evening event, I had instead planned an intimate breakfast for 20 friends, journalists, influencers and thought-leaders. The café I had chosen was quite literally the closest one to our house to make it as convenient as humanly possible. Lexi stayed at home with Iva, and popped down later on in the day when I was hosting a private dining room lunch with some readers.

As part of the book promotion, I had a live TV appearance on a breakfast show. It fell outside of an Iva day and Wade had a business commitment he couldn't move – so I called Alana, my publicist at my publisher Hachette Australia, and asked if there was any chance she could watch Lexi while I did the interview. Luckily, she was happy to help. It was a pretty epic mission to get Lexi and me out the door and to the north of Sydney to make the 10 a.m. call time, and due to a clash with Lexi's nap, her morning sleep had been canned.

The interview went very well and (side note) my hair looked fabulous after the hair and make-up department's magic. Alana got the sweetest photo of Lexi watching me on TV from her pram, and seeing that photo made me realise the point of the whole thing. For Lexi to see me doing this stuff, and to be integrated into those experiences with me, made me appreciate that I was being the role model I wanted to be for her.

Doing an interview used to be fairly straightforward for me (book it in, prep myself, turn up), but it now involved a pretty intensive coordination exercise and compromise from both Lexi and me, plus some help from Alana. However, we did it. And my seven-month-old girl got to see her mama on TV.

A couple of weeks later Wade, Lexi and I set off for a week of book promotion. Wade had suggested that instead of doing his regular Wednesday with Lexi, he batch his days together so he could travel with me for a week while I hosted book launches and also held some interstate mentoring sessions.

We spent a few days on the Gold Coast and while we were there we had one last look around our soon-to-be-house before we exchanged contracts. We then flew to Melbourne and stayed with our friends Sabri and Shalini and their one-year-old daughter Melia.

By the time we got to Melbourne, I was feeling tired. After a four-hour mentoring session on the afternoon of our second day, I was exhausted.

Hitting the eject button

Back when I was contemplating what life post The Remarkables Group would look like, Wade had asked me what I'd do if I could do anything at all.

'I just want go to Bali with Lexi, dye my hair pink and wear an ankle bracelet for a while,' was my response.

After that conversation, I had remembered a first home buyer's bank account I had put some money into four years previously, at a time when the government was offering a special interest deal if you saved some money towards your first pad. The deal had since been wiped, so the account was sitting there dormant. With the ongoing monthly revenue from my Mastermind mentoring group and this sum, I calculated that I could spend two months in Bali doing some much needed decompression with Lexi.

I booked the flights over the Christmas break – eight weeks of delayed maternity leave with my baby girl. The plan was that Wade would use our time away to get his head down in his business, and would come to visit us three weeks in – and again if he could manage it. My mum and sister also booked to come visit during our stay.

But while in Melbourne I received news that would threaten to derail all our plans. Sitting in my inbox was a letter from the Australian Tax Office, informing me of a six-figure debt owed. This tracked back to a grant consultant I had engaged when running The Remarkables Group in 2015, who secured tax relief for the business based on a new concept we had just launched. The PDF attachment I read with rapidly increasing panic as we inched down a packed Victorian highway told me that the 2015 tax grant was invalid, and the business would need to pay back the tax relief, plus a 50 per cent penalty and interest.

That day, we had just put down the initial deposit on the house. In order to bring together the full deposit, I was using a significant proportion of the proceeds of the business sale and all of my savings. In the space of a day, I had gone from being the most ahead I had ever been financially to being the furthest behind I had ever been.

The next day, while Lexi had her morning nap, I spoke to my tax accountant, the ATO, my lawyer and a couple of tax experts my lawyer recommended. Of course, this entire goatfuck (to borrow one of Wade's armyisms) was complicated by the fact that I didn't actually *own* The Remarkables Group anymore. Natt did, and she wasn't even in the business when this tax grant had been received.

As unfair, painful and intensely demotivating as it was, I knew I needed to take on the debt personally and remove any liability from The Remarkables Group's balance sheet. At the same time, we had progressed with the house sale on the Gold Coast – we were committed now and we would stand to lose even more money if we pulled out of it. Thankfully, my parents offered to lend me a very generous and significant amount of money, which would hopefully give me enough leverage to negotiate a reduction in the penalty with the ATO if I paid the amount immediately.

But what about the trip to Bali? I felt strongly that I should cancel it – who was I to be hippy-tripping around Bali when I was now in the most amount of debt I'd ever been in my life? Surely I should be power-mentoring over those two months and sending my Bali travel fund in the ATO's direction instead? However, I knew that this window of time would not come again. I felt dried up, brittle and really quite broken from the events of the previous year. It was all catching up with me – and I feared for both my mental and physical health if it did. How could I care for Lexi if I went to pieces? I decided I could take care of the ATO situation from Bali, and so I hit the eject button and boarded a plane for Denpasar one Wednesday afternoon with an eight-month-old baby and 30 kg of luggage.

I found a wonderful nanny who came to look after Lexi for a few hours four days a week and, in between calls with my Mastermind mentees, I managed to liaise with my lawyers and tax accountant on slow hotel internet. My response to the ATO was sent by my lawyers two weeks into the trip, and it felt like an axe waiting to fall over my head. Four weeks later, I had a call from the contact at the ATO. They accepted my offer of an immediate payment in order to reduce the fine by 33 per cent – so I gratefully took up my parent's offer and clawed whatever amounts of money I could from my bank accounts to cobble enough cash together and pay the amount. As abysmally shit as it felt to pay that money over that day in our Bali hotel room – paying for the total lack of integrity that someone who I had never met had run their business with – it also felt good to finally reach some resolution.

Bali was, for the most part, heavenly. The time to actually just *be* with Lexi was a balm to my stressed out soul, and I enjoyed yoga classes and massages, and I saw healers.

My biggest learning from that trip was that I needed to trust myself, and my baby, more. We sometimes question our own abilities and instincts as parents, and get sucked into other people's opinions of what we are doing or want to do. Doing that trip was one of my greatest decisions to back myself, and to back my child. And I am so very glad that we did it. It made me realise that when I trusted her, she trusted me.

Time for the tree change

We finally got to the Gold Coast – and Wade flew back to Sydney two days after. I set about creating our new Queensland life – discovering where to get our food from, taking tentative steps to making friends, test-driving a new yoga studio. We hired a wonderful nanny, Nikita.

When I started a second business – Remarkability Australia – a few years before, it was my side hustle of mentoring, books and speaking. Now that it was my 'full' hustle, it was time to build it into a business. With the energy and focus boost from my Bali trip and our tree change – it really felt like we were living in paradise – I began to bring to life the ideas I had for the business.

But our plan for Wade to be in Sydney four days a week didn't work. Given the requirement for him to be in Sydney over weekends for business commitments and to travel interstate and overseas, it became more like him being with us at home for a week and then being away for 2–3 weeks ... a very different proposition to what we had planned.

It wasn't an option for Wade to spend more time with us. His business was going through a very rough patch and for a number of weeks was hovering on the brink of bankruptcy. After the cage-rattling experience with the ATO earlier that year, neither of us could fathom the possibility of dealing with that. Fortunately for us he masterminded an epic save of the business, but it took many hours of calls and meetings with his business partners, and intensive legal and admin requirements.

Initially I found the stretches of time apart to be manageable. I'd sprawl out in the king-size bed, go to bed as early as I wanted, work late if I wanted to and revel in watching the shows that I adore and Wade doesn't. This got old pretty quickly though, and I started to actively fear the long stretches alone.

Our dream of bringing the rather-abandoned garden back to life and living off the land proved more difficult than we expected. With all that was going on in our businesses, we just didn't have time to educate ourselves on gardening – never mind actually getting out there! The terrifyingly aggressive Queensland weeds ran riot and we started to have major guilts and overwhelm about how we were going to get the whole thing under control. A flourishing garden started to feel like an impossible dream. We had to admit that our lifestyle was much more suited to going to the wholefoods market and loading up our shopping basket.

I connected with a couple of like-minded women around me, but I didn't invest the time and energy I could have in building friendships as I was focused on getting the business going.

And if I'm very honest, I felt shy about getting out there and meeting new people. There's something deeply unsettling about being in a whole new state on your own, and I realised how much of my identity was knitted into being a Sydney resident. It all felt so overwhelming, and I missed the easy familiarity that comes with very old friends.

One of my wise mentees Jenny Donnithorne (who did the interstate move years ago) articulated this perfectly for me. 'Friendships need history,' she said. 'With new friends, you need to create that history. And the thing with history is that it takes time.'

I started to feel myself sink into what is the closest to depression that I've experienced. I felt constantly sad and would burst into tears numerous times a day. I started working with a therapist, and had the opportunity to talk through how I was feeling – not just at that time, but working through stuff dating back to my childhood.

I missed Wade, I missed my friends – but most of all, I missed myself. I felt my sparkle was gone, and that I was a dulled-down, low res version of myself. I went from one end of the week to the other without wearing make-up (this is not me) and lived in my activewear and Uggs. My hair was a mess. To sum it up with a total Irishism, I looked like boiled shite.

As a way of digging myself out of the rut I was in, I implemented a Make Lorraine Great Again plan – and this helped enormously. I tended to my gut health (as I believe our emotions come from our guts), got my hair done, invested in some new skincare products and began to wean Lexi. However, the pinnacle of MLGA was a week spent back in Sydney kicking off an entrepreneur's mentoring group, filming and spending time with my Mastermind group.

The day before Lexi and I were due to fly down, I noticed that my mood was immeasurably better. I felt bouncier than I had in weeks, and that bounce intensified as I stepped off the plane back in Sydney – and continued for the whole week.

Returning home to the Gold Coast, I could feel the heaviness descend and Wade commented on how quickly my mood had deteriorated in the space of a couple of hours. The heaviness stayed, then Wade left again for another stint of three weeks away.

On the Thursday morning after he got back, I was meditating and it was clear what we needed to do. It was so simple that it was elegant: we should move back to Sydney. It hadn't even occurred to me before that point, and now that it had, there was no doubt in my mind that it was the right thing to do. I ran up to our bedroom to Wade and told him what I was thinking.

What ensued was a long, intense, emotional conversation about *where* we were at. He was concerned about how us moving back to Sydney would look – perfectly understandable given us moving to Queensland was a core element in his team's plan for the business. He was also very worried about the cost and logistics involved in moving interstate for a second time in just six months.

I felt – and still feel – bad about pushing for the move to the Gold Coast. Wade made a lot more sacrifices than I did in order for us to pursue our tree-change dream. He missed out on time with Lexi and he didn't feel settled in either of his homes. As a Cancer, home is deeply important to him and he found it incredibly unsettling not to have one solid base to operate from. He was also on a plane pretty much every week.

That night, we ran some numbers on the cost of moving back and also did a comparison of living expenses on the Gold Coast versus Sydney. Reducing our living expenses was a big motivator for us to move to Queensland. Our mortgage was half what we were paying in rent in Sydney and we thought that food, petrol and general living expenses would be less up north.

The reality was that yoga/gyms/petrol/food cost the same as in Sydney, and the costs involved in essentially running two households was negating any potential savings. The big difference if we did move back to Sydney would be childcare for Lexi. Having the space for a live-in nanny in Queensland meant that our childcare costs were approximately half what they would be back in Sydney.

However – aside from the outlay of shifting all our stuff back to Sydney – there wasn't a compelling financial argument to stay where we were. And as I constantly say: 'You can't put a price on your happiness.'

The decision was made – we'd aim to be back in Sydney by the beginning of September, six weeks later.

I think the only thing that kept us borderline sane doing two interstate moves in six months was breaking down the move into three steps – and not letting ourselves jump ahead until each step was completed.

Step 1 – Rent out our house on the Gold Coast

This was done within a week via the network in our local area. We were on!

Step 2 – Find a house in Sydney

I was extremely worried about finding a rental back in Sydney – the competitive urban rental market stresses me out and we didn't want to get panicked into paying more rent than we'd budgeted for. Plus, we only had a week in Sydney to househunt, which intensified my stress.

The area we were looking in was Sydney's Eastern Suburbs and its surrounds, but we had one Inner West wild card on the day we searched (six houses in four hours – boom!) and that was The One. The rent was a good 40 per cent less than we were planning to spend, it had harbour views and a magical old-cottage feel.

Step 3 – Coordinate the move

This was where we came unstuck! We were super-organised our end, given the logistics and stress of the move north in February. But our removalist proved to be inept/corrupt/non-communicative ...

Enter stage left an epic save by Wade – he drove our car down to Sydney, got straight back on a flight to Queensland and drove back down to Sydney with a van full of stuff the removalist had left behind. Hero.

Step 4 – There wasn't one! But I should have included it and it would have been: Set up our new life

This has taken a solid three months, but we've got the guts of a new life organised: Lexi is in daycare two days a week and we've hired a nanny for two days. The house is unpacked and set up. We've found a cleaner, a gym, a yoga studio, a farmers' market, a butcher.

Wade and I have been adjusting to actually living together full-time again after six months of regular separations. Life back in Sydney feels familiar, but also brand new as it's a different area for us.

The biggest upside to our failed tree-change attempt is that we now *know* what the tree-change entails. It was always a pipedream, and with those pipedreams come the arrogant assumption that life will be perfect in that dream. We think we'll hit the escape hatch on our lives and somehow find ourselves parachuted into a world that is devoid of stress, worry or tension – where the realities of family responsibilities, businesses and relationships simply melt away.

I guess you could say that we got the tree change out of our system. If we do pursue a more Nature-connected lifestyle again in future (which I think we will), we'll go into it with a much more realistic, educated lens.

We've had moments of feeling a bit stupid. To nail our colours to the tree-change mast so patently, for us to come back to Sydney three months later – well, as Wade said, the optics aren't great. However, I'd much rather be the person who pursues a dream only to find it doesn't work out, than to never pursue it at all.

So what did we learn?

When we catch up with friends we haven't seen for a while and they ask us how the last year has been, we tell them honestly that's it's been the most challenging one of our lives so far – and we have each notched up our fair share of stressful experiences over the years. Fellow parents will almost invariably nod sympathetically and say, 'Yeah, that first year after having a baby is *tough*.'

Wade and I comment regularly on how Lexi was actually the easiest and certainly the most joyful element of this past year.

I know that a first child's appearance is epicly unsettling for most parents, however I feel it almost does her a disservice if we say that. The reality was that she sat patiently holding space for us while her two over-stretched parents felt like they were in a combat zone on multiple fronts – businesses, finances, lifestyle.

Regardless of what was going in our lives, Lexi still needed food and cuddles and sleeps and baths and nappy changes and storytime and a push in the swing – and I really believe that's what saved the two of us from going off the deep end. Her daily routine gave us some much-needed certainty in a year filled with uncertainty.

The simple, pure, unrivalled joy that she brings to our lives acted as a powerful antidote to our stress, and gave us a daily reminder of what's really important in life.

PART TWO

MAKING IT WORK

CHAPTER 10

Fuck The Juggle

In media interviews, in the audience Q&A at the end of a speaking engagement, from Instagram followers, to casual chitchat with a new connection while waiting for an event to begin, one question dominated from the moment Lexi arrived.

This question was one of the very first I was asked, regardless of the context of my relationship with that person. It could be someone I had previously met once who was now interviewing me on their podcast, a close friend overseas in an overdue WhatsApp call, a business associate who I've worked with for years or the person next to me on an interstate plane.

I was quite flummoxed the first time it was posed to me, as I didn't know how to answer the question.

Then it began to incense me.

The question was: 'So, how are you finding the juggle of Lexi with the business?'

Now excuse me friends, while I hop up on this here soap box. And get comfortable – as I have A LOT TO SAY on this question.

I have many problems with the concept of The Juggle. 'But why, Lorraine?' you wonder.

Let me tell you …

The Juggle is impossible

I can bet that whoever you are dear reader, it's very likely that you can't juggle. And I mean the original concept – you know, standing up in front of a crowd and effortlessly tossing 3+ oranges/plastic balls/items of your choosing in the air and from hand to hand for several minutes and not dropping them.

Unless this was a skill that you diligently practised as a kid, or you had the great joy and 'what the hell' experience of running off to the circus for a few years (horrifying your parents in the process), it is a rare ability indeed to be able to juggle.

Yet – for some unexplained reason – the moment a woman births a baby and attempts to then go back to work after having said baby, she is expected overnight to be able to juggle. Whether she'd previously juggled or not.

And the worst thing, in my opinion? That *we expect ourselves* to be able to juggle!

So what we have is millions of women setting themselves up every single day in a vain attempt to master a skill that – unless we book ourselves into circus school or stay up late into the night for weeks hitting play and pause on juggling tutorial videos – we cannot master.

Friends, this is lunacy.

As I write this, I'm midway through Michelle Obama's book *Becoming*. This book is having a major impact on me on multiple levels. One of the most resonant statements she makes in the book is this one: 'Failure is a feeling long before it becomes an actual result.'

It struck me that mothers attempting The Juggle experience exactly this. We can't actually juggle, but we tell ourselves (and society tells us) that we *should* be able to juggle. Then it all feels too overwhelming, we remember that we can't juggle anyway, we begin to feel like a failure, and then the reality of that 'failing' sets in.

It might manifest in us feeling that we're slipping behind in our jobs, that our kids are underserved, that we don't have the superwoman abilities like our friend/sister/neighbour who seems to execute The Juggle, that we can't keep this up for much longer, and a million different iterations and combinations of these.

Spending our lives minute to minute believing that we should be triumphing at something that is technically impossible for the vast majority of us is seriously crazy-making stuff, and I can see why having a career or business and a family is a source of enormous stress for many women.

The Juggle is a really shitty form of self-talk

When I was writing *Get Remarkably Organised*, I included a whole section on the power of self-talk. When I then took the book on tour around Australia with a series of immersive workshops, the first topic I brought up was the importance of self-talk.

I felt it was critical to address this, as how we speak to ourselves is the foundation of everything we achieve (and equally don't achieve) in our lives.

I explained to the audience that I could arm them up with every single trick, life hack and tip in my arsenal to help them get more organised, however every one of these would be completely pointless if they continued to tell themselves negative things in their own heads.

What do I mean by self-talk?

Every one of us has a constant internal dialogue running in our minds. This dialogue takes in what's happening in any moment (Hmmmm there's a lot of traffic this morning), what's happened in the past (Crap I'm tired after Lexi being up at 3 a.m.) and what's happening in the future (I think I'll make risotto for dinner tonight).

This conversation with ourselves runs all day long – from the moment we wake up until we fall asleep at night. And many of us have multiple streams of conversation going on with ourselves at any one time.

This self-talk also gives us a never-ending evaluation of where we're at and how well we're performing in our own opinion of ourselves. I might say to myself: 'Yes! Well done me for landing that meeting with that potential new client – you are so on the ball.' I might also say: 'Crap Lorraine, why did you mess up that email – you're so sloppy!'

Something I explained to the people at my workshop was that if their internal dialogue is saying things like, 'You're never going to get organised', 'Your time management is appalling', 'You're always behind on your to-do list', 'You'll never be like person X – they actually have their shit together', 'There's no way you're going to make this work', etc. ... then that's exactly the reality they will create in their lives.

I got them to write down the most negative thing they say to themselves when it comes to getting more organised. One woman in my Melbourne workshop, who was working full-time, studying part-time and had three kids, wrote: 'You will never finish your uni degree, you're a failure.'

I asked her if she would say this to one of her kids, and the abject horror on her face told me that, no, of course she wouldn't. Yet she would say it to herself – several times a day!

Then I asked the group to reframe that Inner Mean Girl comment (as my friend Melissa Ambrosini would call it) to say something positive to themselves instead. Only by changing the track in their mind, I explained, would they create the environment for themselves to get more organised.

So instead of tearing herself to shreds, my Melbourne friend instead resolved to say: 'I have plenty of time to study and I'm going to ace this semester.'

What's this got to do with our frenemy The Juggle?

Going back to Problem 1 – if we're a) setting ourselves up for failure from day dot by attempting something that's physically impossible, then b) berating ourselves daily for not achieving that impossible feat ... then it's a freaking recipe for disaster.

Michelle Obama is right – we tell ourselves we're failing before it's ever near to being a reality, which then fast-tracks that reality our way.

The Juggle is a word with negative energy

I believe very powerfully that everything around us has an energy: from the people we interact with and the books we read, to the thoughts we have or the words we use.

These things are all on a scale of vibration, from high to low – including ourselves. The combination of these things that we experience in our lives will result in us as people vibrating on a certain level.

If this is all new to you, please do bear with me – I'll get to the point in a moment ...

The vibration these things have is personal to each of us.

Here are ten examples of things that raise my vibration/energy:

1. Relaxed hangs with Lexi
2. A tidy and clean home
3. A powerful, energising, blissful yoga class
4. A long unhurried meal with Wade
5. Cooking
6. Being in flow with work that I love – like writing this book
7. Making proactive plans to deal with problems
8. Having beautiful scents around me – essential oils, candles or incense
9. Time to read
10. A proper soul chat with a friend

Ten things that lower my vibration/energy are:

1. Clutter and mess around me
2. Arguing with Wade
3. Rushing
4. Spending too much time attached to my phone
5. Engaging in lengthy text message conversations with friends/family (refer to above)
6. Feeling overwhelmed with my to-do list
7. Worrying about problems
8. Feeling like I don't look good (dirty hair, broken nails, tatty clothes)
9. Doing work out of guilt or obligation
10. Being on the receiving end of an irate driver

I also firmly believe that words carry an energy all of their own. When we read, think or say them, it impacts our vibration. If the word raises our vibration, we'll feel uplifted, optimistic or energised. If it lowers our vibration, we'll feel sad, deflated or tired.

As a little exercise, read these words aloud to yourself and observe how they make you feel:

- Joy
- Mess
- Encourage
- Stress
- Happy
- Cruel
- Juggle
- Tidy
- Full
- Kind
- Hectic
- Blend
- Crazy
- Calm
- Exhausted
- Busy

While each word will have a unique vibration to each of us individually, there are some words that I believe are universally vibe-lowering. One of those is 'busy'.

In a conversation with Melissa many years ago, she told me how she had stopped using the word 'busy' in her everyday language and replaced it with 'full'. She explained that 'full' had a very different energy – it suggests abundance, focus, positivity. Whereas 'busy' feels almost like we're expending energy with no clear focus or direction.

If I say 'full' I feel grateful for my life.

If I say 'busy' I feel exhausted in my life.

I'm fairly sure that you would agree that 'juggle' is more on the lower end of the vibration scale. If I say 'juggle', I feel immediately stressed and overwhelmed. And I don't know about you, but I for sure don't want to feel like that every day of my life for the next 20 years until Lexi is reasonably (hopefully!) self-sufficient.

Words have energy.

'Juggle' is not welcome as a player on the field and it needs to be firmly kicked to the sidelines.

The Juggle is (apparently) for women only

Wade has his own business as well, and after a few months of fielding The Juggle Question, I said to him, 'Does anyone ever ask you how *you're* finding The Juggle?' He looked at me as if I was crazy.

Not one person had ever asked him.

I actually looked up the word 'juggle' on Dictionary.com and here's what I found. To juggle is to:

continuously toss into the air and catch (a number of objects) so as to keep at least one in the air while handling the others. *Charles juggled five tangerines, his hands a frantic blur … She works full time, juggling her career with raising children.*

That's right friends – even in the dictionary, juggling a career with a family is the exclusive domain of ladies!

Wade and I picked up this conversation over dinner again a couple of nights ago – still, no-one had put The Juggle question to him. He stressed that a lot of people have asked something along the lines of, 'How are you finding having the business with Lexi?', and to him that was the same thing.

I took massive issue with this. In my opinion, they are *not* the same thing. He is expected (in society's eyes) to *have* the business and a family. However, I – as the female – am expected to *juggle* the two. And that pisses me off.

In her exemplary book *How To Be A Woman*, UK writer Caitlin Moran shares her simple rule of thumb in deciding whether something is sexist or not. She writes:

> Are the men doing it? Are the men worrying about this as well? Is this taking up the men's time? Are the men told not to do this, as it's letting the side down? Are the men having to write bloody books about this exasperating, retarded, time-wasting bullshit? Is this making Jeremy Clarkson feel insecure? Almost always the answer is no. The boys are not being told they have to be a certain way, they are just getting on with stuff.

My husband does not worry about juggling and has never devoted even one single brain calorie to considering it in his life. And I can bet that most men are exactly the same.

Therefore, The Juggle is sexist.

If we have a situation where one half of the parenting population are set up for something that's achievable (i.e. *having* a career and a family) and the other half are set up for abject failure (i.e. *juggling* a career and a family), well it's pretty easy to spot which half are going to be unhappy, isn't it?

As a little scientific-ish experiment for yourself try typing 'woman juggling' into the search box on Google.

Then type 'man juggling' into the search box.

What you'll find for the female search is a bunch of strung-out looking women juggling everything from laptops to baby bottles to pets.

For the male search, you'll find men juggling ... well, stuff. Fruit, vegetables, bowling pins. You know, stuff that *should* be juggled.

The Juggle brings in-built Mum Guilt

I have a whole chapter coming up on Mum Guilt (Chapter 14), but it needs to be addressed within the context of The Juggle as well.

Imagine yourself being handed three palm-sized bean bags – one has Family written on it, a second Career and a third Home.

I need to point out here that most women could have ten bean bags and would still need more bean bags to accurately represent the many areas of their life they're expected to 'juggle' – but this is Juggling For Dummies so let's keep it easy for now, yah?

You start to juggle them.

First up in the air is Family. You keep it in the air (going with our Dictionary.com definition) and almost bore a hole through it, so intense is your gaze on keeping it going – ignoring the other two bean bags completely.

You successfully catch Family in the next hand, then Career is up in the air. Again, you train all your attention on Career, hoping that Family and Home will be able to look after themselves for a few seconds.

Inevitably, you drop one – or even all – of the bean bags. Maybe someone distracted you, and you threw the Home bean bag higher than you planned to and that upset the careful equilibrium you had going, or two more bean bags got added into the mix (maybe Health, and Relationship With Partner).

How do you feel?

I'll take a wild guess ... Guilty.

Guilty that you were so focused on successfully transitioning Health to your second hand that you dropped Family with a thud on the ground. And there they are, your precious child or children on the floor – all because you didn't do your job of juggling properly.

Attempting The Juggle is a double-bind: we take on an impossible feat, then feel guilty when we can't achieve it.

I repeat: this is crazy-making.

My child and career are too precious to juggle

For 15 years before I became a mother, my career was my biggest focus by far. I spent three years doing a bachelor degree at university, then committed another six months and the equivalent of $6000 to undertaking a post-graduate diploma and internship to finally land my first public relations role.

I moved to London to advance my career and was willing to start again at the bottom of the ladder in a much bigger, much scarier market. I went into the office on Saturdays to catch up on my to-do list, volunteered for extra-curricular responsibilities and took many a round of constructive feedback on the chin.

I called in sick for the first and only time in my life to attend a second round of interviews for a new role, and when I got that job flung myself headfirst into a totally different type of client and style of PR for a year.

Deciding to get more global experience under my belt, I moved to Australia and got a job covering a maternity leave contract in a small PR agency. I was in way over my head – with a team of ten for the first time, a very hands-off MD and one team member who scared the bejaysus out of me.

Two weeks after the woman I was covering for returned from maternity leave, I was made redundant – which stung for many years afterwards. But I dusted myself off and spent the next month of Sydney winter sitting at my desk in my cold bedroom searching and applying for jobs from 8 a.m. to 6 p.m.

I gripped up the job I got with all the fervour I had. I was determined to make a success of my second role in Australia and became Ms Yes to every committee, organising group or extra hand required in the business. I rebuilt my confidence as a leader and took great care of the (thankfully for now, smaller) team I had under me.

I discovered a passion for the burgeoning blogosphere and attended events outside of my work hours to feed that passion. I ran evening workshops in my own time to help bloggers, finishing long after everyone else in the agency had gone home.

Personal development became a huge focus for me and I spent many weekends sitting in windowless hotel function rooms learning about Neuro-Linguistic Programming goal setting and – most importantly – myself.

I decided to start my own business at the age of 29 and walked away from a job and agency that I loved in the hope that this risk paid off. I built a first-to-market business from my spare bedroom and rolled with the inevitable punches that that attracted.

I diligently built a thriving culture for my team, one that saw many of them feel like family – even now when it's years since we worked together, we pick up like it was just yesterday we were in the throes of an exciting project together.

We attracted a shitload of awards: from Entrepreneur of the Year, to Emerging Agency of the Year, to getting onto the annual list of BRW Fast Starters. We made great money – and I could treat my team to $5000 surprise bonuses, hot air balloon rides and overnight stays at Taronga Zoo.

The business I created became the primary source of income for dozens of influencers over the years – some sent their kids to private school, some had long-dreamed-for overseas holidays, all got to make a living doing what they truly loved.

On a number of occasions, I backed myself to make some pretty momentous decisions in that business: resigning a client, resigning all our talent and repositioning the business, exiting a hire that just wasn't working out.

I committed myself to becoming a confident public speaker (this having been one of my greatest fears), and developed that skill to a point that people pay me thousands of dollars to speak on stage for 60 minutes – and fly me to beautiful parts of Australia to do so.

I seamlessly brought on a wonderful business partner and got the business to a place that it could live without me for a few months while I had Lexi.

I listened to my internal whisper and sold that business when I knew there was something else that I was needed more urgently for. As I write this, I'm six months properly into that new business.

In that time I have launched a comprehensive mentoring program for ambitious entrepreneurs, hosted nine women on a life-changing retreat to Bali (life-changing for them, and me too), travelled to four states on a national workshop tour, written half my third book, run an eight-week program to help people get more organised – and written countless pieces of content, been interviewed for many podcasts and had meetings and phone calls with dozens of new and old contacts.

I'm not telling you any of this to impress you.

I'm telling you this to acknowledge that I have worked fucking hard on my career in the last 15 years. And also to acknowledge the work that you, darling reader, have put into your career. That we both continue to put in.

Those hours of learning, growing, schmoozing, improving, deciding, committing, u-turning, developing, meeting, speaking, listening, following up, connecting … all of that combined is our greatest asset as professionals.

And I'll tell you something – that asset is far, far, FAR too precious for me to chuck up in the air because society tells me I should be 'juggling' it.

Then there's Lexi.

A whole different type of precious.

Tony Robbins once said that, 'Progress equals happiness.' I could not have prepared myself for the pure happiness that comes from seeing my child's progress. From the first time she reached for my face as we settled into a plane seat when she was a couple of months old, to just this morning watching her try to get her shorts on herself.

Since her birth I have discovered within me a very pure sense of contentment that comes from being her mama, and an equally fierce tigress who will do anything – and I mean fucking anything – to protect her, and any other child as well.

So do I want to fling Lexi up in the air like a palm-sized bean bag? You bet your ass I don't.

Asking women to juggle their career – that they have built painstakingly over the years – with their precious children is asking them to put either and both of those entities at risk, which I don't believe any woman would be, or should be, comfortable doing.

Juggle no more!

But what's the alternative?

Of course, it's all fine for me to ask you to ditch The Juggle – but that's not overnight going to make this any easier, is it?

I'm not saying that if we simply stop telling ourselves we're juggling that things will immediately get immeasurably easier. I'm also not saying we just dump our kids or our careers. However, we *do* need to set ourselves up for success.

Taking on The Juggle is like clinging on to the deck of a sinking billionaire's yacht trying to tip out water with an eggcup to keep the whole fancy boat – infinity pool and 2000-thread count sheets and all – afloat. And The Juggle comes with a whole ocean's worth of expectation, societal norms, self-flagellation, sexism and sheer bloody pressure.

Once we begin to wean ourselves off the J word, we start to wean ourselves off the myriad challenges and juxtapositions it brings with it.

It's not realistic, though, to simply ban the word and reduce to nothing this attempt to bring our careers and babies together, as it's a very real, very potent challenge that many women are facing every day. A challenge that called me to write this book. But if we don't call it a juggle, what *do* we call it?

I've got a suggestion for you, a word that dropped in for me when Lexi was about five months old and I was starting to find my feet with this new normal of being a working mother.

The word is *blend*.

From the day it came to me, I never once referred to myself as juggling again. Instead, it was all about The Blend.

What's the difference between juggling and blending?

Well, first of all, blending is actually possible for every person – circus experience or not. I can guarantee that you have followed at least ten sets of instructions or recipes that required you to blend in the last 12 months alone, and I also guarantee that you didn't give it a second thought.

For my fellow weekend cook-up fans, we probably blend at least three different times in the space of a two-hour kitchen love-in. During my own cook-up this weekend, I blended the wet ingredients with the dry ingredients to make bread. I blended mustard, bone broth and apple cider vinegar to make a sauce for the pork. I blended whipped cream and cream cheese to make a cheesecake. Blending is possible. Juggling is not. Blending is easy. Juggling is not.

Blending, in fact, is *so possible* and *so easy* that most of us even have a kitchen appliance that can do that job for us! I have yet to hear of a juggling machine, and nor do I want to – it stresses me out even thinking about it.

Blending also has a much more positive energy about it. For me, it conjures up a visual of bringing really great things together, to make something even more great. Think about wine blends, coffee blends, liquor blends. Would Baileys Irish Cream be as nice with just the whisky bit? No! It needs the gorgeous smooth creaminess of the fresh cream added to it.

I would much rather blend my beautiful daughter with my exciting career than juggle the two, as well as the several other commitments I have in my life.

Blending the lot together recognises that each element of my life is wonderful in its own right, and blending it with the other areas makes the end result even better.

In fact, one of the sub-definitions of 'blend' on Dictionary.com is 'to form a harmonious combination'.

Blending also helps with my self-talk. If I have a long business day where I don't see Lexi until bedtime – that's ok, as it's more of a business blend today.

If Lexi doesn't have her nap and so I don't get my inbox to zero while she sleeps – that's ok, it's more of a baby blend day.

At a recent event, Laura Macleod (one of my mentees) shared a great word she uses. She says from day to day she 'tilts' between her family and her business. I loved that – for the simple reason that we can all tilt. We can't all juggle.

The marvellous thing about blending, and also tilting, is – and I hope you're sitting down for this next bit, Society – *men can do it too!*

I know! What a revelation!

This book is geared at sharing my experience of The Blend in my life, and I tell you very honestly that psychologically ditching The Juggle has been the biggest revelation in the whole experience. Just like getting remarkably organised, it has provided a solid, tangible, achievable foundation for me on which to approach my life with newly added baby to the business picture.

CHAPTER 11

Filling the tank

One of the exercises I like to do when I'm mentoring or speaking is called the Wheel of Life. This exercise is the most efficient way for me and the people I'm working with to get a handle on where they're at with the different elements that make up their life.

The idea is that you pick ten elements of your life and score yourself out of ten for each area, then you chart that score on a wheel. When all the areas have been rated and charted, you have a visual outline of a wheel that tells you very quickly which areas are humming along nicely, and which areas need some urgent attention. (I talked about this exercise in *Remarkability* and you can get the worksheet on my website.)

When I began working with this exercise, there was a segment called Fun – to represent those things that the person does just for fun, and has no agenda/motive attached to it. I began to notice that when my mentee was an entrepreneur – without exception – the Fun segment was always rated one of the lowest, if not *the* lowest.

I realised that when you have your own business, the time, need and desire for Fun drops quite significantly. I know I have experienced this firsthand myself. It's not that I don't *want* to have as much fun, it's more that I actually have a lot of fun in my business.

In addition, time to just chill out or kick my heels up also doesn't feel as abundant as it did before starting my business, as start-ups have a way of permeating a good chunk of your waking time, even when you're 'not technically working'.

I also think that when you're in the throes of the first few years of a business (and beyond!), the idea of just having fun can seem somewhat … wasteful? Or pointless? This is not necessarily a good thing. I know myself when I prioritise play – doing things I love just 'cos I love doing them – that my stress levels drop, my ideas flow abundantly and I overall feel a lot more contented in myself.

I addressed this Fun issue by instead giving that segment a new title. 'Fun' got crossed out and instead it was renamed 'Filling Your Tank'. This moved it away from being a superficial waste of time and gave it a purpose – to charge you up so you can give more to your business and family.

Another oft-used analogy is borrowed from aeroplane travel. We get told in the pre-departure safety briefing that 'in the event of a loss of cabin pressure [etc. etc.] … if you are travelling with infants or small children, please put your own mask on first.' Justine Flynn (Thankyou co-founder) puts this eloquently:

> I have unfortunately learnt the hard way that time and money are not your greatest asset, your energy is. If I have time to spend with Jed, but don't have energy, I cannot have meaningful moments and connections with him. If I have so many hours to put into work, but don't have energy, it is extremely unproductive and leaves me just playing things safe and not doing things that are bold, daring and risky, or putting off the big things that sometimes need more pushing uphill.

Before Lexi arrived, filling my own tank was something I did a lot of. I could see that – as the founder – the business was dependent on my energy to succeed. During the times that I was flat, burnt out and resentful, the business struggled. In fact, I wish I had charted my business revenue with my own mindset over the years, as they dance intimately, with one never far behind the other. Revenue would take a nose-dive when I wasn't in a good place mentally, emotionally or spiritually. Once I hauled myself out of my funk, revenue would climb upwards rapidly.

And so I learned that I needed to fill my tank. This could be:

- Setting out for a long, meandering walk around Centennial Park – with no set time I needed to be back
- Kicking back on the sofa on a weekend afternoon with a slab of homemade cake and one of my favourite magazines
- Taking myself on a retreat – from a long weekend locally, to a one-week spiritual getaway, depending on my schedule
- Going for a Saturday morning yoga class, then having breakfast while I read the paper in a café
- Indulging in any number of beauty or spiritual treatments
- Shopping for gorgeous things just for myself
- Booking, planning and enjoying weekends away with Wade and friends

God, writing this has me practically salivating onto the keyboard! The concept of having such an abundance of time to myself honestly feels like accessing some insanely titillating portal of fantasy.

I can see very clearly that the time, money and energy I invested in filling my tank up so high was one of the direct contributors to the levels of success my first business enjoyed. And so it's something I recommend that all entrepreneurs do.

And then Lexi arrived.

One of the biggest adjustments for me since becoming a mother is accepting that those long stretches of time to fill my tank are much more difficult to come by. For someone who sets such store by that time, it has felt like a sacrifice I have made. Wade has also experienced this, so I don't think this is the sole domain of mothers.

When Lexi was a newborn, she obviously needed me constantly. However, she also slept a lot, so I could leave her snoozing in her pram while I got a chiro adjustment, had my lashes done or went shopping. She would feed underneath the gown at the hairdressers, and I even took her to a facial when she was five weeks old – she slept propped up on my legs, so we both had our own version of pampering.

We did long walks together, once I had recovered post-birth, but they were a very different proposition to me jumping in the car with just my keys and a water bottle. Now they required the pram, a fully stocked change bag, the baby capsule and were timed around sleep and feeding schedules (hers, not mine).

Also, the opportunity to really relax and lose myself in my own thoughts was not available during these tank-filling activities, as my number-one priority was making sure Lexi was contented and safe. So I was still constantly 'on' – monitoring her needs, nappy performance and hunger levels.

As she got older, toting her along became more difficult. This was offset by the fact that she was taking the bottle, so I did have more than two hours at a time to get things done.

Even now, and even as someone who lauds the magical powers of having a full tank, I find it very difficult to justify paying a nanny to look after Lexi while I go 'pamper' myself, or cracking into our limited time as a family by leaving her with Wade at the weekend. When Lexi is in care, I feel that's my time to be in business – and I am still working on overcoming that guilt that I'm not 'being productive' if I dedicate some of that time to filling my tank.

However, it became painfully obvious to me that, in order for Lexi to thrive, I had to keep my tank full – literally. Lexi had her first cold around the time of our move to the Gold Coast, which I believe was caused by me feeling so rundown, stressed-out, broken and brittle. My milk supply had dropped significantly since the New Year break, which coincided with

Lexi starting to have three solids meals ... or so I thought. But one Monday during all the madness that was our lives at that time, I left Lexi with her nanny and took off to fill up my tank. I had an acupuncture session, followed by a sauna, and then pumped *twice* the amount of milk I had been getting.

For me, it was a clear sign from my body that when I filled up my tank, it would be able to give more to Lexi.

Just a month ago, I hosted my first retreat in Bali, with nine businesswomen who were seeking the breakthroughs and bliss I had experienced myself a few months beforehand. We weighed up the option of taking Lexi and her nanny with me, but with all that has gone on in her/our lives Wade and I decided that she'd had enough disruption so she would stay at home with him.

So I found myself in the airport – solo! – one Wednesday morning. No baby, no baby carrier, no pram, no bottles, no snacks, no books, no toys, no nappies. There wasn't even one baby wipe on my person! (Or so I thought, until I found one stashed at the bottom of my handbag, and I felt like *such a mum* when I did.)

Weirdly (or maybe not), I clocked every baby changeroom as I moved through the airport and even took a mandarin from the lounge for Lexi before I realised she wasn't in fact with me.

I had flown solo for business a couple of times since she was born, but never with ten baby-free days ahead of me. It fully blew my mind. It was the most crazy, surreal experience. Like a timewarp back to pre-baby when I'd just flippantly zoom through the airport and settle into my plane seat. I even read the in-flight magazine.

It amazes me still how an experience that was so vanilla, so standard, can transform to being so very different (different, not better or worse), then you step back into the experience as it used to be ... and you can't quite believe how that was just *normal* before you had a child.

When I checked into the hotel I unashamedly squealed with delight that this entire room was *just for me*. There was no baby kit to unpack, no portacot at the foot of the bed, no sleep routine to oversee. Even better, I had two whole days to myself before the retreat began (you can picture it: sunset swims, baths alone, room service, stretching out in the king-size hotel bed).

Just as luxurious was Time to Think. Time that didn't have one eye on the clock to get back for a nanny/Wade/Lexi feed. Time that wasn't bookended by the end of one nap and the start of the next one. Time that wasn't simultaneously accompanied by a mental running commentary of what Lexi would be eating for her next meal, how nappy stock levels were, what food needed to be bought, what the current state of play with laundry was ... and the endless thoughts that run through my mind when I'm at home.

One afternoon, I sat by the pool with my notebook and a pen to do some assessment on my business. In just 60 minutes and minus any spreadsheets, financial reports or wifi, I got more clarity than I'd had in months on where it was at.

For 16 months, I had devoted hours every day to nurturing Lexi and running our home, as well as the other significant hustle of starting and operating my second business. To have just two days to be in my own world, on my own schedule, and have time to fully tune into my thoughts ... Well, it was transformational.

It reminded me of how powerful this tank-filling time is, and also how bloody little I appreciated it before I became a mother!

Give yourself permission

A couple of months before my solo trip, I had run a Get Remarkably Organised workshop in Melbourne. In the workshop, I talked about the need for time to fill our tanks – whether that was getting up an hour before the kids did for a gym session or walk, or committing to getting a massage once a week.

A woman in the group got quite visibly upset when I shared my you-must-fill-your-tank spiel. I asked if she was ok and she said – with no small amount of panic in her voice – that she had absolutely nothing in her life that filled her tank. She said that she couldn't even imagine having that kind of time with her full-time business role and three children. I actually read in her words that she didn't think she *deserved* that time.

Oprah talks quite often about an experience she had filming an episode of *The Oprah Show* in the 1990s. Her guest on the show was talking about how women don't prioritise themselves – instead giving all their time and energy to their families and jobs. The concept of self-care was so radical back then (and we're only talking 20 years ago) that the audience actually started booing!

I know self-care is something that simply wouldn't have been in my mum's vocabulary when she was raising my sister and I, and also working. However, I also think that she had a lot more support around her – I'm pretty sure I spent at least one night away from home a week for the majority of my childhood, with adoring – and at that point, childless – aunties and uncles, who were all too ready to spoil me.

I firmly believe filling up our own tanks (or the more oft-used term of practising self-care) is one of the greatest gifts we can give to those around us – not just our kids, but our partners, our extended family, our friends and our colleagues.

Marissa Mayer, former CEO of Yahoo, famously gave an interview to *Business Week*, in which she said she doesn't believe in burnout. She said that we *crash out* when we're feeling resentful. That made total sense to me. Me filling my own tank heads off any seeds of resentment that I might start to feel about my role as a mother and its associated responsibilities.

Talking about her interview with our girl Oprah, Brené Brown recalls her experience of the morning that the segment was filmed. Brené was (understandably) pretty overwhelmed at the enormity of what was about to happen. She was a bigtime fan of Oprah and had flown in the night before the interview was due to take place. Her daughter phoned her that morning, checking in on a permission slip that Brené had written for her before she left that would enable her to attend a school outing.

Brené had a lightbulb moment – what if she wrote *herself* a permission slip? She was so caught up in her own nerves and perfectionism that she was forgetting that this should actually be an inspiring, fun experience.

So she wrote her own permission slip, which gave her permission to enjoy her imminent interview with Oprah.

I LOVE this idea. For many of us, giving ourselves the permission to fill our own tanks is the most difficult thing. Those around us might gladly give us their permission, however we can't grant it to ourselves.

So I've created a permission slip just for you. You can download it on my website. I want you to print a few out and complete one whenever you need that extra push to allow yourself the time to fill your own tank. It might be to go to a gym class, to sit on the sofa and drink a cup of tea, to book that retreat with a girlfriend, to take yourself for lunch solo. Whatever it is, write yourself a permission slip.

(I'd like you to give yourself the permission, but just in case you get cold feet, I have also personally signed it for you – now you have no excuses!)

The challenge with filling our own tanks is that (predictably) it's the times when we really *need* it that we can't muster the energy or focus to decide on something that would fill us up – a cruel bind!

One of my friends Jules has a list in the Notes app of her phone that includes all the things that fill her up – everything from a really good goats' cheese, to a swim in the ocean. This is a great way of looking after your Future Self.

Some of your filling-up things might be free (like a soak in the bath), others might cost money (a massage at a day spa). Some might take a few minutes (a cup of tea in the garden), or more time (a long solo walk). Having this list written and ready to whip out when you're having a feel-flat day is a sure-fire way to pick yourself up easily. And you'll always be ready to fill up if the chance appears.

CHAPTER 12

The Mental Load

Wade and I are in a family Secret Santa, and this year I got one of the guys, Jai, and he got me. Jai is married to Wade's cousin, Katherine, and they have three kids together. He has his own business and Katherine works at home.

When I found out who my Secret Santa was, my immediate default was to text Kate and let her know what I wanted, and ask what Jai wanted. Then I checked myself – why did I assume that she would be leading the charge when it came to everyone's Christmas presents?

I mean, I was 90 per cent sure that she *was*, knowing that it's how this particular couple divvy up the responsibilities. However, if I cut him out of communications altogether then surely I was just bolstering the expectation that women should be the overseers of all things gifting. And I had just started this chapter the day before!

I actually didn't have Jai's mobile number, so once I got it from Kate I sent him a text putting in my request to the North Pole (a voucher for a homewares store) and asked him for his request.

'Cool cool,' came the reply, 'I'll pass that on to Kate.'

This made me laugh. The experience reminded me – for the 10,000th time – *how very much I would love a wife of my own.*

Imagine sailing through your life knowing that someone else's brain is essentially the safety net to yours? Where you're prompted to buy gifts in time for birthdays. Or even better, the gifts are bought and wrapped for you to give. Where new shoes magically appear in your kids' wardrobes. Where someone else knows when the sheets were last washed, how long the milk has been in the fridge, that the olive oil is almost out?

Now I know that just because someone else is gripping up the detail of the home front, it doesn't mean that life is a cruisey stroll in a rose garden. However, it would make life a hell of a lot easier – and would also free up immeasurable mental energy to focus on other things ...

You know, like a career, further education and having actual windows of time where your brain isn't running the endless mental checklist of keeping the whole show on the road.

Annabel Crabb wrote a terribly well-backed up and dreadfully depressing book called *The Wife Drought*. The stats ain't pretty. On studying Australian Census data, she found that 76 per cent of full-time working dads have a 'wife' – i.e: someone who is at home more than him to manage the home and family. For mothers who work full-time, the rate of wife-having is only 15 per cent. As Annabel rather gloomily puts it: 'Australian working women are in an advanced, sustained and chronically under-reported state of wife drought, and there is no sign of rain.'

In 2017, a French cartoonist called Emma created a series of illustrations called 'Fallait Demander' (translated to English, it means 'You Should Have Asked'). Her images – and the message behind them – went viral, with hundreds of websites and news outlets picking them up. She later translated it into English, which you can locate easily by searching You Should Have Asked.

The in-a-nutshell version of the comic strip is that – very often – women shoulder the mental load of the running of a household, a relationship and a family. Men proclaim their willingness to help with the actual execution of tasks, but they essentially spend most of their lives awaiting instructions on what those actual tasks should be.

This means that for most women, they are the brains trust of everything from nutrition to playdates, from household repairs to supplier payments, from wardrobe updates to medical checks, from social calendars to house cleanliness.

Equally, most women live with the knowledge that there is no safety net – that if they don't remember to pay the cleaner/ change Saturday's playdate/buy Johnny new shoes, then no-one will.

Emma's point is that when she got to a certain level of seniority in her career, she could no longer continue to be the 'doer' (i.e. the executor of the work) *and* the 'thinker' (i.e. the project manager of the work). In order for her to be successful at her job, she needed to be able to delegate the doing to her team.

In the comic strip Emma identifies that women mostly hold responsibility for the project management, but still do a lot more than men on the actual task execution front.

We often talk about the Mental Load as the domain of mothers, however this starts much earlier than that. I have argued with Wade about the unfair distribution of the Mental Load in our relationship since long before we became parents. Probably from when the honeymoon period of us meeting and living together had worn off, and I started to resent how much more I was thinking about than he was.

It's important for me to say right now that the actually *doing* of all the stuff required to keep a home operating was a whole different argument. The two, however, are inextricably linked – as anyone who has managed anyone knows, sometimes (and maybe often) it's easier to just do it yourself than brief someone else, give them feedback on how it's been done, and then check the final result.

This means that by merely carrying the Mental Load, women are by default signing up to do more of the heavy lifting with housework, child-rearing and social secretary duties.

The Mental Load has been an Actual Thing discussed in our relationship for at least five years (even if early on there wasn't an actual label for the imbalance that had me seething with resentment).

So how does it play out? Well, for example, I monitor Lexi's wardrobe to ensure that her clothes fit, are season-appropriate and haven't fallen apart/gotten stained to the point that she looks like a cast member from *Oliver*. Wade (I'm pretty sure) couldn't tell you what her shoe size is, or how many onesies she has to sleep in at any given time.

Today we noticed something we wanted to get checked out at the doctor and I went ahead and booked an appointment at our usual medical centre. Our GP wasn't available, so I got a spot with another doctor for this evening. Wade – who obviously wanted to take on some of the load – sent me a message: 'Re Doctors: Can you please let me know if Lexi has a standard GP and I'll organise a time.' He once took Lexi to the doctor on the Gold Coast, but hasn't taken her since we came back to Sydney six months ago. Until quite recently, our family 'suppliers' of cleaners, nannies, tradesmen and ad hoc additional people like window cleaners and gardeners reported in to me.

In the midst of this set-up, I drew the 'org structure' of our family for Wade on the back of a to-do list. I had four 'reports' with an arrow coming at me (our tenant at the time, our cleaner, Lexi's nanny and our real estate agency), and he had no arrows coming at him. I exclusively manage the finding, briefing and management of these family suppliers.

In what was most definitely not a wise thing to say, his comment was: 'Well, why would they contact me for stuff, as they know I wouldn't get back to them?' Dud move, dude.

I need to be fair to Wade here and say that he contributes massively in our home. And he is willing, very willing, and I am extremely grateful. But the fact is that the *bulk* of HQ responsibility – when it comes to the thinking about and running of our house, relationship and family – still rests with me and it's exhausting. And it makes me resentful. And I wonder how the fuck – as a card-carrying feminist and successful (whatever that means) entrepreneur – I ended up with this imbalance.

One of the factors that was key to me in our Let's Start Trying conversation in the Blue Mountains all those years ago was that I wanted us to parent as a team – with 50:50 responsibility for our children. But it's not 50:50. Why is that? I have some theories …

Why are women taking on the Mental Load?

It's all we know

Those of us operating as working women and potentially mothers right now are something of a social experiment. For all of myself and Wade's relationship, we have either earned the same or slightly less or more than each other. This is a very different scenario to our parents' set-ups.

My dad worked six days a week for most of our childhood. My mum worked full-time (five days a week) until I was 11 and my sister was eight, when she went to part-time hours. My dad earned more than my mum, and their agreement – in fact there wasn't even an agreement as it was just assumed that this would be the case – was that Mam would be the almost exclusive manager of the home and children.

Even though she herself was working full-time, the shopping, cooking, cleaning, child-minder recruiting and managing, school liaison, medical appointments and kiddie social calendars all sat with my mum. She would be at work while also mentally ticking through her to-do list at home, and would dash to the shops at lunchtime to get food sorted for dinner. If the child-minder was sick and there was no-one else to look after us, Mam didn't go to work.

I had a few health challenges and needed five operations as a kid, and my mum was the one who took me to most of my appointments, was there when I came around from the anaesthetic and stayed home with me while I recovered.

Occasionally if Mam was out, Dad would cook dinner – grilled pork chops and boiled vegetables and potatoes. I remember this feeling like a special occasion, so it certainly wasn't a weekly or even monthly occurrence.

It's something of a running joke that my sister and I would unwrap our birthday presents and say thanks to our parents – and Dad would smile along, acting as if he had played a hand in selecting whatever the gift was. Geez, when I think about it, my mum has decided on, purchased, wrapped and handed over birthday presents for three people for 36+ years!

Wade's dad has been self-employed for Wade's entire life. His mum only went back to work when Wade was 14, mainly due to health issues.

My point is that neither of us has a model to emulate when it comes to spreading the Mental Load more evenly. All of our parents did the best they could for the time they were living in. Wade's and my generation are essentially guinea pigs trying to unpick an unspoken agreement that has lived in our DNA for generations behind us. And that takes time.

Men don't think there's a problem
When I talk to Wade about the Mental Load, he really does not understand what I'm talking about. He cannot conjure up a picture for himself of how exhausting it can become project managing the show alone most of the time – as he's never experienced it himself … until recently.

As I've mentioned, when I ran my retreat in Bali, Lexi stayed home with Wade. The longest he'd had Lexi solo for until then was two nights over a weekend when I flew to the Barossa Valley for a speaking gig, so ten days was a pretty big deal for all of us.

I was apprehensive about going away – about leaving Lexi for a long stretch of time, and also worried if Wade would be able to cope. There's a very big difference between having her solo for a weekend and ten days when all his work, exercise and other commitments would need to fit around daycare pick-ups and drop-offs, and the nanny's hours. Wade later said:

> Looking back, I can't believe I stressed as much as I did those ten days. Nothing was hard, it was just constant. Being on my own gave me a massive appreciation for the efforts of single parents and for how tough Lorraine must have found it on the Gold Coast. Those ten days also showed me the value of staying 'in the game' with a whole week of Lexi's routine so I would be able to handle it any other time without detailed instructions.

So, all up, a worthwhile experience for all three of us.

Women tend to be the experts

In Malcolm Gladwell's book *Outliers*, he writes that in order to master a particular skill – whether that's as an artist, an athlete or any similar pursuit – we need to devote 10,000 hours of practice to it.

A major challenge with the Mental Load is that – mostly – a woman will stay home with the baby for the first 6–12 months. In doing so, she clocks up 4380 to 8760 hours, so she's already well on her way to being a consummate professional at baby-tending – and likely home-tending, too.

Is it any wonder then that we find it difficult to hand over, or for partners to step in, beyond that point? We have gotten so much practice that it's automatic for us!

I know that Mum is not solely looking after the baby and that Dad is doing his bit often too and that Baby will likely be in some kind of childcare/family care, however for the sake of my argument let's go with it for now.

Women can be perfectionists ...
... including me.

I have a very clear idea of how I want our home, food and lifestyle to be – after all, this is traditionally my domain. I also have high standards for these things, which if I'm honest I wish I didn't sometimes.

Given that, I've also (see above point) clocked up a lot more hours of the Mental Load than Wade has, and I can manage it more easily.

One of the pieces of advice that Sheryl Sandberg gives in *Lean In* is that women accept the standards that their partners apply to child-rearing. In her words: 'Let him put the diaper on the baby any way he wants as long as he is doing it himself.'

I get her point. She's saying that if we women elbow our way in constantly when Dad is trying to do his job, he'll feel less confident doing what he's doing and – ultimately – will decide that there's no point in even trying as he's not meeting Mum's exacting standards.

When I was in Bali, I know that Lexi ate a lot more avocado on toast for dinner than she would have if I was at home – however, that's a pretty unremarkable trade-off for me not to have to think about goings-on at home for ten days so I could focus on creating a wonderful experience for my guests.

It's a very fine line we women – and society as a whole – need to tread when helping dads become more proficient at doing the do when it comes to the Mental Load and raising families.

The hapless, clueless dad is an archetype that has been dialled up for any number of TV commercials, movies and literary butts of jokes. Think of Homer Simpson or the characters in the movie *Daddy Day Care*. It entertains us to see the hopeless dad trying to do his bit, or worse, we patronise him.

While I was away, my friend Leila said that on a few occasions she was about to text Wade to see how he was doing, but stopped herself as she didn't want to buy into the assumption that he wasn't coping.

We get guilty

Every so often, I'll say 'fuck it' and resolve to just not do something and wait for the shit to hit the fan so that Wade will see the full implications of what happens if I drop the Mental Load ball.

One year, I staged a Christmas gift strike – where I decided I wasn't going to run around like a crazy thing selecting and buying presents for his family, who we would be spending the festive season with.

Christmas Eve rolled around and Wade is frantically last-minute shopping for his parents, and of course I'm there helping him as the thought of sitting there on Christmas morning without anything for them made me burn up with shame.

Women are raised to be good girls. We get a tonne of positive reinforcement for anything 'womanly' that we do – whether that's nurturing our smaller cousins, helping our mothers clean up after dinner or selecting a thoughtful gift for our sibling.

Over Christmas, Lexi was playing with her teddies and covered them with her blankie as if she was putting them to bed. Someone leaned over her and said: 'Well done Lexi, you're such a good mummy.' My blood boiled and I had to chomp hard on my tongue.

Men – to a large extent – get a hall pass from this. They aren't expected to be looking after their personal space and the people around them, as – well – they're off doing 'boy things', like playing sport, wrestling anyone who will wrestle them and finding mud.

Any time I perceive myself dropping the Good Girl ball – like when our house isn't tidy and sparkling clean when visitors come over, or we haven't got the perfect gift for a family member's birthday – *I feel so guilty*. As if the Good Girl Gods might smite me down on the spot.

Even if the reason I haven't gotten those things sorted is that I've been interstate on a speaking tour, launching a new campaign within my business or putting the finishing touches to a book, I *still* feel I've failed as a Good Girl.

Last night, I was watching my guru-of-tidiness Marie Kondo's Netflix show *Tidying Up* and the episode featured Katrina and Douglas and their two kids. Both parents work full-time; Katrina as a hairstylist and Douglas as a musician. Marie tours the family's compact apartment – there's musical instruments strewn around the living room and the kitchen is disorganised. Douglas demonstrates how the glasses are piled into the same cupboard as the seasonings. He says the kitchen stresses him out so much that he can't even go into it anymore and he doesn't do any of the cooking. He explains that only Katrina knows where everything is in the apartment, and says: 'Katrina bears a lot of the weight of keeping the house organised and helping us to keep it organised, because we don't know where things are.'

Their teenage son chips in. When he's home alone and can't find what he needs, he'll text his mother, constantly. He says it can get to the point where 'I just spam her phone until she answers. That's how much I depend on her.'

Katrina breaks down in tears. She explains that she feels she's failing as a mother by not getting the home tidied up, alongside her simultaneous duties of doing all the cooking, cleaning and laundry for the family. Plus, of course, working.

'Mom is meant to make the memories, Mom is meant to make home home,' she sobs.

What Katrina is experiencing is the shame of falling short of being a Good Girl.

This stuff is endemic in us as women and it will take time, patience and a hell of a lot of self-awareness as we begin to shed this load. I really do hope that it's our generation that achieves this, but the realist in me believes that this will take a couple of generations to phase out.

The cost of the Mental Load

There are numerous ways that carrying the Mental Load has a negative impact on a woman's life: resentment of her partner and the ensuing relationship difficulties that creates, mental exhaustion and – in extreme cases – longer term mental health issues like depression and anxiety.

Sex and relationship counsellor Susie Tuckwell says:

> On any given day, many more women than men are depressed and anxious. Fatigue and depression may be expressed through irritability and pushing people away, or criticism and low self-esteem. Relaxation, fun and play, time to talk intimately without interruption, time away just as a couple – all of these bonding experiences are often sacrificed as she responds to the tsunami of responsibilities.

However, in my opinion, the greatest impact of all is the opportunity cost of that time and energy being consumed by keeping track of all the moving parts of a household. In my role as a business mentor, I talk a lot about opportunity cost.

Helping my mentees or workshop attendees identify opportunity costs is one of the first areas I tackle when helping them map out their plans for global domination – where are they devoting time to what could be tasks that aren't moving their businesses forward?

For example, providing high-touch service to a low-paying and difficult client. This client is taking up valuable time and mental calories that the business owner could devote to landing a client that would pay ten times the fee of the pain-in-the-ass client, and be a lot easier to work with.

Or personally responding to every customer service enquiry. This task would be much better delegated to a virtual assistant or employee, so that the business owner can free up time to actually improving the service their business is providing.

With the Mental Load, the opportunity cost is a hefty one. It steals focus from the things that actually *do* light us up and move us forward in life – from agenda-free, pure play time with our kids, to going the extra mile on a business project we're leading that puts us right in line of sight for that next promotion.

So what can we do about it?

There have been a few measures that Wade and I have taken that have eased the Mental Load somewhat. I talk more about our relationship in Chapter 13, but here are some of the things we've been doing to ease the burden of the Mental Load on me.

Structured communication

Before Lexi came along, Wade and I would endeavour to have a weekly planning meeting at the weekend – the idea was to compare diaries for the week ahead and divvy up any household jobs that needed to get sorted. Given travel, one of us being out or us just not feeling like it, this meeting actually happened about 50 per cent of the time.

Now with Lexi in the picture, this meeting has *got* to happen. Recently I interviewed one of my closest friends Jules, who is also an entrepreneur, also has a toddler daughter (and now a baby boy) and is also married to an entrepreneur.

We talked about the need for a weekly planning meeting with our husbands, and what the week looked like if that meeting didn't happen. I said: 'A total shitfight.' She said: 'A constant negotiation.' I get what she's saying.

In myself and Wade's Sunday evening chat at the kitchen/ negotiating table, accompanied by our laptops, it's one big negotiation session as we map out where each of us is going to be for the following seven days so that Lexi is cared for. So

I'll do Monday's daycare drop-off and pick-up, while he does Friday's, and so on.

Structured communication like our weekly meeting means that we co-create the plan for the week. If that didn't happen, then I know it would be a lot more of me carrying the plan in my head and reminding myself to speak to Wade to help me execute that plan – meaning we would negotiate daily rather than getting everything sorted in one hit at the weekend.

Project planning meetings

This is a relatively new approach for us, and was born as a result of me getting overwhelmed with managing the detail on major life events. Most specifically, trying to organise an interstate move from Sydney to Queensland while also doing some of the most intense work weeks of my career to date. I have rarely been as stressed as I was in those weeks. I had a few meltdowns and thankfully Wade arranged a back-up moving plan.

Since then, we have tried to sit down and work out together what needs to be done for key projects. 'Projects' sounds like a funny word to use for our second house move or making plans for Christmas, but that's exactly what they are.

To prevent the disaster of the first house move, when we decided to move back to Sydney we sat together and worked out a list of everything we would need to do – and who was going to do it. We booked in dates for myself and Lexi to go to Sydney for house viewings and our ideal date to move. We created a budget for everything we would need in order to rent out our house on the Gold Coast and get to a point where we were moving into a rental in Sydney.

Basically, we both shouldered the Mental Load together – and it made a huge difference to my stress levels.

Last Christmas, we forced ourselves to sit down for our weekly chat at the kitchen table. Wade had just gotten back from two and a half weeks on business in the US and the familiar

Christmas gifting/logistics pressure had been building for me while he was away. It was a week to Christmas Eve and in that time we needed to buy gifts for his family and each other, clear and clean our house as we had tenants over Christmas, and make our plans for the two-week Christmas break so we could arrange Lexi's childcare.

So we made a list of who we needed to get gifts for and what they were getting, bought a couple that could be purchased online, booked in Thursday afternoon for the two of us to tackle the house together, and tacked on our usual weekly planning session.

As a result of that 45-minute conversation, I immediately felt that the responsibility to make Christmas happen lifted from my shoulders and became more of a shared project – which makes it something I'm infinitely more excited to be part of.

Clearly delineated roles and responsibilities

A relationship coach we worked with in the past gave us a (lengthy) handout that was geared at helping couples to reduce arguments over household chores. We never completed it, and thus ensued another few years of chronic catfighting over who does what – or more to the point, who doesn't do what!

The idea is that if each partner knows *exactly* what sits in their realm of responsibility, it becomes very clear if someone isn't lifting their fair share of the weight. It also means there's less scope for ambiguity and assumptions, and that (hopefully) everyone can play together much more nicely as a result.

Thankfully Wade had scanned in the sheet and saved it on his computer system, so we recently blew the digital dust off it and finally powered through all 102 tasks that are required to keep a household running.

We covered everything from who cleans windows (answer: no-one, hello grimy windows), to who organises medications for the family. The goal with the exercise is to allocate as many tasks as possible to just one person (i.e. not to both of you), as you're trying to get rid of unnecessary ambiguity – which leads to assumptions and inevitable let-downs. It also avoids doubling up, and lost time in future negotiation.

For Wade, that's the garbage bins, general insect removal (this is Australia after all), dealing with our real estate agent, maintaining and cleaning the car, and managing our finances (which, thankfully, he has automated to a large extent).

For me, I oversee anything to do with food, Lexi's clothes and health, and the family social calendar.

I have created my own list of household responsibilities that can form the basis for some more evenly shared household tasks, which you can download from my website.

Playing to our superpowers

I can create a meal plan, knock out the resulting shopping list, do the food shopping and pack it all away in less than four hours.

For Wade, this would take close to double the time. He doesn't have the natural passion for all things food that I do, and he tends not to be as ruthlessly efficient as I am on getting tasks like this done.

So it makes sense that I 'own' the food end of our household.

Wade is extremely good at automating the detail in our lives. He has streamlined our finances with an elegant system that means our money comes in, moves around, and lives in certain pots so we know we are constantly saving and also have money set aside for travel and occasional extravagances like a staycation in a hotel.

He will manage detail in a way that I cannot bear to – like setting up our shared Google Drive folders, eliminating a mould issue and getting me out of overwhelm mode with an action-orientated task list.

Identifying what each other's superpowers are has been extremely helpful in accepting each other's natural strengths – and trying to orientate our responsibilities around those strengths. It also means that all of Wade's responsibilities aren't part of my Mental Load.

Being conscious of the models we're creating for Lexi

In her book *Fed Up*, Gemma Hartley raises the vital point that our kids need to see both Mum and Dad operating the household and raising the children.

Wade and I want Lexi to see *both* of us contributing – in the external world of business, community and family, and in the internal world of our home.

I love that Lexi was in my belly while we spoke to hundreds of people at a time onstage together and that she saw me on TV from the green room when she was seven months old. I want to maintain that throughout her life … yet that's not going to be possible now that she's older.

The problem, of course, is that she's happily playing at daycare while I'm running a workshop for 40 people at a corporate, and Wade's leading an all-day offsite training for his team. Or she's at the park with her nanny while I'm mapping out a new business product and the required timelines, contractors and revenue models, while he's at a meeting with a key university stakeholder.

She's not privy – and nor should she be – to the daily agenda that each of us have as business owners. Therefore it's critical for her to see that both Mama and Dada are thinking about, and managing, the home – as that's our world together.

She needs to see Dada, as well as Mama, hanging out laundry or picking her clothes for the day. She needs to see Mama and Dada proactively making plans for the family together, and sharing the workload of implementing those plans, even if it's arranging a barbecue date with friends.

I believe very powerfully that Wade's and my generation has the responsibility to be the circuit-breakers of traditional gender roles in the home, and we need to make equality as patently obvious to our children as possible.

Accepting that done is better than perfect

I have long advocated when I'm coaching entrepreneurs that *'done is better than perfect'*. What I mean by this is – if we didn't have to do it, and it was done reasonably well, then we should not concern ourselves with doing that task ourselves.

For many entrepreneurs who are in the early days of building their team, delegating is a skill that is difficult to adopt. We care so deeply about every element of our business that we are wary of handing over control to even trusted team members – assuming that they won't do it as well as we will. And they won't! They'll do it their way, which we often think isn't as good as our way as it's simply been done differently. But if it gets done well enough without us having to do it, it's better than perfect.

Wade and I have been working to get him across Lexi's styling aesthetic. It must be so weird for a very guy's guy who has never even interacted with a doll or Barbie to all of a sudden be charged with the hair and wardrobe of a tiny, wriggly human.

One day I left for work early and he got Lexi sorted in the morning and dropped her off to daycare. I picked her up that evening and was scratching my head at what she was wearing – a T-shirt, a pair of woolly tights and her gumboots. I asked one of the daycare team if Lexi had lost her skirt, and she said, no – that's how she arrived that morning.

Sure, Lexi wasn't dressed as I would dress her. And yes, I did cringe that she had been rocking that look unbeknownst to me *all day long*. However, the fact is that I got the chance to start work early that morning, and she was dressed.

This one is still very much my classroom and I am trying to be more self-aware of my perfectionist tendencies, and also cutting Wade more slack when things aren't done exactly how I would want them.

Outsource what you can

Outsourcing of home tasks has become wildly popular in recent years, and there are entire batteries of apps, home delivery services and other models to help relieve the Mental Load at home, such as Airtasker, Jarvis, Hello Fresh and even Uber Eats. Getting that task off your/your partner's list by bringing in an efficient third party means that you both buy back energy and time to do things you're more excited about. I myself launched a Cook-up Club this year, as I found that meal planning, recipe sourcing and meal preparation was a huge mental burden for my online community.

In closing

Yes, the Mental Load is fucking exhausting, and can make us quite crazy with resentment. However, it's also a privilege to have it. Wade and I have come a long way on this front, and I hope we continue to work on this together. Both sexes are doing a lot of figuring out when it comes to what our roles are as guinea pigs of equality.

I asked Wade for his perspective on this and he says:

> There are inherent, natural strengths and weaknesses of each sex, as well as real differences, but we need to keep working away at overcoming the challenge of male/female roles. I see a whole generation working at this – I think it's about awareness and we all just need to get on with it.

In closing this chapter, I want to share with you this quote. I saw it as a total reframe of the Mental Load. In *A Woman's Worth* (required reading for every woman in my opinion) Marianne Williamson writes:

> Women will continue to be oppressed, socially and politically, until we recognize the roles traditionally associated with women as being among the most important in our society.

Someone's got to take care of the house and raise the kids. The *I Ching* says that if the family unit is healthy, then society is healthy; and when the family falls apart, society falls apart.

Recognising the value in all the teeny-tiny things that I occupy my brain with day-to-day immediately made me see the overall ROI of what those seemingly insignificant things are doing – they're the glue for our family. And while business is exciting and dynamic and enables me to influence many people, the most important sphere of influence is our little family and the environment it's creating for Lexi to flourish.

CHAPTER 13

Relationship with Wade

I'm starting the first draft of this chapter on a cool, drizzly December morning in Sydney. Last night, Wade and I had our first date night in a month. We watched *Love Actually* at the open-air cinema with a group of friends. We had fancy snacks and snuggled up and giggled together through what is quite possibly my favourite movie. Life felt pretty perfect.

Then, on the drive home, things took a decided turn for the worse. It started with Lexi's childcare plans for next year.

We recently found an awesome nanny who has been looking after Lexi on Tuesdays and for the first half of Thursdays, then Wade is with her on Thursday afternoons. On Mondays and Fridays, she's in daycare – and Wednesday has been my Lexi Day for the last six months.

Unfortunately this new nanny isn't available on Tuesdays or Thursdays next year, so while Wade has been on his US business trip over the last few weeks I've been trying to figure out how we restructure Lexi's care to keep the nanny and make sure that the weekly rhythm still makes business sense for myself and Wade. Lexi adores this nanny, and I wanted to do my best to keep the person who lights up her life so much.

The solution I had gotten to was that I would swap my Lexi Day to Thursdays, we could get Lexi into daycare on Mondays, Tuesdays and Fridays, the nanny would do Wednesday, and Wade could pick up Lexi from daycare early on a Friday to still get his time with her. (Don't worry, you're not required to expend brain calories on understanding this set-up!)

Once I had run through my not-uncomplicated plan, I asked Wade for his thoughts. He communicated that he felt he needed more time to work on his business, in order to make it as successful as he wanted it to be. He said he wasn't getting nearly as much time as he wanted to for it, and wanted to increase that time next year.

'But you've just been away for two and a half weeks with the business,' I said, 'and you already get a hell of a lot more time to work on your business than I do with mine.'

And so it was on.

As he manoeuvred the car through Sydney CBD, he waved a hand in the direction of some office buildings and said: 'There are guys sitting there working right now [this is at 11.30 p.m. on a Tuesday night], and *that's* why they're successful.'

I replied: 'And who do you think is at home looking after their kids while they do that?'

He said: 'They probably don't have a family.'

And I said (ever so maturely and not meaning it *at all*): 'Well maybe you should explore that option.'

This heated discussion turned into a full-blown shouting match at home once we had despatched the babysitter. Wade's points:*

- There was nothing stopping me from working in my business more, I can have as much time as I want to do that.

---

* These points were not delivered in so measured and articulate a fashion as I have outlined here.

- He was fully supportive of me and my business and has never stood in my way of doing anything in it.
- He is prepared to help as much as he can with Lexi and house responsibilities.
- He cannot understand why I am so against him spending more time in his business, which ultimately would deliver a result for us and our family.

My points:**

- It's not necessarily more time I need to make my business more successful, it's mental bandwidth (the fact that I was fired up from writing the Mental Load chapter last week probably didn't help here).
- For him to spend more time in his business directly correlates with me spending less in mine – something has to give in order for him to do that.
- I don't need him to execute more tasks, I need him to take over more of the thinking – he wasn't the one liaising with daycare and the nanny for the last two weeks, I was doing that.
- I resented the fact that he could spend a total of seven weeks away from home over the last six months, compared to my two weeks.
- How could he help out more at home if he was spending more time in his business?

This argument declined rapidly over its one-hour duration and included me slamming the bathroom door (repeatedly) and storming up and down the stairs.

Wade flung the picnic basket onto the kitchen floor, and grabbed his pillow from our bed and stormed to the spare

---

** Neither were these ones.

bedroom to sleep. This is a significant occurrence as he needs to be really triggered to either throw stuff or sleep in a different room to me. I, on the other hand, with my Celtic temper, do not.

It is a blessed miracle that Lexi slept soundly during this ruckus.

We didn't exchange one word this morning before he left for the office, and a conversation will need to be had this evening to try to resolve the events of last night.

I was going to delay starting this chapter until Wade and I were on firmer ground, but that felt dishonest. As ugly as last night was, this is the reality of two deeply imperfect entrepreneurs adjusting to having a child added into their equations. And it would do you, my valued reader, a disservice not to share that reality honestly with you.

From conversations with some friends and mentees, I know that Wade and I are not unique in having these feelings and arguments.

Wade and I are not stupid. In fact, I would place a fairly confident bet that we are both of above-average intelligence. We have both proven that we can run businesses that turn over seven figures a year. We are both considered leaders in our fields and can problem-solve a business challenge quickly and effectively.

Figuring out how to find an even keel where both of us feel we have the freedom and mental capacity to pursue our business ambitions *and* be the parents we want to be? Fucking impossible. And the fact it feels like that is a source of immense frustration – and if I'm honest, shame – for me.

Over pizza one night when Wade and I were in the midst of another tumultuous period, my friend Jules put it so well: 'It's like you and your partner have been running this race together for all these years, hustling in your careers. Then you have a baby, and your partner's still running. You've now got the baby, but you're still in the race. You just have to run twice as hard to keep up with your partner.'

She's right and the incredible unfairness of that cuts me to the quick.

As much as we can have weekly meetings and he can be fully supportive of my business (and he is), things have changed for me in a way that they haven't changed for him.

If I go to work for eight hours, I'm also in parallel thinking about our childcare arrangements for next week and what Lexi needs to have for dinner. I'm also checking in with the nanny if it's a nanny day and fielding any questions that she might have.

Wade does not do this. He goes to work and he's at work. He does not *really* even think about home responsibilities until he steps back in the door.

This is obviously the reality I'm creating for myself.

On a health retreat several years ago, I fell into step with two women on the morning bushwalk. Both of them were mothers and one shared that her husband had pretty much insisted she take the weekend at the retreat for herself. She revealed that she was at breaking point with working and having chief responsibility for their two children.

'The problem,' she said, 'is that men don't keep score like we do.'

And they don't!

The hardest thing about writing this chapter is that Lexi herself has not generated any of this. We have not been sleep-deprived. She has not cried for hours without good cause. She – quite honestly – has not pushed us to the point of real frustration or anger once in her 18 months.

I married a very good man, an amazing man, in fact so much so that I call him my Mr Amazing.

He has never once grumbled about his responsibilities to his family. Becoming a dad has softened him in the most beautiful way. He's an affectionate partner to me, but he is next level affectionate with Lexi. I have never seen someone's heart cracked open so wide as his is with her. He has had my back over a year that I'd quite like to not have repeated. He has provided unwavering support for me, my businesses and my books.

And even with that, our relationship has struggled.

It's a double whammy. Because what I've realised is that it's the relationship with Wade that provides the safe place in the craziness that is a) life with a new baby, b) part and parcel of growing a business and c) dealing with the inevitable stressors that life will send my way. Yet it's that relationship that becomes the shock-absorber with all the other stuff going on.

I know that we are not alone in the challenges we have been trying to navigate together – sometimes successfully, sometimes not. However, I do also need to caveat this with the fact that our individual couple story when it comes to becoming parents was also set to the backdrop of 18 months of the most intensely stressful external circumstances of our relationship to date.

We've had family issues, a financial wipe-out, near bankruptcy, a business sale, a new start-up for me, a rapidly growing start-up for him, oh and let's fling two interstate moves in there, too.

Aside from the competing attentions of two businesses and how we navigate that, there are also a few other key factors that are potentially more universal to other parents when a baby comes along. So, with sometimes painful honesty, let's talk about these.

New-baby challenges for couples

Reduced intimacy

First up, the reduced opportunity for intimacy. Of course, sex is a factor here, but setting that aside for a moment, intimacy is so much more than that.

It's the cuddle on the sofa, the spooning in bed at night, the hand-holding walking down the street. That's the physical intimacy.

Then there's the emotional intimacy – sharing the thoughts you don't share with anyone else in your life or having a partner hold space while you have a meltdown.

If we think about a relationship like a bank account, these intimate moments represent deposits of cash in the account. Over time, the deposits build and accumulate interest, building a relationship that is strong and resistant to external – and internal – stressors.

A baby comes along and for many couples, the opportunity to create new deposits is dramatically reduced.

I remember noticing this on the very first night that Lexi was at home with us. She was 22 hours old when we settled into our bed as a new family – Wade on one side of the bed, me on the other, and between our two pillows, there was now a teeny-tiny baby in her little baby nest. It was a crazy pinch-me moment.

I also realised that I couldn't reach Wade in bed without stretching over Lexi. For years, we had fallen asleep holding hands and most of the time my legs were draped over his. For the next six weeks that Lexi slept in bed with us, that didn't happen.

We still snuggled down on the sofa, but the star of the show (rightly so) was now this little 3.4 kg bundle of cuteness. Rather than Wade and I entwining on the sofa, one of us now held Lexi and we spent most of our time gazing at her sleeping face or listening to her ickle-baby sounds. We were – and are – smitten.

Cooking and eating dinner in the evenings used to be an opportunity to connect after each of our days and a hug, a touch on the hand or shoulder as we passed each other in the kitchen was exchanged almost unconsciously. We'd talk about the minutiae of our days and the other would chip in with a suggestion, pep talk or question.

Now, as new parents, one of us would be holding Lexi while the other tried to get dinner on the table as quickly as possible. The focus shifted from being about time for us to be intimate, to getting the task at hand completed.

In the final weeks of our pregnancy, I asked my Instagram followers what Wade and I should be making the most of before we stepped into our new roles. 'Hold hands' came my friend Roisin's reply. I wondered then how the hell you couldn't hold hands just because you'd had a baby!

When Lexi arrived, I realised what she meant. If the three of us were out and about, one of us would be pushing the pram – meaning one hand generally wasn't available to hold the other one's hand. It became almost a novelty when Lexi was in the Ergo and we could hold hands!

Another factor, of course, is that there's an addictively cute new person who is capturing probably hundreds of kisses, cuddles and 'I love yous' that previously were sent your partner's way. Wade and I put a rough estimate that Lexi gets a minimum of 50 kisses from both of us every day (sometimes more) – and she's 18 months old.

We have found that our intimacy has been dramatically reduced since we had a baby. As a result, the regular cash deposits that we had been lovingly putting into our relationship bank for the previous 7.5 years dropped immediately.

Reduced time to do the things that make you you
A few months ago, I was doing a mentoring session with someone who wanted to start her own business, and also wanted to have a baby over the next couple of years. Her ideal strategy was that she'd get the business established, and so would have more flexibility than her current corporate job offered when the family came along.

'The problem,' she said, 'is that I just can't find the time to focus on getting the business started.'

At this point, I put my pen down, put my palms flat on the table, looked her square in the eyes and said: 'You have so much time right now. In fact, you have *no fucking idea* how much time you really have.' (No-one chooses to work with me for sugar coating.)

Before Lexi was born, my evenings and weekends stretched out in what (comparatively) seems like endless hours filled with potential. I would set off on a walk around Centennial Park on a Saturday afternoon – no phone, no agenda, and walk for hours processing through my thoughts, connecting dots and problem-solving issues in the business. I'd come back filled with 'aha' moments and ideas to share with Wade.

I was committed to travelling overseas every year to immerse myself in the marketing industry so that I could come back laden with insights and global case studies for our clients at The Remarkables Group. I would jet to NYC with a month's notice as there was a conference I wanted to check out, and while I was there run around Manhattan having coffees with people whose perspectives I wanted to hear. I would come home itching to share my downloads with my long-suffering husband, and we'd talk for hours about what I had learned.

Wade – having been in the full-time Australian Army – has since been in the Army Reserves for five years. He would regularly go out bush for a weekend or week with the Reserves. Getting rained on, sleeping on hard ground and being surrounded by dozens of other men who have also not showered for days is (amazingly) his happy place. He would return home with his face still smeared in war paint (as I called it – it's actually called 'cam cream'), dirt from head to toe, with a sack of disgustingly smelly clothes – and he was quite literally as happy as a pig in shit.

His participation in those exercises has fallen off a cliff in recent years, mostly due to his business commitments, but also as Lexi is with us now. If he's going to use his 'away from home' credits, then he feels he should put them to the most sensible cause, and devote them to growing a business that will provide for our family.

I listened to a Goop podcast episode recently, in which Gwyneth Paltrow interviewed intimacy teacher Michaela

Boehm. Michaela explained that what creates attraction and intimacy in a relationship is 'polarity' – so two opposites coming together. I guess like magnets!

By me going off doing my international study tours, or even a long walk in the park, I was investing in all the things that made me, well, me. Ditto for Wade as he lost himself in army exercises in the bush. After doing those things, we'd come back to centre together with an abundance of fresh ideas, energy and interesting new things to say to each other.

The dramatically reduced time we now have to do those things has meant that they have dropped in priority and accessibility. It's not to say that we *can't* do those things now. I did, after all, just go to Bali for ten days to run my retreat and Wade had a business trip to the US two weeks later. However, in order for us to do them, it requires a logistics effort that didn't previously exist – as well as a simultaneous pull on the other one's time and energy.

So you have a situation where the opportunities to create that polarity are less present than they were, and that has a knock-on effect on the dynamic of the relationship.

More life complexity

Then there's the fact that life is just more complicated when you have a small human, or multiple small humans, to keep alive.

Until their age is in double digits, they can't be left alone for five minutes. They require constant cleaning, feeding and monitoring. For years, they're asleep more than they're awake in each 24-hour period, which requires them to be at home in their bed, being listened out for in case they wake.

Everything their parents need to do – work, exercise, socialising, time with each other – needs to be designed around their existence, as a Small Human's needs come first, as they should.

This makes life complex.

My family are all in Ireland and Wade's family are in Port Macquarie, so the only support we have had is paid childcare – nannies and more recently daycare. Having no support around us means that the pressure on each other is peaked, making life even more complex.

Once we were back from Europe and Lexi was three months old, I took my yoga studio membership off pause and committed to getting back into a regular exercise routine. The challenge was *when* I'd do the three classes per week that I had committed to, as I needed to be home when Lexi woke between 6 and 7 a.m. to breastfeed her, and again between 6 and 6.30 p.m. for her bedtime feed, while three days a week I was at the office until 4 p.m.

Wade and I discussed it and decided that my only option would be to do a class at 6.45 p.m.

He would work right up until the last safe moment at the office, then he'd hop on his bike and cycle the ten minutes home. I'd put Lexi down at 6.30 p.m., run to change into my yoga gear and be standing at the back gate watching for him riding up the street – at which point I'd race to yoga to make my class. He never once was even a minute late as he knew how important it was to me to make that class.

Pre-baby Lorraine would just decide on the spur of the moment to grab a yoga class – a very alien concept to me now!

For such a small person, Lexi has increased tenfold the complexity of what I know were already above-average complex lives. Simple things like an exercise class, coffee with a friend or a date night don't just happen anymore – they require planning, negotiating, coordinating and careful execution. Logistics, logistics and more logistics …

And the problem is that logistics are not sexy. At all. Revisiting our idea of things that raise our vibration and things that lower it, I would be surprised if any person said that managing household and family logistics raised their vibe!

So what can we do about this state of affairs?

Over the last 18 months, there have been a few things that have helped a lot:

The weekly planning meeting

To a large extent, this means that we can knock over much of the weekly logistics in one hit. It also means that we're both aligned heading into the week and that we minimise surprises (like me factoring in a yoga class on Thursday night assuming he'll be home, when he's actually got a team dinner on).

Split Saturdays

We did this during a hectic period round the six months' old stage and it worked brilliantly. Wade would take Lexi for the first half of Saturday so I could have a morning to myself. I'd do a yoga class, have breakfast on my own and maybe get a massage. It was heaven. I'd get back for us to have lunch together (and give Lexi her lunchtime feed) then Wade would go do his thing while I spent the afternoon with Lexi. Usually Wade would go to the office, but sometimes he'd add in a gym session or catch-up with a friend. We'd have Sunday together as a family, with myself and Wade both feeling topped up from our few hours to ourselves the previous day.

Gold stars

As I have already mentioned, for me these are critical. Since having Lexi, I have developed a deep-seated need for Wade to give me grown-up gold stars. I need him to see all the things I'm doing to keep her thriving, our house in order and my business growing.

This flummoxes him. In his mind, we're each just getting the shit done that we need to get done, and the appreciation and acknowledgement of the other's contribution is assumed. He genuinely looks bewildered when I thank him for putting out the bins or for sitting with Lexi till she falls asleep when she's unsettled.

I'll say it again, I need my gold stars. Coming from the business world where my output was measured in terms of revenue, media coverage and awards, transitioning to the world of invisible achievement was a shock.

No-one gives you a high-five for helping your baby gain 100 grams in their earliest days. No-one takes you to a bar for a drink for managing business and Baby for a week. No-one pats you on the back for staying calm and collected with your child, even though it's 3 a.m. and you have a full schedule of meetings the next day.

So give me *allll* the gold stars, damn it!

It's the deep work that we really needed ...

As I come back to the second draft of this chapter, we are wrapping up the first working week of the year after a two-week break over Christmas and New Year.

Rather than going away somewhere after a Christmas spent with Wade's family, we decided to stay at home and spend ten days getting our act together as a couple.

We were coming off the back of the toughest year in our marriage, with the external stressors of some intense financial pressure, selling/growing businesses, an attempted tree change and a lot of physical separation between us.

One of our major – in fact, the most major – goals for the Christmas break was to get right down into the weeds of where we were at individually and together. Over a series of days, we examined every area of our lives and our relationship, and started to piece it back together into a plan to move us forward.

The exercises we did were:

Vision and values

We had a long discussion about what values we held to be most important for us as a couple. We have both set values with our teams in our businesses, but never thought to do it for ourselves.

We got down to six values, which are now the guardrails for our interactions, activities and goals.

We also articulated what our vision for our life together is, and what the purpose of the whole thing is. Our lives are nowhere near as complex as some couples we know, however they are definitely on the more complex end of the spectrum – so knowing WTF the point of it all is has been a gamechanger.

Wheel of Life

This gave us a good base to compare notes on where each of us was at, and what areas we wanted to focus on over this new year and beyond. You can get this worksheet on my website for free.

Five-year vision and one-year vision

Using my Setting Your Vision worksheet (also on my website), we individually worked through our own visions, then shared them with each other over a delicious lunch (food is always a help with this work – ha!). Beyond that, we identified our goals, and knowing the other one is onboard with what we want to achieve means we are so much more likely to hit those goals.

Perfect Week

This one took *hours* for us to agree on. We are both growing businesses, and we both want time with Lexi. We don't have family around us, so in order for one of us to be at work/the gym/yoga/out with friends/anything outside of Lexi's daycare hours or our nanny day, requires the other one to be back at the ranch taking care of her and doing the daily grind of running a household.

This meant that every one of our goals and desired weekly commitments needed to be negotiated with each other and planned into the week. Before she graced our lives, a change like me increasing my weekly yoga classes from three to four (one of my health goals for this year) would have been simple. Now, it requires Wade being onboard, and careful scheduling in both our calendars. It also requires a heavy focus on life systems, more of which I'll cover in Chapter 16.

We eventually got there with our Perfect Weeks and the clarity and focus that has given us has been incredible. Wade led the charge with diarising everything as recurring calendar invites, and this is the new rhythm. It's been revolutionary.

Striking a deal

Over the course of our talking last week, I realised the source of much of the resentment I held last year – since we had Lexi I feel that my life has changed in many ways that Wade's hasn't. For me to go to Bali for ten days was A Very Big Deal for both of us, whereas he has spent weeks travelling and it's accepted without comment.

We are both growing businesses and have equal financial responsibility to our household, but I also have the title of Main Caregiver for Lexi. As an out-and-proud feminist, this has rankled me – particularly last year when there were many other intense external stressors that we were trying (and often failing) to deal with.

If I'm honest, it felt like we were in competition for much of last year, with bucketloads of resentment on both sides. We spoke very honestly about this last week, which was painful and scary. However, we hit upon A Deal and it has immediately made our playing field clear.

The deal is that Wade will work double the hours that I will this year, and I will retain my role of Main Caregiver. In return, he'll be Acting Main Caregiver for five weeks this year so that I can run some business events, tour my new book, and have some time away on my own and with friends.

Each week, he'll also spend one morning and one evening with Lexi so I can do a breakfast meeting and get that fourth yoga class in, and he'll take her on Sunday afternoon so I can have some chill time.

On the surface, it seems like I'm still taking on a lot more than he is, but I realised that he hadn't had the benefit of five years child-free to build his business like I had with my first one. And between you and me, I've set myself a target to earn as much as him even with half the hours to devote to my business each week. We women are nothing if not resourceful and I'm doing this one for us girls!

Assigning household responsibilities clearly

We talked about this in Chapter 12, and having a clear delineation – and accountability – for who does what has removed a lot of unnecessary communication and angst.

Diarising the crap out of everything

Wade has spearheaded getting our new Perfect Weeks in the calendar – so things like his morning and evening with Lexi come up as recurring diary notes each week. We also have a day together booked in to keep our conversations going from last week, and to bank an adventure together – the idea is that this will keep us on track and feeling connected like we are now, regardless of how hectic our year might be looking.

Also in our diaries are our quarterly visits to interstate friends (one of our Friends Goals) and our holidays. This means that there is always something to look forward to – a tip I picked up from Global CEO of Business Chicks Emma Isaacs' book *Winging It* – and that there's quality time together to create space between the weekly rhythm we've designed.

Getting out of the house to get deeper

I do think it's important that this deep work is done outside of the wallpaper that is our homes, at least in part. We went to a new beach, walked around the city, did a bushwalk and revisited all our old homes together. This triggers happy memories, and summons in fresh energy to think big about our lives together.

We got to conversation topics that we probably wouldn't have sitting at our kitchen table the whole time, plus – as Wade wisely pointed out – I didn't get distracted with household tasks like flinging on a load of laundry or prepping food!

It's not easy, but my God is it worth it.

The rewards of deep work

The benefit of doing this work goes far, far deeper than a band-aid weekly date night. We needed to get aligned, seriously aligned. It amuses me to think that two people who run successful businesses and spend an inordinate amount of time on building the vision and culture of our teams have never thought to apply that same approach to our relationship with each other!

Having done that work last week – and, of course, it is still early days – we both know precisely where we stand. We know what each of us is bringing to the table. We know where we're going. And we know the checks and balances that will keep us on track.

If there's more friction than frolicking going on in your relationship now, then I suggest you consider working on some of these exercises together. Even better: do them *before* a rocky patch.

If the time isn't available to work through this process (ours all up took the guts of a week), then picking off more accessible exercises like assigning the household tasks and striking your own version of A Deal would be a good – and productive – place to start. But honestly, I think the Perfect Week exercise is a non-negotiable.

So what has Wade got to say about all of this? Let's hear from him ...

Combine reduced sex with the loss of intimacy, reduced face time, increased logistical burden and reduced flexibility to respond to other areas of life – especially business – it appears to be all doom and gloom. Before we had Lexi, some people said, 'Your life will be over.' I can appreciate why they said it, but I don't agree with it at all. Lexi has been the best thing that ever happened to me and I love everything about having her in our lives.

What we've learned

My biggest relationship insight from this entire journey we've been on together is this:

It is so damn easy to prioritise kids (and let's face it, they don't give us much choice!) and our businesses/career – oh and the machinations of running a household.

The fact is that it's our romantic relationship which provides the safe cushion for us to rest our heads in the maelstrom that is all of the above. It's the oil on the cogs, the smoothing of the waters.

When Wade and I are firing on all cylinders – time together, working as a team, hot and connected sex – life is infinitely better. My business hums along with effortless ease, my mood is bright and sparkly, time at home is fun and refuelling, money flows steadily into my life. I stand up straighter, my whole energy is lighter.

And when we're the opposite?

Well, life is the opposite. And the worst bit is that it's really, really fucking lonely.

Placing the much-needed spotlight on my partner in life has stepped up my life on every level – and that's how I want it to stay. And how we need it to stay for Lexi.

CHAPTER 14

Mum Guilt

Once I joined the Mum Club and became privy to conversations with other mothers, I was shocked at how much guilt women carry about how they perceive themselves doing as a mother.

Mum Guilt is a thing.

And it's making millions of women unhappy every single day.

One blogger – Kate from Hurrah for Gin – even gives Mum Guilt a persona: The Shitty Guilt Fairy. In her comical illustrations, Kate claims that 'The Shitty Guilt Fairy' rocks up for the first time to a new mum during her labour, announcing her arrival with 'Congrats Mummy! I'm here to make your life suck.'

Getting to work straightaway, the Shitty Guilt Fairy proceeds to add her own commentary to the birth – whispering 'Junkie' in a mum's ear as she has an epidural, or 'Cheater!' in another's ear as she has a caesarean.

One of my mentees Kristy Goodwin shared a joke with me a while back: the gist of it was that the injection that women can have after their baby is born which speeds up the delivery of the placenta (also known as a 'managed third stage of labour') isn't *actually* to get the placenta moving, it's – in fact – a shot of Mum Guilt.

With my 'fellow mum' hat on, and also with my 'business coach' hat on, I have had probably hundreds of conversations or references to Mum Guilt. And it pisses me off.

Five reasons why Mum Guilt pisses me off

1. The men aren't worrying about this one either!

Quelle surprise – Dad Guilt is hardly a thing. A Google search for it throws up 10,100 results.

Tap in 'mum guilt'? That's got 62,900 results. And 'mom guilt' garnered 381,000 results.

Mum Guilt is mostly a ladies-only club. Like a random email newsletter that drops into your inbox, that you have zero knowledge of signing up for, Mum Guilt sneaks its way into your life and pervades a scary amount of real estate in your already over-stretched brain.

Going back to our top chick Caitlin Moran's definition of sexism: 'Are the men doing it?'

The boys most definitely are *not* worrying about their crushing Dad Guilt, therefore I take great issue with the fact that women are expected to worry about it – and, worse, *expect themselves* to worry about it.

I'm not saying that many men would not like to have more time with their kids. However, they are not losing sleep or crying into their pinot noir with their BFF about how guilty they feel about the fact that little Harper hasn't seen him for breakfast for two days running, or that he had to take a call while he was supposed to be having quality time with little Jack.

Men are black and white ... enviably so. A man will accept that this is how things are right now, then that's how things are. Whether that's not being home for bedtime, or missing his child's birthday as he's on a business trip. In a man's eyes, that's the way things are. End of.

As I write this, Wade has just come back from more than two weeks in the US for business. Sure, he missed Lexi while he was away. However, he never felt *guilty* for being away from her. He had a job to do while he was there, so he did that job. He came home early from work to have dinner with her the day after he got back and generally drowned her in affection. End of.

Women will angst about these same things, telling themselves that they're a terrible mother, that their kids must feel unloved/neglected, or are going to grow up to be homeless/drug addicts/reprobates as a direct result of the day-to-day choices their mother is making.

I think we could learn a lot from men.

2. It's a waste of brain calories

I learned about the concept of 'brain calories' from entrepreneur and entrepreurial mum poster woman, Tracy Harris – she of Mums with Hustle.

During an interview for her podcast, we discussed my various hacks for getting more organised – the goal being that we flow more effortlessly through life and feel significantly less frazzled.

Tracy built on what I was saying, with the insight that we 'save brain calories' by being more organised. I told her I was going to steal that, and I'm staying true to my word!

If we're choosing to limit our daily calorie intake, we have a set amount of calorie 'credits' to use for the day. If we set ourselves a limit of 2000 calories, then we might choose to expend 500 calories on breakfast, 500 on lunch, 500 on dinner and 500 for a couple of snacks or a glass of wine over dinner.

The idea of 'brain calories' is that we more than likely have X amount of mental bandwidth to use each day – and those calories get used for our work, kiddie logistics, meal planning, social plans with friends, remembering items X, Y and Z that's required for that meeting/school day/accountant tomorrow, troubleshooting a problem with a client, weighing up the red dress or the jeans/cami combo for the party next week, daydreaming about a future business to create, wondering why our sleep wasn't so good last night, and endless other things.

I try to limit the amount of sugar I eat, as I get sugar-high scarily quickly, and the ensuing comedown is not fun. So when I do plump for gelato, a doughnut or chocolately dessert, it's a big treat – and it needs to deliver.

Wade is familiar now with the look of disappointment that flashes across my face when I have the first spoonful of sugary treat. 'Not worth the sugar?' he'll ask. 'No,' I'll reply as I shake my head sadly.

The reason it makes me sad is that I've allowed myself the sugar hit, but if the taste and enjoyment factor doesn't live up to the hype, then I've essentially wasted that sugar hit – that could have been spent on something fabulously delicious. It's the ultimate opportunity cost.

Mum Guilt is an absolute waste of brain calories. And as A Busy Mum (oh don't you love that stereotype – anyone heard of A Busy Dad?), we do not have these calories to waste.

3. It makes us feel that we're always failing

From the questions I've asked working mums, I've learned that the biggest 'fuck you' that Mum Guilt delivers to them is that they feel like they're failing in both areas of their lives. They feel their work is suffering as they're a parent, and that their kids are suffering as they're working.

As we already chatted about in Chapter 10, from our Lady Hero Michelle O, failing is a feeling before it's ever a reality. Shouldering the burden of Mum Guilt every single day is only taking us in one direction. *Hint: it's not to smouldering success on both the work and home front.*

If we allow ourselves to be consumed by Mum Guilt, we will eventually manifest that reality in our lives – whether that's by falling behind in our careers (not having the confidence to go for that promotion, playing small in our businesses as we don't feel worthy of the revenue or team size we'd secretly love), with our kids (resenting them and their needs, losing our tempers) or our partners (snapping at them, stewing on our issues with them).

As I write this in a café in Ultimo, out the window I can see a woman helping her little boy walk along a raised garden bed. He's gorgeous, blond and looks the same age as Lexi. He's taking tiny tentative steps as he walks along the foot-high garden bed, coaxed by his mum. He just got to the end of it and she swung him in the air, much to his delight. Now she's scooped him up onto her hip and they're happily walking down the street.

Seeing them, I'm not feeling guilty that I'm not doing the same thing with Lexi. She's at home with her nanny as I type. I get to be here, hopefully writing a book that will help thousands of people. And that's pretty cool.

4. It doesn't serve our kids

Pop quiz time!

Which of these is going to be better for a child?

Option 1: a mother who embarks on her work and parenting with a sense of confidence and respect for herself, and acceptance that she is blending her work and family day-to-day.

Option 2: a mother who spends significant portions of her days (and nights!) worrying that she is falling short as a mother and business owner/employee.

I've said before that our generation has a role as the change-maker between The Old Paradigm (traditional male breadwinner set-up, woman's career takes a radical back seat to his career while she has sole responsibility for family and home) and The New Paradigm (women creating successful careers/businesses alongside a family and more even distribution of responsibilities for family and home between male and female partner).

I truly hope that Lexi doesn't have an expectation placed on her that she should be guilty about – or worse need to choose between – her successful career and having a family.

The evolution from where women are now to where we could be doesn't take place with the advent of the #MeToo or #TimesUp movements, trail-blazing protest marches, government lobbying and online petitions. Those things are amazing and have a key purpose, but they don't percolate down to the humdrum that makes up all our day-to-day lives.

It starts in our homes. In the tiny threads that make up the tapestry of the everyday.

There is some pretty scary research that shows that a child's blueprint for their entire life is formed by the age of four. Yep, their blueprint for how relationships should be, how successful they are (be that at sports, reading, art or music), what work represents to them ... everything.

Discovering this has made me hyper-aware of what behaviours Wade and I (and me specifically, given that Lexi is female) are modelling for our child.

At the age of 18 months, Lexi sits next to me while I do my make-up, swatting my make-up brushes at her perfect, juicy little cheeks. She grabs the kitchen cloth and wipes down her little table after her dinner. She (much to Wade's annoyance) reacts with horror to cockroaches, as that's exactly what she's seen me do – true-green, wimpy Irishwoman that I am when it comes to Aussie creepy crawlies.

When I was preparing for my ten-day trip to Bali, I started to feel the twinges of Mum Guilt about leaving Lexi for so long. I shared my feelings in an email to Katherine Pinner, one of my guests on the retreat, who was leaving her 2.5-year-old and eight-month-old daughters back in the UK to come join me in Bali.

'We want to raise independent women and what better way than to show them!' she wrote back.

That put me in my box pretty firmly, I can tell you!

Do I want Lexi to see me feeling guilty about leaving her to go to work, knowing that's the blueprint she'll carry through for her life? Hell, no.

In an interview for her podcast, coach and all-round Earth Mother Claire Obeid and I discussed how important it was for our daughters to see us excited by our work. Claire described how she explained to her toddler daughter Soleil that Mummy was going to work, and conveyed how excited Claire was to do the work she was about to do.

This is important stuff. Seeing us, their mothers, collapsing under the weight of Mum Guilt sets a benchmark for our kids for the rest of their lives.

Remember also that 93 per cent of communication is non-verbal – and kids are scarily good at picking up on energy. This Mum Guilt Revolution begins by us actively choosing not to subscribe to the burden that it brings in our own minds, and radiating that out into our lives and – more specifically – our interactions with our kids.

So let's do it for the kids and ditch the Mum Guilt.

PS: If you're reading this and Mum Guilt is something that you struggle with, this particular point is not aimed at making you feel even more guilty!

Mum Guilt is our Inner Mean Girl at her nastiest

My gorgeous friend Melissa Ambrosini dedicated her entire first book to the delights of our Inner Mean Girl. She's a bitch – the Mean Girl, not Melissa.

In *Mastering Your Mean Girl*, Melissa writes: 'Your Mean Girl is that voice inside your head that is constantly feeding your negative chatter. She lives in a perpetual state of fear and is always telling you you're not good enough ... She's all about judgement, labels, comparison, roles, masks, expectations, fear and fitting into a neat little box ... None of which are the truth of who you really are.'

5. It disempowers our kids

I've just finished reading US writer Anne Lamott's book *Operating Instructions*, about the first 12 months of her son Sam's life. She was a single mother and recovering drug user, who wrote a warts-and-all account of what that first year was like.

Anne was beating herself up endlessly for the fact that Sam wouldn't have a dad, that she wasn't in a financial position to give him the lifestyle she would have liked to, and that (in her opinion) her mental health was questionable.

She shared her feelings – or Mum Guilt – with her friend Larry in a phone call. Larry said to Anne that she was 'just an opening for Sam to come into the world, that I wasn't supposed to be a drug for him. I was just supposed to be his mother.'

This resonated with me. As mothers, we can often see our roles as being to protect our kids from every painful emotion, negative interaction with another person, or situation where they may be in danger.

It's hardwired into our DNA – from right back to thousands of years ago, when we needed to fiercely protect our cave babies from being stomped on by the stray foot of a woolly mammoth, from being gobbled by the cannibals of the neighbouring tribe, or from falling into the smouldering embers of last night's cooking fire.

The idea of Lexi ever being hurt, or even vulnerable, quite literally hurts my heart. I want to protect her from ever being in that position. However, that's just not realistic. I cannot be with her 24/7 to keep mean kids away from her, protect her from the bite of a mosquito or stop her tumbling off her little chair (even though its seat is only 15 cm from the ground, she still manages to do this ... frequently).

Last week at home, she fell off her little chair, headfirst into a wooden cube. She cut her forehead and needed a cuddle for 60 seconds before she trotted off to seek out more toys from her bedroom.

On Sunday, I was at a new playground with her and an older little girl out of the blue pinched Lexi's arm. Lexi squealed and looked to me for reassurance – I told her she was fine and the little girl later came and apologised to Lexi, who was more interested in the little girl's dog.

Yesterday she was on the receiving end of a cuddle from a child in her room at daycare. The hugging child lost their balance, toppled them both over, and Lexi knocked her cheek on an abacus (as you do). She cried for five minutes in the kind arms of one of the daycare team, and promptly forgot all about it when lunch was served. I was greeted at daycare pick-up by a pretty bad graze on her cheek, which hopefully will resolve itself before Santa photos in a few days time.

Back before Christmas, Wade's dad sent us both a text asking us to bring a stair gate with us for our stay at their new home, in his words 'to protect Lexi'. I wrote back saying that we'd taught her to go up and down the stairs in our new house, as we figured that was easier than watching her like a hawk constantly as she adjusted from bungalow life to the steep stairs of our old cottage. As a result, she flies up and down the stairs like a little spider monkey, only sometimes accepting a lift from one of us (which is only offered to speed up our exit from the house!).

In a recent YouTube video, *12 Rules for Life* bestselling author Jordan B. Peterson says (on how we can protect our kids): 'You don't get rid of the vulnerability. You teach them to be strong.' I love this perspective and subscribe fully. If a core factor in Mum Guilt is us worrying if our kids will be ok without us, it is much more useful for our kids (and kinder to ourselves) if we focus our energies on building them up to be independent, adaptable little humans. Beating ourselves up for not being around more doesn't empower them, or us.

Kids are endlessly resourceful, independent and robust, and I believe we need to give them credit for that, rather than being fearful that they're somehow going to go to pieces if we're not around. If we're ok, it's infinitely more likely that they'll be ok.

So how do we deal with Mum Guilt?
I've got a short answer and a long answer to this question.

The short answer: We opt out of it altogether
I'm serious. In 2015, I was a speaker at the Business Chicks inaugural conference, 'Movers and Breakers', at Uluru. As a speaker, I got to go along to the other sessions with the conference guests and a highlight for me was seeing Global CEO Emma Isaacs interviewed onstage. One of the questions posed to her was, 'How do you deal with Mum Guilt?' Emma's response was that, well, she didn't.

She went on to explain: 'Guilt is a wasted emotion that serves no-one.'

To have someone that I respect enormously dispelling Mum Guilt up on that stage was a pivotal moment for me, although I didn't realise it at the time.

This was before Wade and I had had the Let's Start Trying conversation, and kids were not on my mental horizon at all. However, Em's comment was clearly internalised for me, as it made me realise that guilt is something that we can consciously choose not to buy in to – whether society expects us to or not.

If I was to put my (horribly uncomfortable, by the way) Mum Guilt hat on, there are many, many things I could probably allow myself to feel guilty for:

- Let's start with the fact that I wrote a book when Lexi was a newborn.
- That I toted her along to meetings in London when she was 11 weeks old.
- That I left her with a nanny or her dad for three days a week when she was three months old.

- That she had been on 30+ flights before she was a year old.
- That I left her with her dad for a weekend while I attended to business in Adelaide when she was 14 months old.
- That I frequently pay a nanny to take care of her while I do a yoga class.
- That I left her for ten days at 16 months old.
- That she's in daycare rather than with me while I write this very chapter to you today.

If I were to wear my Mum Guilt hat, I could probably go all day at this.

But I try my utmost not to put that hat on – 'cos really, what's the point?

The long answer
Beyond trying our level best to not buy into the Mum Guilt, here are a few tactics that may help you negate the impact that the guilt cycle is having on you in your life:

Remember that your kid/kids chose YOU
I'm kicking this off with a distinctly spiritual bent. Strap yourselves in, we're going deep, people!

We need to remember that our children – back when they were twinkles in our eyes, singular sparks of energy floating around the Universe or little cloth-nappied cherubs dangling from a stork's beak – selected their parents.

They selected them knowing all the weaknesses, scope for improvement, life commitments and general human-ness of those parents. They may even have chosen those parents knowing that those same parents may decide not to bring that baby down into the earthly world, or that one of those parents would be largely or fully absent in their lives.

Our children didn't come to us expecting these perfect humans who would live perfect lives and perfectly manage the blend between their perfect careers and their perfect family. They knew what they were getting in to, and they chose anyway – which is why they're with us now.

The day before I departed for Bali, I posted on Instagram about the feelings of trepidation I had about leaving Lexi ... mainly, would she think Mama had abandoned her?

My ever-wise friend Peta reminded me that: 'She chose you knowing exactly what work you're here to do, and how you're here to do it.'

Whether you're working 50 hours a week in your corporate job, are at home full-time with your kids, or you need to be interstate every fortnight for your business, remember that your kids knew you and knew the work you were engaged in, and they were – and still are – ok with that, even if there are times when it seems they're not.

Be selective with the opinions you take onboard

When Sarah's daughter Cara was less than a year old, she travelled to Melbourne with me for a trip to see influencers and clients. On one of our days there, we had lunch with some influencers who were the same age as us and had kids of a similar age to Cara.

On learning we were in Melbourne for two nights, one of the influencers (with a look of pure confusion on her face) asked Sarah: 'But who's got Cara?'

Sarah was taken aback for a moment before replying (equally confused) with: 'Well ... she's with her dad.'

After lunch we marvelled that the question came from a woman who was also a working mother, and discussed in depth if there was some kind of veiled (and totally unintended) inference that Sarah shouldn't have left her infant daughter to travel for work.

Most women will have comments like these aimed at them – and often the comments are packaged up as being 'well-meaning'. These comments might be related to the number of hours they choose to work, or the age their kids are when they choose to go back to work, the food they feed their family, the fact that they travel for work, or any combination of other life choices they make for them and their families.

I'm reminded of a Christmas meme that went around a couple of years ago: 'Tis the season to have your life choices mocked at the dinner table.'

Many of us – sadly – feel that we're constantly defending our life choices when it comes to our family, and – probably even more sadly – to those who are close to us, or who we feel should be more understanding of our position.

To help combat this – and combat is absolutely the right term to use here – we need to weed out anyone who consistently makes us feel like shit about how we're choosing to live our lives.

I've spoken to many business owners who felt on the outer perimeter of their local mothers' group, as the other women just didn't 'get it' that they needed to work even though their babies were tiny.

This isn't solely related to business owners either. We all know people – especially fellow women – who make us feel less than. And often those people are directly related to us ... which makes it pretty difficult to exit them from our lives!

In just the last month three women have separately shared with me that their own mothers make them feel most guilty about the fact that they're working mothers. No doubt this is due to the fact that these mothers are probably looking at their daughters as if they are aliens, compared to how they themselves raised their kids a generation ago.

One of the women who shared her thoughts comes from a traditional Italian family. Her mum is completely disinterested in the fact that her daughter runs a business – even being unaware of the fact that her daughter has a real office with real staff, and that the business hit $1 million revenue in its first year – and is constantly berating her daughter for not spending more time with her kids.

Obviously it's not possible to give these people the red card from our lives, so the strategy here is to employ our forcefield from Chapter 3. When I feel like I'm on the receiving end of some not-so-endorsing opinion, I'll visualise my forcefield coming down around me – and Person X's opinion bouncing off that forcefield.

Maybe it's because I've mostly surrounded myself with people who accept my life choices around business and family, or because the forcefield over time has stopped people from sharing their 'observations' on my life, but I rarely – if ever – am on the receiving end of judgey comments now.

I also 100 per cent believe that if our own self-acceptance is high and we're not self-flagellating ourselves for how we are raising our families, that the opinions and comments of others just don't fan the flame or trigger us as much as they would if we're already operating in a place of self-doubt and questioning our decisions.

Recently I listened to Oprah interview NBA star Dwyane Wade and his wife Gabrielle Union. The major topic of their conversation was around the couple's struggle to conceive, and ultimately their decision to have their daughter via a surrogate.

In one part of the conversation, Gabrielle shares some of the negative (and indeed, obnoxious) comments that had been left on her own social media channels and online media stories about the birth of their daughter.

Oprah exclaims: 'But why would you even read those comments?!' And she goes on: 'You're reading them and it's hitting the nerve that you already have. The comments can't affect you unless you already think it yourself.'

We are dramatically more resistant to – and probably tolerant of – guilt-inducing comments or opinions when our own self-image is robust.

Find your tribe

Connecting with like-minded women who build us up and make us feel like rockstars is another effective weapon in banishing the Mum Guilt from our lives.

The fact that I have women in my inner circle who are both fellow entrepreneurs and fellow mothers makes me feel normal, and accepted, and valued. If I didn't have those women in my life and instead I felt I was constantly going against the grain to those who didn't make similar choices to me, then it would be a hell of a lot harder to assuage the Mum Guilt for myself.

That's not to say that if we're entrepreneurs we can only have fellow entrepreneurial mums in our tribe. My friend Jules – an astute businesswoman – counts her friend Jessie as one of her BFFs. Jessie has chosen to be a stay-at-home mum and has no plans (at this point) to start her own business. Yet the two of them are truly great friends, there for each other for the highs and lows of their journeys through life.

Acceptance is one of our deepest human needs, so surround yourself with people who accept you for who you are.

Celebrate what you are doing well

As I listed earlier in this chapter, there are many things that I could potentially feel guilty for in my relatively short history as a mother so far.

The first thing I can do is reframe that list into positives.

For example, leaving Lexi with her nanny Iva for two days a week when she was three months old could be reframed as: 'Isn't it awesome that Lexi gets to hang out with someone else who adores her each week, and that she gets lullabies sung to her in Czech?'

Or the potential guilt that Lexi has flown so much and been in multiple time zones: 'How cool is it that she's so familiar with aeroplanes and airports and that she gets exposed to the new sights, smells and people of other cultures?'

The second thing I can do is celebrate all the stuff that I have done super-well: breastfeeding exclusively until she was 13.5 months (no easy thing to fit around working), feeding her incredibly nutritious food (yesterday I counted that she'd had nine different fruits or vegetables by lunchtime), creating an environment whereby she's open and trusting of new people, or making sure she lives in a clean and (kind of) tidy home.

If you're reading a book like this, I know that you're committed to your own personal development and to that of your family (or future family).

If you have kids, I know that you are doing things – tiny, apparently insignificant things – every day that no-one but you probably knows about.

You might whisper a certain phrase in your child's ear every night as you take them to their bed like we do, make sure that their favourite food is stocked in the fridge for the week ahead, or greet their classmates by name at the school every morning.

You're also doing big things, like moving house or changing jobs to work around your family.

I have a quote stuck up on the fridge, which reads: 'With gratitude, all fear disappears.' Taking a similar philosophy, we could say that: 'With recognition for yourself, all Mum Guilt disappears.'

I've created a worksheet that you can grab on my website to help you banish the Mum Guilt, by helping you firstly identify what you're specifically feeling guilty about, and secondly to help you recognise yourself for everything you *are* doing well – and I know that you are.

CHAPTER 15

On expectations

Last week, I received a direct message on Instagram from one of my followers, Jess. She wrote:

> You've been a total inspiration to watch! Although I feel a bit like I cannot possibly do half of what you've achieved on nine months of broken night's sleep. Do you think that makes a difference? A baby that sleeps through versus never slept through, and how that impacts on energy and motivation? I keep questioning why I don't feel I can achieve the same! It's the comparison hangover of Instagram, too.

I have so much to say on this topic – a whole chapter, in fact. To me, Jess's question and all it encompasses – comparison, the pressure we put on ourselves, questioning our own abilities – all boils down to expectations; and mostly our expectations of ourselves.

First of all, let's talk about sleep

Yes, it *does* make a difference.

There is zero doubt in my mind that without decent sleep I would not have been able to launch and complete the various projects that I have since Lexi was born – including moving house interstate (twice, for our sins), selling my first business, running a retreat in Bali, hosting a national workshop tour and even writing this book. No doubt at all.

When it comes to my wellness and my sanity, sleep is the absolute foundation that everything else is built on.

As sleep expert and founder of The Kind Parenting Company Kylie Camps points out:

Sleep truly is a pillar of health and wellness, not just physically but also mentally and emotionally. When our sleep is compromised we are impacted. It is not a matter of pushing through. Sleep is as critical as food and water, we simply need quality rest to function. When comparing the side effects of sleep deprivation against the list of symptoms for postnatal depression, they are similar.

I've already shared that we have been inordinately lucky on the sleep front with Lexi, and managed to dodge the extreme sleep deprivation that many parents experience – especially when their little one is fresh out of the oven.

I am (obviously) no expert on this space, but something I did on the advice of my Auntie Ellen was to get Lexi used to putting herself to sleep when she went to bed. Of course, many times she fell asleep on the boob and it was deadset the sweetest thing I ever did see. However, as much as possible I would try to put her into her bassinet dozing but awake so that she got used to the experience of falling asleep on her own.

That is not to say that Lexi has not impacted our sleep negatively – she has. For us though, it's more of an occasional big night than a constant occurrence.

Just last Sunday night, Wade slept in the spare room while I took a teething, coughing and feverish Lexi into our bed. She woke up distraught at 10 p.m., then hourly until 1 a.m., did a solid wailing stint from 2 to 3 a.m., woke up again at 6 a.m., and finally at 8 a.m.

We finally arose to a room strewn with baby painkiller, teething powder, snotty tissues, wet face cloths, various bottles of coconut water/milk/water, vomit-stained towels and clothes, and a very very tired toddler and her mama.

Lexi was in no fit state to go to daycare on Monday, so I parked any aspirations to work on the launch of a new business product and set up for a day of sick-baying. I was seeing stars and wondered how we'd make it through the day.

To add to my anxiety, I had four jam-packed days for the rest of the week, that included launching a new product within my business, a two-day training event for entrepreneurs, two interviews, and three half-day sessions with my one-on-one mentees.

Miraculously, Lexi had a 4.5 hour sleep – bless her, she was equally if not more wiped than me – and I powered through as much as I could of my new launch. I quite honestly surprised myself that I was able to produce quality work given the state I was in. That night, Wade was on duty while I slept in the spare room. And of course, she slept through.

I can tell you that if we were experiencing ongoing sleep challenges, I would be hiring in the big guns with no hesitation whatsoever. In my opinion, babies need their sleep just as much, if not more, than grown-ups. They've got a whole lot of playing and growing and exploring to do – and they need sleep to do that.

I know myself that when I'm really exhausted, I don't function anywhere near as well as I would with a decent sleep under my belt. I don't eat as well, I'm snappy and most definitely over-emotional. Why would children be any different?

I have had friends whose lives have changed as a result of getting some help with sleep training their kids. Without exception, they have wondered why they didn't tackle their kid's sleep issues earlier.

Teaching our kids to sleep is one of the greatest ways we can help them. I shared a great quote on Instagram recently: *'If it makes you feel like shit, change it.'* This – I believe – 100 per cent applies to helping kids sleep so that their parents can sleep, too.

Of course, broken or chronic lack of sleep is going to hamper your efforts to build your career or business – so set yourself up for success by nixing sleep problems as much as possible with the help of experts.

There are hundreds of people whose life calling is to help sleep-deprived babies and their parents, so ask around and get some recommendations from friends on who you can turn to. You don't have to sacrifice yourself on the altar of sleep deprivation.

One of those experts is Kylie, who says: 'Teaching your little ones the skill of independent sleep when appropriate is truly a gift. Sleep is critical for optimum development and processing for infants and toddlers alike.'

Now, let's talk about comparison

It is very easy to assume that someone else's life as a mother/professional is perfect – and that we are the only ones suffering in whatever way we're suffering at a particular moment.

I adore Instagram as a channel – I have built a beautiful like-minded community on there and the accessibility Instagram gives me to them brings me much joy and fulfilment, not to mention the heroes and heroines I get to access there.

All of that said, I have serious concerns about how many of us make the mistake of assuming that what we see on tiny Instagram squares is the absolute reflection of someone else's life.

I've read it many times that social media is just a highlights reel – and it's true. However, in moments of doubt, or loneliness, or fear, I myself have often fallen into the trap of believing that Person A, B or C's life is blissfully perfect, and that I'm falling short in many ways in my role as a mother, wife, partner and friend. And let's not even get started on not sporting a honed physique as I tote my six-month-old baby on my hip!

Instagram is not real.

Let's say it again: Instagram is not real.

It's a lens applied to a very small part of someone's life, which is then filtered to look fabulous, cropped to hide any mess/ugliness, and generally posted with some kind of wise/funny/insightful caption.

Remember also that even if someone is as honest and authentic as they can be on social media, some things may be going on that are too painful or raw for them to share in real time online.

Yes, I have gotten a lot done in my business since Lexi was born. However, I've also experienced a financial wipe-out, Wade's and my relationship has gone through its roughest patch to date, and I had a horrible period where my parents and I weren't speaking for two months.

As much as I like to share my life on Instagram, each of those things were far too distressing and brought with them a horrible emotional burden of shame, fear, grief, self-hatred, anger, resentment and frustration – and I didn't feel either able or willing to share that with the worldwide web until I'd worked through those challenges myself.

There is an expectation that we should share every bump in the road live with a social media audience, but that's not healthy and it's certainly not realistic.

I have been for lunch dates with groups of close friends who have not asked me one single question about my life as they assume that what they see on Instagram is an accurate representation of what's going on. I fell that little bit more in love with my BFF Richenda when she messaged me one day to say, 'So tell me, what's going on behind the Insta stories?'

Please don't base your expectation of yourself on the pretty squares of someone else's life. You have no idea what's going on in their world, and nor should you. Just as they don't know what's going on in your world, and nor should they.

Comparison will kill your motivation, your self-belief and your spirit.

You won't get as much done as you did pre-Baby

I am all for buying into anything-is-possible and all that great stuff. I really am. It's held true many times in my life.

The fact is that my ability to be productive has changed since Lexi arrived. Obviously, there is a lot more to physically do – feeding, changing, winding, bathing, figuring out how the fuck you get this small child out the door with all the equipment they need just for a supermarket visit. That physical activity requires energy.

During a session with my favourite Bali healer Jimmy Doyle, he talked to me about 'The Trance'. His theory is that a woman's body puts her into some kind of trance when her baby is born – that magicks her into being able to find the time to devote hours upon hours to caring for this tiny person that has materialised in her life.

'How else,' Jimmy questioned me, 'do you think that you – this woman who didn't have time to scratch her own arse [he's not your traditional healer, Jimmy!] before this baby came along – all of a sudden has all this time to cater to Lexi's every need?'

He was right, something powerful, physiological and secret must have been at play.

Then there's also the mental activity. It has blown me away how equally easy and difficult it is to be in the present moment with Lexi.

Easy, as she's utterly bewitching and creates a moment in time all of her own when I'm with her.

Difficult, as we constantly need to be one step ahead of where she's at.

She's about to wake up in the morning? Bottle or boob needs to be ready to roll. She's having her breakfast? Face cloth and dishcloth need to be ready at the table. We're on a morning adventure? We need to be heading towards home by 11.30 a.m. She's having her nap? Snack needs to be teed up ready to hand to her when she wakes up. She's on her way home from daycare? Dinner needs to be on her little table. And so on and so forth ...

This 'staying one step ahead' has almost been a mental muscle that I've flexed over the months we've been together – it's my Future Self principle, but the stakes are much, much higher. Anyone who has experienced an over-hungry over-tired toddler after a day at daycare will be in no rush to repeat that particular episode!

The result is that we require not just physical energy to look after our child, but mental energy, too. Michelle Obama put this so well in her book *Becoming*. She said of her career post the birth of her two daughters: 'I was now more cautious, protective of my time, knowing I had to maintain enough energy for life at home.'

I would not hesitate to identify that I squeezed too much into the first year of Lexi's life, and my friend Peta Kelly did the same. Her little girl Sol is a month younger than Lexi, and there were many parallels between our experience of pregnancy and the first year of the girls' lives – including publishing a book when they were 5/6 months old, moving house (her internationally, me interstate) and launching new businesses.

Comparing notes on where we were at, Peta shared with me that she had gotten her own lightbulb moment from a healer. This wise woman had recommended that for the first 18 months of a baby's life, the parents shouldn't make any major life changes – for the simple fact that 70 per cent of the mother's energy is still required for her baby (whether she's breastfeeding or not). The insight is therefore that too big or too many changes can easily lead to overwhelm for the mother.

Peta and I both marvelled at how we had quite literally done the opposite of what this healer suggested!

When I discussed this with Peta as I was editing this chapter, she added an additional point. For her, she had set her business up so well that when Sol arrived, there wasn't anything that she desperately, urgently needed to fling herself into. However, her body and brain were so conditioned over years of entrepreneurship to powering through and constantly seeking to be productive that she maintained that pattern for months after becoming a mother, until she found a new pace that enabled her to be the mother and the business owner she wanted to be.

My point here is to accept that you are likely not going to be firing on all engines like you were pre-baby – for the simple fact that much of your time, energy and focus is being devoted to caring for your new addition.

Get ok with that – and if you do find that you have the capacity for big business growth or a promotion in those early months, then treat it as a wonderful bonus.

Yesterday I was listening to entrepreneur Jenna Kutcher on her Goal Digger podcast. After two years of painful false starts, Jenna and her husband were finally expecting the arrival of their first baby.

I was blown away when she shared in the episode that she had managed to pre-prepare an entire six months of content – that's podcast episodes, social media posts, blog posts and other material.

Her reason? She didn't know how she'd feel when her baby arrived, so she didn't want to place any expectation on herself to do anything in those early months. Now this, my friends, is great advice.

Saying that, you may surprise yourself

If you had told me that I'd be able to run a half-day mastermind session for six entrepreneurs, jump in the car and eat lunch as I drove, then run another half-day training session for 15 team members from a major tech company on just two hours' sleep, I would have laughed in your face.

But I did when Lexi was ten months old and had us both up for most of the night with travel-induced exhaustion when we had just landed back from our Bali adventure.

Pamela Jabbour was up all night with a colicky Lucas before her very first external meeting she attended after maternity leave (a tough procurement/contract review discussion). In her words: 'I got up, dressed up and showed up. A power suit, lots of make-up to cover the dark eyes and coffee got me through. We secured a new contract for two years.'

We, as humans, have an incredible ability to surprise ourselves with hidden and unexpected resilience, strength or sheer Get Shit Done grit.

And mothers have this in bucketloads. Our bodies are designed to cope with broken sleep, dramatically increased workloads on the home front and moving between multiple – and sometimes conflicting – demands on our time. If we hook this in with doing work we actively enjoy and find flow in, then we really can surprise ourselves on the upside over and over.

The key is self-belief.

Henry Ford famously said: 'Whether you believe you can or believe you can't, you're right.' I adore this quote and have leaned on it a number of times, both pre-Lexi and since her birth.

Honestly?

My mindset on getting up at 5.30 a.m. and creeping around the room so as not to wake Lexi that morning after we got back from Bali was not positive. I was crying, freaking out at how I was going to not let down my clients, stressing about how Lexi would go with the nanny I had hired for the day, and panicking at how I could hide my washed-out face and dead-in-my-head eyes for my meetings.

I realised that if I believed I wouldn't be able to achieve what I wanted to achieve that day, then I wouldn't achieve it.

So I switched my mindset.

I visualised myself smashing both half-day sessions, everyone getting exactly what they needed from me, and Lexi having a brilliant day. And that's exactly what happened.

Yes, approaching business with a baby is more complex and brings its challenges, however our ability to overcome those challenges comes with belief in ourselves.

You're still smart

It makes me sad when I can see a woman's confidence has been dented when she gets back to work after having her baby. Sure, we may have been cocooned in milk, nappies, baby puke and teethers for weeks or months. But we're still *us*. We still have that experience, those skills, those connections.

Since having Lexi, I feel like a softer, more emotional version of myself – but I can still write. I can still speak onstage. I can still build rapport with someone quickly. And I've learned that being a parent is an excellent ice-breaker with any number of people I come across in my work – from CEOs of corporates to new mentees.

Having a baby is an epic identity shift to make, and it stands to reason that that may make us feel wobbly in terms of our own self-worth in the workplace. If you're feeling this right now, remember everything you achieved to get to where you are in your business or career. You're still that woman. You've still got it.

There is no fucking around

Interviewing one of my mentees, Janine Wade, the other day, she dropped this gem. And it pretty much sums up everything there is to say about how work (be it your own business or your job) changes once Baby arrives.

A mortgage broker, Janine had – she thought – set herself up beautifully in her business for the birth of her first baby. She had hired a gun administration manager to deal with the back end of the loans she was managing, and teed up another mortgage broker to take on any deals she didn't have the capacity or desire to manage.

Unfortunately the admin manager fell very short on standards, and Janine had to make the very tough decision to exit her from the business just two weeks before her due date. Janine was now stressing out bigtime – her baby was coming and her business was not ready.

So how did it all turn out? At our interview, Janine shared that she was still managing both the broker hat and admin hat within her business – and running it while her now eight-month-old son Bear had his day naps. She hadn't revised her revenue target from her original admin manager plan, and her monthly revenue was currently sitting at just 20 per cent of what that target had been. Amazingly though, when she worked out her hourly rate for the time she was spending in her business, she was making *significantly more* money.

'WTF?!' I said. 'How the hell is that?'

Janine explained that she had become ruthless with the kind of clients she accepted since Bear came along, as she simply didn't have the time to waste if they weren't going to move her business forward.

This meant that she stuck rigidly to the minimum loan amount that she wanted to handle, and she declined to work with referrals from past clients she had worked with who themselves had been difficult. In the past, she said, she would have felt sick refusing any potential client. But no more! Janine also said that her intuition is stronger since becoming a mother, and that has served her bigtime when it comes to selecting which clients to work with.

I fully agree with what Janine says. Pre-baby Lorraine would gladly say yes to 'can I pick your brain' meetings, afraid of what the other person would think if she said no to their request. Today's Lorraine politely declines these requests with zero compunction. Pre-baby Lorraine would spend days angsting about having a difficult conversation. Today's Lorraine quite literally cannot wait to get that discussion over with so she can free up the brain calories for more worthwhile activities. Pre-baby Lorraine would say yes to commitments like awards judging, unpaid mentoring and vague coffee brainstorms about potential collaborations. Today's Lorraine says no to 95 per cent of these commitments.

The simple math is that I am building a business on approximately 50 per cent less of the time I had before Lexi came along, and approximately 60 per cent less of the mental bandwidth I had before she came along.

So in order for me to say yes to a client, a meeting or a speaking opportunity, there needs to be a rock-solid justification for that yes – energetically and commercially.

Another element of this is that there is an added premium on the quality of decisions I make, as there is less time available to a) explore various options and b) mitigate any potential negative outcomes of said decisions. My friend Jules and I were talking in her kitchen just the other night about how deciding on our next business steps has changed post-kids, and she summed it up with: 'I've made so many dumb-ass business decisions – but back then I had all the time in the world to fix them.'

Dealing with the expectations of others

There are few things that elicit the expression of expectations from others more than the arrival of a new baby – from how others think that baby should be birthed, to how others believe the baby should be fed, when they should be fed, when they should sleep, when they should wean, when they should get teeth … On and on it goes.

I get it. It's part of our basic human psychology to evaluate what others are doing and benchmark it against our own experiences and beliefs. I find myself doing it all the time –

before I catch myself and remind myself that I would hate for someone else to place the judgements or expectations on me that I'm putting on them. In my opinion, this is karma at its best!

The level of expectation others place on new parents is intensified when it comes to the new mother and how she plans on working – or not working – after the baby is born.

British writer, author and podcaster Pandora Sykes posted an ode to her nanny on Instagram a while back – and railed at the expectation that many people had that she wouldn't go back to work, or if she did, that she wouldn't need childcare as she was a freelancer. It read:

> Will you return to work?
> They asked, with tender concern.
> What does your husband do
> (Whispered) *How much does he earn?*

People will often place an expectation on the mother, which is purely based on their own scope of experience and values – and is no way whatsoever related to the mother and her situation.

And this is what we need to remember. Those expectations of others are *in no way whatsoever* related to you or your situation.

Earlier on in Chapter 3, we talked about OPS – Other People's Stories. I shared how I would imagine a forcefield dropping down around me when someone started to enlighten me on how our birth would be, how difficult it would be to live on no sleep, how I wouldn't be able to write my book with a newborn and so on. The result is that I didn't take on that person's stuff, it essentially bounced off my imaginary forcefield.

This is exactly what we need to do with other people's expectations of us. It is for every couple, parent and child to figure out the way of doing this that works best for them. Everyone else can take a flying jump with their baseless, unsolicited and irrelevant expectations.

I'm sure there were people who didn't think I should go back to work three days a week when Lexi was eight months old, who questioned my decision to write my book when she was small, who didn't think I should go to Bali solo with her. But I honestly couldn't tell you who they were, as I had zero interest in their expectations of me, Wade, Lexi and my work.

One of the most powerful allies you can have in dealing with an onslaught of expectations from others is to find your tribe of people who 'get it'. I know many women with their own businesses who didn't feel that level of belonging and acceptance at their local mothers' group – and many who did.

Surrounding yourself with those who a) don't place expectations on you and b) accept you for who you are, brings with it a wonderful sense of relief, support and validation. Find those people – and nurture your relationships with them.

We need to be our own best bosses

Marketing guru and author Seth Godin wrote a blog post back in 2010 entitled 'The world's worst boss', pointing out that – whether you're self-employed or not – you are your own boss, managing everything from your career and your week to your daily emotional responses. I love this idea, as it puts the power for our own lives right back where it should be – with us ourselves. He even says: 'If you had a manager that talked to you the way you talk to you, you'd quit.'

In order to achieve the blend between business/career and Baby, you do not have the option *but* to be your own best boss. That means speaking to yourself in an encouraging way, not smashing your tender self with negative self-talk. It means prioritising the things that should be prioritised, and not frittering time away on things that ultimately aren't important. It's working when you're meant to be working. All of this, of course, needs to be served with a hefty side portion of acknowledging that once we're parents, we may be the boss of ourselves – but our kids are the CEOs!

Just yesterday, I marvelled at how Lexi had Wade and me trailing after her trying to tempt her with any number of tasty foods. She had just come off the back of a solid fortnight of a teething-induced almost fully fruitarian diet, so the two of us were desperate for her to eat something more substantial – and pathetically dedicated at least 30 minutes to presenting her with delicious food options, much to her absolute disdain. We knocked out at least five courses in our amateur-hour degustation dinner – and all to no avail.

It goes without saying that our lives are no longer in our own hands once children come on the scene, however as much as possible we need to be our own best bosses.

Small steps trump giant leaps, always

I have always believed that small steps taken consistently every day will reap more rewards than occasional gigantic leaps.

Small steps are achievable. They're consistent. They do not overwhelm.

Gigantic leaps scare the shit out of us. They require epic levels of guts, energy and time.

With a baby or few babies added to your equation, you might not be feeling hugely courageous. You might be easily overwhelmed. And you might not know where to start – whether that's starting a business, growing your existing business or getting back into the swing of work after maternity leave.

My advice? Figure out where you want to be – make it realistic and achievable with the amount of time and energy you have to devote to it.

Work back from that goal with what you need to achieve this quarter, this month, this week, each day. Then start there.

I would much rather that someone who wants to start a business while on maternity leave spends 30 minutes each day on that business. For example:

- Day 1 – Buy the domain name you want
- Day 2 – Ask for recommendations for a web designer
- Day 3 – Email three web designers
- Day 4 – Review three quotes
- Day 5 – Decide on a designer

At this pace, within a couple of months you'll be ready to roll. Consistent small steps trump haphazard fits and starts. Always.

CHAPTER 16

Life systems

As you can imagine, as someone who had written a book on getting organised, I was pretty organised before Lexi made her sweet appearance.

I was organised as I was starting and growing a business, and given I was wearing all the hats – marketing, sales, admin, project delivery, finance, HR, client management and probably 20 more – I didn't see how I had any option *but* to have my shit together. If I didn't, balls would drop and the whole shebang would come crumbling down around my ears.

Add a baby, my second business, Wade in serious growth stage with his business, and no family support around us, and I very honestly did not know how this would run without some very deliberate and repetitive steps to look after our Future Selves as much as humanly possible.

If getting organised is a specific area of challenge for you, then I would love for you to read my second book *Get Remarkably Organised*.

For the purposes of this book, we've talked in numerous chapters about how we can be more organised as a business person/parent – whether that's how we get ready for Baby to arrive, preparing a business for us to step out of, or coping with those heady newborn days.

I want to talk specifically for a while about life systems, and I'm dedicating this chapter to those – essentially a subset of my overall *Get Remarkably Organised* approach.

In business, systems are all the rage. There are entire teams devoted to creating and building new systems in corporates, and almost every entrepreneur I mentor is seriously focused on streamlining the systems in their business.

Why?

The fact is that systems enable businesses to grow. If every customer complaint response needs to be written or approved by the founder/CEO, then that business is going to grind to a halt pretty quickly.

The CEO will be caught up in investor meetings, recruitment or the gazillion other pressures on her or his time. It's only by building effective systems that they can gradually start to hand over the reins to other people, trusting that the cranky customer will be looked after in a way that they themselves would approve of.

That means identifying a list of common complaints, workshopping appropriate responses/make goods to those complaints, and writing canned responses that can be tailored to the individual complaint.

The founder now knows that they have given their input into how things should be done, and rather than them becoming a bottleneck, they can now just be called in when the shit really hits the fan with a particular customer and only their top-level status can resolve the situation.

How else has McDonald's managed to build a multi-billion dollar business with hormonal teenagers as practically the sole interface with its customers?

How is Airbnb valued at more than the world's biggest hotel brands (including household names like Marriott and Hilton), valued at US$53–65 billion in just ten years?

How has founder of Spanx, Sara Blakely, become the world's youngest self-made female billionaire?

I'll tell you: systems.

Of course there's also a bucketload of vision, purpose and sheer graft behind these success stories. But a willingness to stay up all night or take your team on the journey to what the future could be is worth sweet FA if the founder still needs to be across every detail and function of the business. That's where systems step in and truly enable a business to scale.

'*Yeah yeah yeah Lorraine,*' you may be saying right now. '*But what's this got to do with a kid?*'

My friend Nicola Swankie and her husband Craig are both entrepreneurs and parents, and they shared something a while ago that stuck with me. They said that they run their business like a family, and their family like a business.

When I explored this with Nicola as research for this chapter, she elaborated:

> We are both passionate about family and business. For us to both be able to build our businesses, spend quality time as a family and, just as importantly, look after our own self-care requires strategy, goal setting, resource planning, dreaded but essential budgets and lots and lots of logistics with shared calendars and communication. If we didn't have this business-like attitude to the organisation of our family, and instead let things go with the flow a bit more, I truly believe so much of what we achieve and experience wouldn't be possible. It helps keep us happier as people, a couple and parents!

So running our family like a business doesn't mean that the entire family runs around with name tags on, every day starts with a check-in on the agenda, that we send our kids a message on Slack to say that dinner is ready, or that we dial in on Zoom to family movie night if we're travelling.

It does mean that we get our shit together, just like we would in a business. That we have a clear structure in place to enable every family member's life to run more smoothly and relieve – as much as possible – the intense complexity that comes with having a family, whether we also have businesses or not.

The goal with building these life systems is that we save time and energy (mental, emotional and physical) by reducing or eliminating the amount of thinking and tasks we have on our plate.

In doing this consistently, we free up progressively more and more space to devote to more fun and more productive things – and reduce the friction between us and our partners and our kids. You know, actually enjoying our lives day-to-day!

I'll give you one quick example of this in our household.

For as long as I can remember, when I envisaged a future us with a family, the mornings always looked intensely stressful. Trying to corral kids and get ourselves out the door – for whatever reason – felt to me like it was going to be horrific. I don't know if this was based on the various movies/TV shows/ads we get served to us. It probably was.

The scene generally runs like this: parents are (sometimes literally) pulling their hair out in the mornings while they snatch bites of cold toast in between brushing a wailing child's hair. There is a lot of screaming – from grown-ups and kids – and the adult invariably forgets something urgently required for the day ahead, which involves racing back home and then being late to an important meeting.

It may sound crazy that a first-time pregnant woman was already worrying about the mornings with her growing family – talk about long-term forecasting in the anxiety stakes!

I believe that the two hours after we wake are the most critical for our entire day, as they set the tone for everything that will happen before we crash into bed again that night.

This has been researched and proven over and over again – when our mornings are calm and productive, our days are calm and productive. I was very genuinely apprehensive about how my mornings would change with a small human in the mix, and the knock-on effect that would have on my days, weeks and months.

We have (very) evidently entered the toddler phase – as I write this Lexi is 19 months old. She now has tantrums over what to us seems like utterly illogical stuff.

Exhibit A: this morning she refused to wear the crisp white turndown ankle socks I suggested, and instead wanted to wear one almost-dead pink and white sports sock and one grey knee sock with her shorts to daycare. This kicked off a five-minute 'discussion', and ensuing negotiation – which I lost.

Thankfully, after breakfast and forgetting about the sock situation, she allowed me to swap her back into the much more aesthetically pleasing socks and off to daycare we went.

As we walked into daycare, Lexi's arms swinging with anticipation of the fun to come, I had this moment of very consciously realising how fun and peaceful our mornings are – and what a revelation that has been to Wade and me.

We feel light and playful with Lexi, and each other. We eat great food before we set off on our respective days, and don't feel we're bolting it down. There's time for cuddles, for curve balls (refer to the sock situation) and for cleaning up.

I don't know how long this will continue, but while it does I'm profoundly grateful that we each get to enjoy our mornings and have essentially set up a positive feedback loop that tells us that mornings are easy, fun and calm.

The reason that they're easy, fun and calm is that there's a whole operation running behind the scenes to make them so.

When you visit Disneyworld, everything is happy, bright, uplifting and running smoothly. However, it's an incredibly elaborately choreographed operation, with thousands of cast members (staff), rigorous briefings and rehearsals, and a plan for every eventuality behind the scenes.

The infrastructure of systems – rather than weighing down Disneyworld guests – actually creates the space for them to run carefree through the parks, knowing that every detail has been designed with the express intent of providing a fun, stress-free experience for them and their families.

Because Wade and I want a Disneyworld version of our mornings with Lexi, that requires a Disneyworld level of structure to make it a reality. And that means looking after our Future Selves, bigtime.

Critically, Wade and I know who's doing what so there is zero discussion required about roles and responsibilities in the morning. For us, the infrastructure looks like:

- Our bags and Lexi's bag (if it's a daycare day) are packed for the next day the night before.
- Our food and Lexi's food (if it's a nanny day) is packed and in the fridge.
- Myself and Wade's morning lemon drinks and Lexi's morning bottle are prepped and in the fridge the night before.
- Breakfast is planned and, if possible, prepped the night before.
- Wade and I get up early so we have time to do our own morning routines before Lexi wakes up.
- We are showered with hair and make-up done (me, not Wade!) before Lexi gets up.
- Buffer time is factored in to allow time to leave the house and for toddler curve balls.

There is obviously a lot of work that needs to be completed every evening – however, that hour of prep each evening has such high ROI that I simply couldn't imagine doing it any other way. The structure each of these small systems creates enables our Future Selves to enjoy the freedom of a relaxed morning.

And that, my friends, is why we want systems at home. So where do we begin?

Start by planning your Perfect Week

As organised as Wade and I tried to be in the first 18 months of Lexi's life, things didn't fully click into place until we successfully did this exercise together.

As I mentioned in Chapter 13, we did a shitload of work on our relationship recently and one of the lynchpins was us individually mapping our Perfect Weeks and then negotiating those weeks until we found a fit that allowed both of us to achieve what we wanted to each week.

Once you do this exercise – for yourself if you're a solo parent, or with your partner if you have one – you will be so much clearer on where all the various elements of your life fit together into hourly increments of your week.

Our Perfect Week

We've finally found our groove: a weekly rhythm that flows with apparent ease and nourishes all the most important parts of our lives – Lexi, our relationship, our businesses, our health and our friends. Our current Perfect Week looks like this:

- Lexi is at daycare Mondays, Tuesdays and Fridays, and I do most of the drop-offs and pick-ups unless I have business commitments at those times.
- On Wednesdays I have Lexi Day and that evening Wade does bedtime so I can do a yoga class.
- Saturday mornings are for house admin – Wade does the grocery shopping while I do laundry and tidy the house.
- While Lexi has her Saturday nap, I do my weekly cook-up and Wade goes to jujitsu.

- Sunday mornings are dedicated to a family activity.
- Once Lexi is down for her nap, Wade and I have our weekly meeting then a leisurely Sunday lunch together.
- Wade and Lexi have time together that afternoon while I have some tank-filling time.

For us, it's a great balance of business time, Lexi time (all together, and for Wade and me individually with her), the exercise we want to do, and the activities that fill each of our tanks – him getting strangled half to death by hairy, sweaty men and me by lying on the sofa for a blissful couple of hours reading and mainlining chocolate.

It is very, very rare that the whole thing runs like clockwork, but the endeavour is to get it as close to that as possible. Wade travels for two weeks at a time, and when that happens of course the whole thing has to adapt. And that's fine.

Michelle's Perfect Week

My rockstar business manager Michelle Broadbent is a single mum to Ruby (12) and Tilly (nine) and runs her own business supporting entrepreneurs. Here's Michelle's Perfect Week:

Mondays I can work from home until around 5 p.m. as the girls go straight from school to their activities so my Mummy Uber duties don't kick in until later in the day.

Tuesday mornings I drop Tilly to band rehearsal early (Ruby gets herself to school) and then head straight into the city where I work from a co-working space all day. This is super productive time for me as I don't have any of the domestic distractions that I have at home. My girls stay at their dad's on Tuesday nights so I usually make the most of already being out in the city and meet a girlfriend for drinks or dinner, or go on a date.

Wednesdays I work from home. Because I don't have to get up and get the kids out the door, I start work early and then have a break mid-morning for my regular dance class. Wednesdays are the only afternoon each week that my youngest must do homework, so I finish work at 3 p.m. to collect her from school and supervise. We also have family dinner as both girls are home.

Thursday morning Tilly has a music lesson and then I drop her to school and head straight to a café where I work for the morning for a change of scenery or a work meeting. I drop Tilly to gym after school (a one hour round trip) and tend to jump back into work for an hour or two once I'm back home while keeping an eye on my tween's homework efforts.

Friday I use to wrap up the week and business/personal admin. If I have my kids that weekend I will try to schedule lunch or coffee with a girlfriend so that I get a fix of adult company. I then do school pick up and we always have afternoon tea and an early evening movie, and then early to bed for everyone before we have to get up at 5.15 a.m. for the Saturday gym run.

I spend all Saturday morning driving to or watching their sport, then use Saturday afternoon to prep for the week – washing, making dinners for busy weeknights, prepping lunch box snacks, making all their sandwiches and freezing them. I also get the girls to do their chores and homework while I'm doing the weekly prep. This ensures that we have Sundays for Family Fun Time with no jobs to do. We always have family dinner on Sunday night.

Every second weekend the girls go to their dad's from Friday afternoon and I use this time to fill my tank – exercise, time with girlfriends, beach, reading, dating, theatre. I try to use these weekends exclusively for 'me time' which means I push to get all my grocery shopping (online), washing and other chores done before 9am on Saturday. The only thing I may do is cook on a Saturday or Sunday afternoon as I find that therapeutic.

Naomi's Perfect Week

Naomi Colley runs Lightbulb Studio, a photography business in Canberra, with her husband Brenton. They have two daughters: Abby (four) and Amelia (one). Here's how their week plays out:

Monday: My mum does pre-school drop off and pick up for Abby, and has Amelia all day.

Tuesday: I do pre-school drop off and depending on whether Brenton is shooting or not he will get Abby. If not, I get her. Then one of us has solo Abby time until picking Amelia up from daycare at 4.30 p.m. That night I do Pilates.

Wednesday: Either my mother-in-law takes Abby to or gets her from pre-school. Amelia is in daycare.

Thursday is my Abby and Amelia day.

Friday: My mother-in-law has the girls.

Saturday: A family trip to the markets and whatever social thing we have on. One of us is usually out that night but there's no structure about how/when/who.

Sunday: If we're planning anything social we try to keep it to the morning so we have Sunday afternoon, from 2ish, as a family. I try to do pre-school/daycare lunch prep on a Sunday too.

In amongst the week we take it in turns to get out alone to walk the dog – this is probably twice a week each on average. This time is a little saviour in our week as it gives each of us a break, some exercise and a chance to just be alone, which doesn't happen much.

As far as running the business together goes, we're six years in and still learning to leave work at work. If we drive to work together (rarely) we use it to get on the same page. If we go separately, we have a quick catch-up in the morning to make sure we're on the same page for work/arranging kids for the day. Then, if we need it, we use a coffee break around 9.30 to have a quick WIP meeting.

You can find my Perfect Week worksheet on my website. I'd strongly suggest you co-create it with your partner or ex-partner (if they're open to it) to enable you both to get what you need out of your week as individuals and as a family.

Nail your morning and evening routines

As I already shared, one of the things that I was worried about when we (hopefully) had a family was that my mornings would turn to absolute chaos – and I was pre-emptively stressing about the knock-on effect that would have on my business and productivity generally.

It's vitally important to me that I have a solid morning routine – for a number of reasons.

Firstly, I know that if my morning is focused, calm and productive, then the rest of my day will be.

Secondly, mornings are my window to do the stuff I know keeps me sane regardless of how crazy life may get – a quick meditation and drinking my lemon drink at a minimum, but ideally a 20-minute meditation, an oracle card reading, journaling, reciting affirmations, checking in on my goals, doing a short visualisation exercise with my vision board, and reading ten minutes of a weighty, self-improvement book.

Thirdly, by prioritising myself as soon as I wake, I feel I'm paying myself first with my time. Like probably all of you reading, I spend an enormous portion of my day looking after other people – whether that's a corporate team I'm training or a mentee I'm working with one-on-one.

My ideal morning routine takes me an hour and I cannot adequately convey the sense of achievement and purpose I get when I complete the whole thing. It is quite honestly life-changing.

If you'd like to swot up some more on morning routines, I'd love for you to read Hal Elrod's book, *The Miracle Morning*. I'm pretty sure I've gotten hundreds of people onto it over the years, and it has changed their life as it has mine. It's a super simple and adaptable infrastructure for creating a morning routine that will have you centred, focused and firing on all cylinders for the day to come.

When I speak onstage about my Get Remarkably Organised philosophy, the importance of a great morning routine is always high on my agenda. Before we had Lexi, I could almost guarantee what the first question would be when I went to the Q&A part of my talk. It would go something like this: 'The morning routine stuff sounds great, and I'd love to do it. However, you don't have kids, and I do. How can I make it happen?' I honestly can't remember what my answer to this question used to be, but I know what it is now and I'll share it here.

Making a morning routine happen with kids
Get up before your kids do

There is no chance in hell that I could do my morning routine post Lexi arising from her overnight slumber. In fact, when she has gotten up mid-Miracle Morning, oracle cards are tossed around, beautiful bound journals are doodled on and my carefully laminated goals are bent into some kind of baby-attempted origami. Currently she wakes between 6.30 and 7 a.m., so my Miracle Morning needs to be done by about 6.45 a.m. so I can get her up.

If you have early risers, then I know that this is not without its pain. However, I know of many very smart and very successful parents who are getting up at 4.30 a.m. so they have 'their time' in the morning before the household is up and about. Entrepreneur Kylie Camps gets up at 4.30 a.m. and her twin boys get up between 6.30 a.m. and 7 a.m. – a routine she has maintained since the boys were 3–4 months old. In that two-hour window, she practises mindfulness, has a coffee and listens to a podcast while she does her hair and make-up, and gets dressed. She then reviews what's coming up that day, makes school lunches, checks her emails, replies to comments online and uploads content to social media.

Thankfully I only need to get up at 5.30–6 a.m. to do my routine, but I very honestly would not hesitate to move my wake-up time earlier if I needed to work around Lexi's own wake-up. That time in the morning is too valuable for me to miss.

Of course, there are nights where I've been up and awake with Lexi more than I've been asleep, in which case I will allow myself to sleep until 7 a.m. if my body needs it.

If you have a challenging sleeper, go back to my thoughts in Chapter 15 where I strongly suggest you engage some help from an expert. Of course we pay the price of feeling constantly tired when we're having broken sleep ourselves, but the double whammy is that we don't have the motivation or energy to commit to and maintain a morning routine for ourselves.

And maybe this will make you feel better ... One of my Instagram followers Brenda messaged me last night to say that she's watching a mother of ten on YouTube, who gets up at 2.35 a.m. (that extra five minutes would make a hellova difference!) and studies and works out before her family gets up at 6 a.m. Then she goes to bed at 8.30 p.m. and starts the whole thing again. Hats off.

Do what you can

It took me years to build a consistent morning meditation practice, and when Lexi was born I was meditating at least four mornings a week for 20 minutes at a time as part of my 60–90 minute Miracle Morning.

Then she arrived, and I didn't meditate once for three months. At that point I decided to make it happen again, and picked up meditating again. After a few weeks I added in my oracle cards and also my journaling. This new slimmed-down routine took me about 30 minutes in the morning, and that's what it was like until just six weeks ago – when I decided at the start of the year to recommit to my full Miracle Morning.

I'm not saying that 45–60 minutes is available to everyone – I know it's not.

So do what you can. This might be a five-minute shower visualising a successful day. It might be sitting at the dining table in blissful silence for ten minutes before the rabble wakes up. It might be doing a short guided meditation in the carpark before you start your working day, or even doing ten full-belly breaths.

Whatever it is you can do, do that and do it consistently.

Enlist your other half

If you have a partner, see if you could tag-team the mornings so that you each get to devote even a small amount of time to a morning practice for yourselves. My friend Jules and her husband Josh have a neat system that means both of them get some quality time for themselves each morning.

Josh wakes up at 5 a.m. and is at the gym for 5.30 a.m. (the same gym as Wade!). Jules gets their daughter Tali up at 7 a.m. and gives her milk and a cuddle. By now, Josh is home and he dresses Tali and gives her breakfast while Jules does a short meditation, has a shower, gets dressed and does her hair and make-up, before having her own breakfast and taking Tali to daycare.

If carving out a window of time just for you each morning is a key priority of yours, have a chat with your partner and see if you can come up with an arrangement like this.

Three boxes every evening routine should tick

The evening routine is also a key one to consider, as it's our evenings that set us up for the next day. I go into a lot more detail on evening routines in *Get Remarkably Organised*, but I will quickly say that there are three core things that every evening routine should deliver.

They are:

1. Closure on the current day

This should be some kind of practice that draws a line under the day you've just had. For me, it's writing my to-do list for the next day and capturing any loose ends from the previous day on there that need to be actioned tomorrow. For you, it might be doing a brain dump in a Word doc of floating thoughts/actions you've accumulated over the day.

2. Preparation for the next day

As you can see from our Perfect Weeks, prepping for the next day is a key element of our evenings. Doing as much for the next day as possible the night before means that our mornings flow so much smoother and are infinitely less painful than they might otherwise be. This means prepping lunches, lemon drinks, office bags, daycare bags, picking out clothes and anything else we can think of. It's a pain at the time, but so very worth it the next day!

3. Gearing up for great sleep

Setting the scene for a restful sleep is a key part of my evening routine. This means that ceiling lights are off from 8 p.m., lavender essential oil is diffusing in our bedroom, phones are banned from 9 p.m. and I usually have a shower and douse myself in magnesium oil afterwards.

Delineate household roles and responsibilities

One thing that gamechanged myself and Wade's week was us knowing exactly who is in charge of what in the house. I shared our approach to this in Chapter 12, but it needs a name-check here as well – because clearly articulating who does what is one of the best systems we can bed down in our homes.

I'll give you a quick example. We order 15 litre bottles of water to drink at home, which we store in the courtyard downstairs – bringing up a new bottle and taking the empty down whenever we run out. I can carry them myself and all-up it takes less than three minutes to do, but they're bulky and heavy and are often dirty from sitting outside, and well – I like my clothes to be clean …

There's also the small matter that given Wade's biceps are probably three times the diameter of mine, he also finds it much easier to navigate the hair-raising manoeuvre of tipping an open 15 kg bottle of water upside down and simultaneously getting the neck smack-bang into the ceramic holder.

In the past, I would see the water gradually running out and make mental notes to swap it myself or nag Wade to do it. It would get to the point that it was all out, and even tipping the ceramic pot thing over would yield only a trickle of water.

I would then redouble my mental note-making, intensify the nagging, and eventually get so fed up with myself, Wade and my raging thirst, and go change the fucking water bottle.

When we recently did our strategy work around us and what we're doing with our lives, one of the responsibilities Wade took on was to swap the water bottles. This means that if there's no water, it is 100 per cent, unequivocally his job to sort it out. Really, by allocating clear roles, we're creating a nowhere-to-hide scenario!

On my side, my role is to meal plan, write the weekly shopping list and make sure we all have food when each meal-time rolls around. If dinner hasn't been sorted, that's totally on me.

The amazing thing about having such clarity around each of our jobs in the house is that it has slashed unnecessary communication and mental energy. We both know that Wade's job is to do the water, therefore I don't expend valuable brain calories on reminding myself – or him – to do it.

We don't need to exchange multiple WhatsApp messages each day brainstorming ideas for dinner that night. That was my job (which I do on Friday evening for the week ahead).

Obviously Lexi is still a little on the small side to be flinging her into domestic child labour, but as soon as she is old enough to understand and complete simple chores – like making her bed and tidying her room – we will be extending this out to her as well. To us, it's important that she plays a part in running the household she lives in, just like my sister and I had allocated jobs when we were growing up. Mine was to do the household ironing each week and vacuum the house. Jenny's was emptying the dishwasher and dusting the surfaces.

On my Bali retreat, one of the women attending was at breaking point with running her business and a household of five people. During our sessions together, interior stylist Amanda Smythe realised just how much she was doing for her partner and three kids (aged 12, ten and seven). One of her actions post-retreat was to have a family meeting and clearly allocate certain chores to the older kids, in order to immediately alleviate the somewhat hefty workload she found herself with. We joked that I'd be getting hate mail from her kids post-retreat! I checked in with Amanda six months later as I was writing this chapter and she said:

I went home after the retreat determined that things would change. What I can see very clearly is that everyone pulling their weight more effectively makes us all better human beings. Me because I get more time to do the things that 'fill my cup', as Lorraine says, such as exercise, and I don't feel like the resident slave. And my children because it makes them more responsible young adults and capable of looking after themselves. They are no longer looking to me to constantly 'save' them and realise that they need to be more responsible for themselves. There was an article in the Sunday paper last weekend about 'Concierge Parents' that spend their lives running around after their children and never let them fail, and how detrimental this is to raising our children. I felt very glad that I was finally on the right side of this.

Keep everything as close to home as possible

It may be an unusual kind of system, however trying to contain as much of your life as possible to a few kilometres from your house will make life *immeasurably* easier. Obviously if you're living in Outback Australia and depend on fortnightly food deliveries via light aircraft, this won't apply to you – but with careful planning and perhaps a little sacrifice, it is possible for most of us to minimise the time spent commuting. For us right now, our house is:

- 600 m from Lexi's daycare
- 650 m from my yoga studio
- 900 m from Wade's gym
- 1.6 km from Wade's jujitsu place
- 1 km from the local farmers' market
- 2.5 km from the shopping centre
- 2.5 km from Wade's office
- 3 km to my coworking space

I cannot even tell you how much easier it makes life that practically all of the places we need to go to on a weekly basis are less than ten minutes away.

As I said, this may need to be a longer-term strategy for you, but it is one of the best things you can do to help life run that bit easier.

Emma Isaacs also subscribes to this approach, saying in her book *Winging It* that: 'I'll do almost anything I can to avoid a commute' and advises readers to draw a 10 km circle around their home and try to get everything to fit within that.

Have less stuff

As I write this, Japanese tidying expert Marie Kondo's show is going crazy on Netflix, with people all over the world caught up in eliminating every bit of clutter lurking in their houses.

I read her book *The Life-Changing Magic of Tidying Up* when I was pregnant with Lexi, and Wade and I promptly ripped our house apart in the spirit of sparking as much joy as possible.

I've long advocated the physical, mental and spiritual benefits of offloading excess stuff, but it's an absolute must-do with Lexi in our little family equation. I read a fascinating study when I was doing research for my second book, which found that mothers' blood pressure spiked when dealing with the physical possessions of themselves and their families.

The more stuff we have = the more stressed we are.

Purely as it's more crap we need to lug from A to B, then back to A again.

Wade and I have found that streamlining our physical possessions makes life a hell of a lot easier. It means the house is easier to keep tidy, it means we need less storage space, it means we have less stuff to keep track of and we can think more clearly without corners packed with clutter.

A great example is Lexi's clothes. Back when we were still in the days of poo explosions, constant spit-ups and getting our heads around solids, we needed to have available at least eight onesies (babygros for my Northern Hemisphere friends) – as often she would get through two or three in just one day.

Now she only wears onesies to sleep in, so having three on rotation is more than enough.

Make mundane tasks as easy as possible

Every household will have small tweaks to ease the daily monotony of chores. As my business manager Michelle Broadbent mentions in her Perfect Week on page 218, she makes and freezes sandwiches for the week to save time on making school lunches. Emma Isaacs and her husband Rowan have a rule in their house that no-one is allowed to go upstairs without taking something that needs to be put away.

Wade and I group the cutlery in our dishwasher basket (all teaspoons in one section, all forks in another) to shave five minutes off emptying the dishwasher. We soak our porridge grains the night before so breakfast is ready in half the time. We have pantry supplies in clear glass jars so it's immediately clear what needs to be replenished. And Lexi's nappies have been on subscription for the last five months, arriving on our doorstep every two weeks – I genuinely cannot believe how much time and mental energy I devoted to planning nappy purchasing for the months before.

My friend and co-founder of SWIISH.com Maha Koraiem Corbett uses a hair straightener to de-crease her clothes rather than going through the laborious process of setting up the ironing board and iron. Her sister Sally Obermeder bought a hanging shoe organiser for her seven-year-old daughter Annabel's wardrobe, with each tier labelled with a day of the week. Each weekend she packs it with the relevant uniforms/backpack/library book ready to roll for the week ahead.

I put it to my savvy Instagram audience to share their tried and loved life systems and my did they come up with the goods!

- Katie Tilden has a laminated schedule in her seven-year-old daughter Sophia's room and on the fridge, which details the uniform, books and sports gear required for each day so Sophia can follow along and organise herself.
- Atlanta Bell uses a Kanban board to keep track of meal prep, cleaning and maintenance.
- Lyndal Halliday and her husband use the Cozi family organiser app to help them stay on top of the moving parts of their family.
- Liz Hayward has shared smartphone notes with her husband so they can collaborate on shopping lists.
- Kylie Miller packs childcare bags and picks her kids' outfits the night before to save on crazy mornings.

- Emeline Roissetter swears by online food shopping and automated payments for bills.
- Emmy Santari labels everything – the baby's drawers, kids toy storage – so there is no excuse for not knowing where to pack something away.

Bedding in your life systems

I hope this chapter has given you some ideas you can take into your own life, home and business to reduce the day-to-day hassles that come with The Blend. The very *very* last thing I want you to do, having read this chapter, is to go hell-for-leather trying to implement every damn thing I – or someone else – has suggested. Instead, I implore you to pick one thing that you feel would have the most immediate and lasting effect, and focus on making that a reality in your life. Once that's bedded in, pick the next thing, and so on.

I've said before that small steps practised every day are more sustainable than massive life overhauls. Try this in small increments, test what works and doesn't work for you and your unique situation, tweak the system and keep tweaking. A more contented life awaits!

CHAPTER 17

Building The Village

For the majority of our lives as parents (which – granted – has been short so far), Wade and I went it alone.

My family is in Ireland, a casual (not) 24-hour flight away. His parents are a five-hour drive away, his cousin (the closest he has to a sibling) is a three-hour flight away. Until very recently, our friends were spread all over the country, and our Sydney friends were evenly dotted to quite efficiently cover most of the key areas in the city.

The only support we had for a long time was paid nannies or babysitters, which again started to be prohibitive when weighing up whether I should attend a certain event – or even a yoga class. By the time I load the $20 yoga class with the $20 babysitter, and the logistics required to coordinate the babysitter, it's that bit more difficult (and expensive!) to do things.

To go see any of our friends we need to drive for at least 20 minutes, and when you're working around baby nap times, the significant kit required to leave the house and city traffic, even that relatively short drive starts to be prohibitive.

In Australia, the public health system creates local mothers' groups – where women with similar-aged babies are bunched together when the babies are six weeks old. There are four weeks of organised talks/education with a health professional and after that the groups run self-sufficiently.

For most of my friends, who like us don't have family around, their mothers' group is where they find their tribe – and given the group is assembled for specific suburbs, this tribe mostly lives within walking distance of each other. My friend Sarah, for example, is still very close to the mothers' group she found herself in when her daughter Cara was born – and Cara just started school last week.

Wade and I took Lexi to Europe the week she turned six weeks old and we were away for two months, meaning I missed the first month of the mothers' group I would have been in. So no tribe for me there.

All of this is the direct opposite of how I grew up. My mum is one of nine siblings, and my dad is one of seven. My mum's family is especially close, and up until the age of eight, we lived in a housing estate in the village, with my grandmother and six of my mum's siblings within a 15-minute walk away (and four within a three-minute walk!). My sister Jenny and I were constantly in someone else's house, and it would be unusual for us to spend seven nights of the week at home.

At eight, we moved out of the village to a house on its own land and from then on, we needed to drive everywhere. However, we still saw my aunties, uncles and cousins at least four times a week, with cousins staying at our house and us at theirs.

We holidayed together – sometimes with up to 20 of us staying in a European holiday resort. When a family went away on holiday, someone would drop them to the airport and pick them up – and they would return to their house cleaned and with groceries in the fridge.

Family get-togethers saw each of my aunts bring their signature dessert (Dorothy's scones, Paula's coffee cake) and the uncles did the clean-up. Sometimes this clean-up was too thorough, with my dad painstakingly scouring my Auntie

Dorothy's new frying pan till the silver shone – only finding out later that it was a new-fangled non-stick pan!

Clothes were handed down, medicines were shared, garden tools were borrowed, dresses were swapped for weddings, firewood was shared around, and there was not just one adult to call in an emergency, there were 15.

This stuff is key once we have kids – and even more so if we're endeavouring to have said kids and pursue a career at the same time.

Hillary Rodham Clinton wrote *It Takes A Village* about parents' need for a support crew when raising their children. The title is based on the African proverb: 'It takes a village to raise a child.' In it, she writes: 'We are all in this together.'

When I compare how I grew up (and the utopian village from Hillary's book) to myself and Wade's experience as parents, you probably could not get more of an opposite picture.

We book ourselves an Uber to get to the airport, clothes we don't need anymore go to an anonymous charity store, if we need an appliance or tool we go buy a new one (even if we'll only need it a couple of times a year) and catch-ups with friends are at hipster cafés. We have 'close' friends whose home we haven't been to in several years.

The village for us, until very recently, was non-existent.

A few years ago Wade shared an online article with me that discussed this breakdown of the village in modern society. It made for devastating reading, as so much of it we could see in our own experiences. It's as if recent generations are blockading themselves into a self-sufficient bubble – needing no-one and helping no-one.

That's not to say that I haven't had tantalising glimpses of what The Village *could* be. My friend Jules, for example, is – in my opinion – a one-woman village.

When Lexi was only a week old, she arrived at our door with bags of baby clothes that her daughter Tali had outgrown, a bag per size. She still passes on clothes now, the deal being that we save what's worth saving, combine it with our clothes, and pass the lot back to her if she and her husband have another girl. She is like a walking Rolodex of nannies, and we found Lexi's first nanny Iva through Jules.

For my part, my signature gesture when BFF has a new baby is to drop a full roast dinner on their doorstep. However, that's about all I've done – as, well, life has seemed to get in the way, and driving 30 minutes to drop off that meal makes it a lot more logistically challenging when time is short, and even more so since I became a mother myself.

I can see that a large motivator behind the attempted Gold Coast move – for me anyway – was to seek out a Village. A big attractor to the place we tree-changed to was the community vibe it had. There was an internal email system for people to pass on clothes or items that weren't needed anymore, or a surplus of fruit or veg from the garden, or to request a loan of a kayak, saw or trailer. When a family in the community experienced a birth or death, a cooking rota was set up to keep them in hot dinners for two weeks.

I made a friend nearby who also had her own business and had a little boy the same age as Lexi. We were both equally excited to have a friend within walking distance, though we only got to see each other every couple of weeks or so as we were both working whenever the babies were asleep. I can see now that it was ridiculous that nurturing a fledgling friendship didn't have the same ROI that our businesses seemed to promise. (Note to self: revenue isn't much of a substitute for real human connection.)

When Wade and I decided to move back to Sydney, we had a challenge deciding where to live as our friends were still scattered across the four corners of the city and its suburbs. In the end we opted for the house we're in now, based on budget and proximity to Wade's office.

It's been one of the greatest revelations of my life to realise that we have – albeit very belatedly – found our Village.

It started with a morning coffee date with Leila Lutz, an Insta-mate who had connected with me as she was four weeks behind me in her pregnancy. When we found out we had gotten the house as we were masterminding our move back to Sydney, I was thrilled that I'd have a friend in the suburb, and that Lexi would get a friend, too.

All of those Insta comments and DMs thankfully materialised into a real-life connection and there was an instant bond between us. We catch up every few weeks, which is nowhere near as much as I'd like. However, to know that she's a ten-minute walk away in itself feels good.

Then we made friends with Gemma and Oscar next door, who have two little boys – the youngest being a couple of months older than Lexi. After walking past their house en route to the park and playing with their patience-of-a-saint cat for six weeks, I finally got to say hello to Gemma while she was standing on the doorstep of her house. Instant ease with her – she's super-chilled, funny and kind. Lexi immediately barrelled across the doorstep (she likes to do this) and got busy exploring their house.

Next up – after much cajoling – Jules, Josh and Tali decided to make the move from the beaches of the east to a bigger house a ten-minute walk away from our house. To say we were over the moon is an understatement.

And then. One of Wade's army BFFs Ryan, who had been studying in Paris since he left the army, told Wade he was moving back here with his wife Annmarie (who I adore) and their toddler son Basil. Ryan's work, Annie's work and Basil's daycare were all in northern Sydney but somehow Wade's powers of persuasion tempted them to our suburb. In fact, it tempted them to the house directly opposite ours!

So in just five months, we have gone from our standard set-up of having zero friends near us to having four awesome like-minded couples within ten minutes of our house.

Leila passed on their cleaner's details, gave me the inside track of the best markets and butchers in the area, and we split a delivery of raw milk. She and her husband Shaun invited us to have Thanksgiving lunch with them, and when she was having a very rough month between sleep regression and teething, I left a bunch of flowers on her doorstep.

When Wade was in the US two months ago, I had filming all day on Monday, and my nails were a shocker. I messaged Gemma to see if she could take Lexi for an hour while I pelted it up to the nail salon for a mani/pedi – and she said yes!

The following Sunday, Oscar was also away so Gemma sent me a text inviting Lexi and me over for a baby-friendly early dinner. I had already sorted dinner for Lexi and me, but I told her we'd bring what we had and toted dinner, Lexi and her high chair next door.

Sitting out in their garden, we shared a total mish-mash of a meal: fish and chips, chicken soup, beef skewers and a salad – Lexi tripping out on the company of the boys, and Gemma and I buzzing from having an actual adult conversation. After dinner, we bundled the three kids into the bath together and I carried Lexi home wrapped in a towel.

When Josh and Jules moved into their new place, Wade and I took Tali for most of the weekend so that they could focus on fully unpacking. When we dropped Tali home, we also took them dinner for that evening. A month later, Lexi had her first sleepover at their house while Wade and I had a 12-hour staycation – our first night in a hotel, just the two of us, since Lexi arrived.

We also helped out Ryan and Annie when they moved in, taking dinner for them on their first proper night in the house. Basil came to hang with Lexi for dinner and bath-time for a couple of nights while Ryan power-unpacked, then he'd collect Basil fed, bathed and ready for bed.

A few weeks later when Wade and I were trying to get our shit together to travel to Ireland for three weeks, Ryan and

Annie returned the favour. They brought over winter clothes for Lexi and me, provided all of our luggage after we realised ours had mould in it, and Annie took Lexi for the morning so I could pack and organise the house for friends who were staying while we were away.

Wade travelled to a wedding in Thailand while Lexi and I were still in Ireland, so he was away the night Lexi and I arrived back. Ryan drove our car to pick us up. He pushed our heaving luggage trolley to the car, installed Lexi's car seat, drove us home and carried a sleepy Lexi and all of our bags into the house. I could have wept with gratitude.

There's a 'Village Ladies' WhatsApp group and we girls had our first dinner locally last week. I know this will be an ongoing thing. The novelty of sitting down for dinner with smart, funny, no-BS women – *and then walking home!* – was special.

Often I'll come back from an errand on a weekend morning and find that Lexi is at Annie or Gemma's house. We love that she's so comfortable in new surroundings, and that it's teaching her to be ok with the apron strings being more elastic.

I had resigned myself to us not having people around us to lean on, and to be leaned on, and assumed that we'd just have to hack our way through as an autonomous family. To have found this small but mighty support network feels like the most revelatory thing.

And the best bit? That everyone else appreciates it, too.

Gemma never joined a mothers' group either as she was running her own florist when she had her first baby. Leila moved away from her group. Annie had Basil in Darwin where Ryan was posted, and they moved to France when Basil was six months old – as a non-French speaker in the freezing Northern Hemisphere winter, she struggled a lot with the isolation and loneliness.

So we're all soaking up this Village thing together, bigtime.

Life as an autonomous person or couple can get intense. When Wade and I are having challenges – external to us with businesses or family issues, or internally between us – it can feel like we're oscillating in a negative feedback loop, with only each other for support.

This has intensified a hell of a lot since we became parents – life is more complex, there's less sleep and we need to rely on each other more than we did when we had the luxury of being totally self-absorbed entities with carte blanche to do whatever the hell we wanted to (within reason, obvs).

When tensions arose, we bounced back and forth between each other and there was no shock absorber. We also almost exclusively leaned on each other for emotional support and reassurance.

Having a Village around us has eased that pressure on each other. There are other people who get the challenges we're experiencing, and – somehow – it helps us just knowing they are there.

As Australian author, entrepreneur and activist Constance Hall posted on Facebook:

> Guess what the silent cost of our lack of village is? Our relationships. Because all the things we should be getting from our village, we expect from our relationship. Our cups are empty and we need them filled, only society has structured us to only rely on one person. Our partners … If we could open our doors to the community, have company and help each other all day, our cup would be 80% full before we even reunited at the end of the day with our partners.

One Saturday a few weeks ago, Wade and I had an argument and the last thing we wanted to do that night was sit in each other's company watching Netflix like we'd planned. Ryan and Annie invited us over for dinner, but I declined as an evening with a clearly feuding couple would not have been fun for anyone. Wade ended up going to theirs on his own, I had a night on my own with Netflix, and tensions had eased by the next morning.

It's early days for our merry band, and with time comes trust. However, I already know that these people will have our back – and us theirs.

Let people in

While reflecting on the discovery of this village relatively late in life, what I've come to realise is that by being this self-sufficient creature – 'I've got this myself, don't need no help, thank you very much' – I was in fact avoiding intimacy.

To have someone in your home and be welcomed into theirs requires intimacy, and I don't think I was ready for that until we came back from the Gold Coast. It's almost as if I needed to move 800 km away in pursuit of The Village to come back and be fully ready to welcome it in.

I believe that true intimacy is something that we start to lose once we couple up and (those dreaded words) 'settle down'.

Hungover Sunday mornings draped across the sofa with housemates, mascara still smudged from the night before, are replaced by shiny bright Sunday morning brunches at cool cafés where we discuss wedding plans and – later – pregnancies. Increasingly, having friends over becomes A Special Occasion that requires house cleaning, fancier-than-normal wine bought in and organised fun.

In *Everything I Know About Love*, Dolly Alderton speaks to one of her BFFs and begs her to promise Dolly that they won't end up like their mothers – who would clean frantically for the arrival of a friend in the house.

Having a friend arrive unannounced is almost a thing of sacrilege now. It would quite honestly never occur to me to pop into a friend's house 'just because I was passing' – yet that's exactly the fabric that The Village I grew up in was woven from.

We then have the extremely mixed blessing that is social media. Yep, we can access hundreds of people from one tiny handheld device, but how many of those people will we ever connect with IRL? Constance Hall writes on Facebook, 'Our village has been replaced with four walls and an iPhone.'

Rather than a long phone conversation or a quick chat with the neighbour over the back fence, we now scroll our Instagram feed seeking inspiration, but company as well. I know that my own usage of social media goes up exponentially while Wade is travelling, as I lean on it for company in the hours between Lexi's bedtime and my own.

We compare our lives with those of the filtered, cropped people in the small squares of Instagram. We feel less than them, which pushes us back even further into our self-sufficient bubbles.

I know that many parents – coupled up and single – are feeling so fucking lonely, and are leaning on a smartphone to offer some semblance of The Village of yesteryears. In fact, never mind parents, *people generally* are feeling it.

You don't need me to tell you that anxiety and depression are through the roof in modern developed societies. My friend's partner is a GP who for years practised in Sydney's western suburbs with patients from a so-called low socio-economic demographic. The most common problems were physical, such as diabetes and heart problems. He moved to a new practice in Sydney's affluent eastern suburbs and those physical afflictions were dramatically less evident. They were replaced with mental health issues – most especially anxiety and depression.

I have this visual of each person, couple or family existing in a clear plastic cell. There are other people, couples and families all around them – above, below and beside them. However, each of them is also in a cell, and true connection is next to impossible, or at least that's how it feels.

The answer to this sad-as-fuck epidemic is not to get online more, but to seek out real human interaction. Let people in so they can let us in. Build our villages – to nurture our kids, but to nurture us as well.

So where do we start?

Firstly, try to live near friends. I know that the set-up we now have is pretty unusual, but it's not impossible. With some longer-term planning, it can be done. Having lived with friends nearby now for a few months, I would dramatically bump proximity to friends or at least people of a similar lifestage up the priority list if we are house-hunting in future (the far future, hopefully!).

Secondly, be the first to ask for a favour.

Before I took the leap to start my first business, I worked for two years at an agency called Naked Communications. One of the co-founders was wild-haired genius and consumer psychologist Adam Ferrier, who shared with me that one of the quickest ways to get someone to like you is to ask them for a favour. Sounds nuts, right?

He explained that when someone is asked to do something by someone they hardly know or don't know at all, they will most often say yes as that's good social etiquette. Their brain then needs to rationalise why they've said yes to helping someone they may not know from a bar of soap, and their brain figures that they must like them!

So be the first to ask to borrow a slow cooker or hedge shears. It makes people more likely to like you. And – critically – it gives them permission to ask you a favour in return.

Thirdly, focus on what you can give rather than what you receive. It's an extraordinary privilege in this village we've found ourselves in to be helped, however it's even more of a privilege to be able to serve others.

To be trusted with someone's kid for a weekend, or for them to welcome you into their box-stacked, messy AF home they've just moved into and they're make-up free with their hair in a messy bun ... well, that's special.

And lastly, have parameters. My Auntie Ellen told me that she and her husband Vincent had a babysitting swap in place for years with another couple on their street. The deal was that she or Vin would go to the other family's house every second Thursday so that the couple could go out. The parameters were that there was a curfew (given it was a working and school night) and that it was Thursdays only – cutting out the 'we can't do Thursday in two weeks, can you do Tuesday instead' mess-around. Use it or lose it was the policy!

While it's wonderful having the close relationship with Gemma, Oscar, Annie and Ryan on our street, we're not sitting on each other's laps. We'll chat when we meet on the street, but if Lexi is having a post-daycare meltdown, it's a quick wave and we're into our own house pronto.

Having healthy boundaries in place means that everyone knows where they stand and the scope or likelihood of specific parties taking the piss is dramatically reduced.

If you've found your Village – good on you.

If you're still seeking, keep seeking. From my experience, I can promise you it's worth the wait.

CHAPTER 18

Travelling with Baby

As I start this chapter, Lexi is 20 months old and in her cot sleeping off her jet lag from our three-week trip to Ireland. Wade's wedding commitment meant that I needed to fly solo with her back to Australia from Dublin, which I didn't give a huge amount of thought to until I got back and the comments came: 'Superwoman!' said Sarah on Instagram, 'You are to be congratulated,' wrote Judith. 'I flew to NZ with an 18 mth old. Longest three hours of my life.' Leila sent me a WhatsApp message saying I was 'seriously fucking brave'.

It seems that travelling with babies and toddlers is an experience charged with fear for a lot of parents, which is why I wanted to share the perspectives and hacks I've picked up over the 50+ flights that Lexi and I have taken together. Let's be clear, I don't deny that travelling with kids is a lot more logistically intense, a lot less productive and a lot less relaxing than travelling solo. Bingeing on movies, flicking through magazines and mapping out business strategies in my notebook is most certainly not happening while I've got Lexi in tow. I am constantly monitoring her and caring for her, and (more recently) sharing all of my food with her. However, I haven't found it to be *as* daunting a task as I expected.

Travel with Baby Lexi

Lexi – in her short amount of time earthside – has done a lot of travelling. Our adventures started with getting her passport. We were booked to take her to Ireland to attend my sister's wedding when she was six weeks old, and even with the express passport option, we were cutting it fine to have her fully documented by our departure date. Time was a-ticking.

When my mum and I went to get her passport photo at the age of seven days old, I realised the Australian requirements for babies are pure lunacy. I wonder if anyone at the passport office has tried to get a sleepy, floppy-necked newborn to simultaneously have their eyes open, have both ears showing, have their mouth closed *and* have a 'neutral expression'. Oh, and not have any visible props or parents' hands in the photo ... Stress levels were high and we came away with me sobbing, Lexi happily asleep and no passport photo.

In all my emotional, post-birth exhaustion, I couldn't face returning to the post office again so Wade took on the challenge (while I got my lashes done, bless him). The man was on a mission. I still don't know how he did it, but between him and the teenaged assistant in the digital photo store, they got the shot. Lexi looks rather startled; the photo still makes us howl with laughter. But we were on our way.

I was so caught up in the preparation to depart on our eight-week trip that it was only when we'd checked in and were walking through Sydney airport to the departure gates, Lexi tucked onto Wade's chest in the Ergo baby carrier, that I fully realised we were getting on a plane with a six-week-old person.

On the plane, Lexi was the star attraction – everyone wanted to stop and coo at her, and one woman rushed up to where we were sitting and exclaimed 'Wow, you're game!' when she saw how ickle Lexi was. Having travelled with a newborn, I am fascinated at this attitude. What we have now realised is that the newborn stage is the very, very, *very* easiest stage to travel with.

We went to Ireland for five weeks all up, spending a week in Italy for a holiday and two weeks in London for both our businesses as well. Lexi was aged six to 14 weeks on that trip, and she basically just ate, weed, pooed and slept – that's it. No snacks, no toys, no books, no shoes required. I was feeding her, so we didn't need to bring bottles with us. And she was on her own newborn schedule, so was totally unaffected by time zones. She slept in her pram or snuggled in her Ergo whenever she needed to, so we didn't need to be back at home base for naps and could fill our days with whatever activities we wanted to. I practised peeing with her in the Ergo, which turned out to be a skill I made maximum use of over the months of travelling that followed. It was so bloody easy.

Looking back, I'm so glad that we did that trip as it forced us to overcome any travelling-with-baby nerves early on – and we realised that we could still do things with Lexi in tow.

During that trip we got eight flights with her, took her in taxis, trains, tubes, rental cars, even boats and an open-air bus, ate at countless restaurants, and navigated all the other usual logistics of travelling.

We had mishaps – like Lexi's attempts to sabotage our romantic dinner in a gorgeous Italian restaurant. Rather than sleeping in her pram like we briefed her, she instead wanted to be on the boob for most of the meal. So I gave up trying (and failing) to eat grilled octopus with one hand and just fed her while I enviously watched Wade speed through his meal. When we finally got her down into her pram, we realised she had done an epic poo explosion that required us to push the pram onto the street next to the restaurant and a two-man job of cleaning, changing and re-dressing her ensued.

Then there was Wade's stand-off with the cabin crew on our 14-hour flight from Sydney to Abu Dhabi. When the 'fasten seatbelt' sign comes on, airplane protocol says that you need to take your sleeping baby out of their bassinet and strap them back into their seatbelt on your lap. We must have had the world's most cautious pilot, as he had the seatbelt sign on for 70 per cent of the trip – even though there was sweet FA turbulence.

When we had lifted a snoozing Lexi out of her bassinet for the third time, Wade lost his shit. 'I'm happy to take on all liability if anything happens to her, but we are not taking her out of her bassinet again. There is absolutely no turbulence and she needs to sleep.' This was addressed to a perplexed cabin crew member. After the situation was escalated up three levels of seniority of cabin crew, I lost my nerve. 'Babe, it's fine, I'll just get her out,' I muttered to him, mortified at the scene we were causing.

When Lexi was five months old, I took her on a solo business trip for the first time from Sydney to Melbourne. Natt and I were in the midst of a major new business push, and had teed up meetings with key potential clients in Melbourne. I was pleasantly surprised at how easy the airport security was to navigate on my own. The staff were super-helpful and gave me a little padded bed to rest Lexi on while I strapped myself back into the Ergo and put her back in.

We stayed with Natt and her family, and Natt had a rented car seat fitted at a place next to the airport before she picked us up. Her 16-year-old daughter Maddy, who was on school holidays, accompanied us around town while we did our meetings – I'd feed Lexi, then Maddy would push her around in her pram while we had our meeting, then we'd meet her again afterwards. I was lucky to have Natt and Maddy's help on this occasion – we just did what we needed to do in order for me to be at those meetings.

At eight months, Lexi and I headed for Bali for our mama-baby *Eat Pray Love* adventure. I'd be crazy if I wasn't nervous about eight weeks of shepherding the two of us around solo – even knowing that Wade, my mum and sister would be joining us at points in the trip. The responsibility of it felt crushing. As it turned out, we coped beautifully well together – it felt like the best team effort as we navigated the different logistical challenges each day.

We had booked a wonderfully welcoming hotel for our first seven days in Ubud, then the plan was to move to self-catering accommodation so I could cook Lexi purées (she had only been eating solids for two months when we left). On a recommendation, I booked what was described as 'simple' accommodation on the other side of town. The hotel driver had to park on the other side of a stream when we arrived as there was no road access, and he helped me carry the luggage along a narrow pathway to the accommodation. There was no-one to be seen in reception – it was only on hunting out a back room that I found someone who could check us in.

What I saw had me instantly in tears. The bathroom was beyond basic and had no natural light. The bedroom was cramped, packed full of furniture. The 'kitchen' was more like an outdoor camp kitchen and was accessed down the side of the building. It had an ancient fridge, a sink and a handful of random dishes and cutlery ... not quite the hygienic conditions I had envisaged to prepare Lexi's meals!

I took out my phone and – in floods of tears – called the hotel and asked if they had a room for us for the night, and if they could come get us. Praise be, they had and they would. I needed to get all of our luggage back out onto the road to meet the hotel driver again, and Lexi was starting to get agitated in the Ergo – it's a wonder she lasted so long with the heat, constant moving around and being bolted into her strung-out Mama's energy field.

I started to lug our stuff in batches, up and down steps and along narrow, bumpy pathways. In total I had two suitcases, one travel cot, one travel cot mattress, two prams, my carry-on bag and Lexi's change bag. Oh, and Lexi. Luckily, some locals from up the road helped me out.

We arrived back at the hotel dishevelled and distressed. The staff were beyond helpful, magicking us to a new room and bringing me a pot of tea and cakes to aid the recovery process.

It's funny to tell this story with the benefit of a year's hindsight, but it really was very traumatic at the time. I had gotten us into a messy situation, and there was only me to get us out of it – in a strange country and with a small baby to protect. I seriously questioned my sanity on attempting this trip with Lexi, and was furious at myself for not looking after us better.

That afternoon, I decided that our safety and happiness were of paramount importance and so I increased the accommodation line item of our travel budget. I struck a deal with the hotel to stay there for the remaining four weeks of our stay in Ubud, until my mum and sister arrived, and I found a company that prepared fresh, organic baby food and delivered it frozen in cooler bags (genius!).

My two biggest learnings from this accommodation misfire were:

1. I could get us out of situations if I needed to – with my Balinese SIM card, some cash and some resourcefulness, I was able to extricate us from a pretty bad situation. It was obviously stressful as all get out, but I got us back to a better place relatively quickly. As disempowering as the experience had been, the upshot was that I felt confident in my ability to pivot us out of undesirable situations if they arose again.
2. It is *not* easy to do basic accommodation with a baby – Wade and I could have managed ok if we needed to, but to have Lexi there was too high a price in terms of my sanity and our safety. There's adventure, and there's adventure!

Travel with Toddler Lexi

By the time Lexi hit her first birthday, we totted up that she had done just under 40 flights – sometimes with Wade and me, but mostly just with me. These were a lot of hops up and down between Sydney and the Gold Coast when we were moving/tree-changing/moving back or other interstate trips for business.

As much as our ability to navigate travel together had bolstered my confidence, I was nervous about our latest plan – travelling 24 hours back to Ireland with *an active toddler* – especially when friends shared horror stories of their own trips.

My friend Richenda Vermeulen and her husband Kyle travelled around the US, North and South America for six fantastic months when their daughter Ashna was aged 4–10 months old, but Richenda said that the two-hour Melbourne–Gold Coast flight when Ash was a toddler was more challenging than all the flights on their six-month adventure put together.

Sarah had travelled to Ireland with their 18-month-old daughter Cara. On their way back, Cara had been hit by a stomach bug and spent the nine hours from Dublin to Abu Dhabi projectile-vomiting over Sarah, her husband Kris and the aeroplane surrounds. The Etihad jingle still traumatises her (Sarah, not Cara).

Fellow Villager and friend Annie's little boy Basil is two months older than Lexi, and she informed me the week before we departed on our trip that flying back to Sydney with Basil and her husband Ryan from Paris was 'the hardest thing' she'd *ever* done as a parent.

While Lexi had a few flights under her belt, it had been more than 18 months since she'd done the Europe mission as a new born, and she also hadn't been on a plane at all for the last five months. We knew this trip would be a very different proposition!

So how did it go? Armed with a back pocket overflowing with tips from friends and my Instagram audience, it was *fine*. Even the trip back solo with her was better than I expected it to be. We had one rough, two-hour window at the halfway point between Abu Dhabi and Sydney, during which Lexi bawled and simply wouldn't settle – even in the Ergo, which is my go-to for Code Red situations. But truly, the rest of the trip went so smoothly. So, if you're wondering if you should travel with your baby, I'd say do it. Definitely.

My biggest travel lessons

I'm about to unpack my best tips for travelling with babies and toddlers, but overall my biggest lessons in travelling with Lexi have been:

Jump in early

I know that not everyone gets the privilege of travelling – and I don't take it for granted that we've gotten to explore Australia and the world to the extent that we have with Lexi.

I would say that, if it's at all available to you, start travelling early with your kids – whether it's a four-hour flight to Fiji or a four-hour car journey to visit friends.

In our experience, travelling early with Lexi has had many benefits. Firstly, it boosted our confidence and self-belief that we *could* travel with her, and secondly it got her used to the disrupted schedule and alien environments that travelling necessitates. To a certain extent, travelling became normal to her, and as a result she didn't have a huge reaction to trips we took her on.

Over-prepare, then wing it

This gem of advice was passed on to me by one of my mentees, Sarah Nguyen. It was shared with her in the context of birth, but I think it's super-applicable for travelling as well. Being as prepared as we possibly can boosts my confidence that we've got a plan for all eventualities, even though we can't know what those eventualities will be.

While I was still pregnant, I was booked to do a speaking gig in regional Victoria when our future baby would be around four months old. The plan was that Wade would travel with me so I could do the gig, and we'd tack on a couple of days in Melbourne for business and friends.

We hired a car and a baby capsule from Melbourne airport, and set off towards Bendigo. I fed Lexi when we pulled into town, then grabbed lunch and headed straight for my pre-booked hair and make-up appointment, while Wade took his turn to have lunch with Lexi in her pram.

A couple of hours later and freshly zhooshed, I met them at the venue. Lexi had another feed in the theatre's green room, then I handed her back to Wade while I got dressed and did some last-minute prep with the event organisers.

The plan was that I'd give Lexi one last top-up feed before I stepped onstage (I had carefully organised a button-down dress for the occasion!), then she'd sleep in her pram in the green room with Wade while I did my talk, signed books and held a VIP Q&A. Later, we'd all travel back to our hotel together.

Lexi clearly wasn't a fan of that plan and screamed blue murder as I was slipping into my heels before going onstage. Wade took her into a soundproofed dressing room, but she was having none of it, and in the end he left a message with one of the event organisers for me and piled the two of them into the rental car. He spent the next two hours pacing the hotel room with her, while I focused on the group at hand. I got a lift back to the hotel later to find a peacefully sleeping baby and her exhausted Daddy in the room.

Surrender to what may happen

Travelling – particularly plane travel – is an exercise in relinquishing control of what's happening around us. We can't control delays, turbulence, the food available, the people we come in contact with, or the behaviour of our children – and (let's be honest) our own behaviour. Particularly embarking on the trip back to Sydney with Lexi this week, I consciously reminded myself to surrender to whatever events would unfold.

As it turned out, we had almost on-the-hour nappy changes, she made a great friend on both flights, we both slept very little, she charmed the cabin crew, all meals were split 50:50 (or more like 70:30 in Lexi's favour) and I paced the plane for at least two hours singing songs trying to get her to sleep.

Other people have your back

It has constantly amazed me how much support and encouragement we've gotten as we travel together as a family. Older people have done it themselves, fellow parents give us a knowing nod, and even the young and childless somehow appreciate the mission we're on. I've found aeroplane cabin crew especially to be supportive.

One of my friends Nikki Price travelled solo with her six-month-old son and said that she must have asked a dozen people in the airport to hold Arlo while she sorted out bags and got him in and out of his baby carrier – everyone she asked was happy to help (of course, she sussed them out first).

See it through the child's eyes

Travelling is stressful enough as an adult, and we fully understand why/how/what we're doing with it.

For small kids, they have no idea what's going down around them, and that can stress them out. I've had a few moments of WTF on our travels, and trying to see a particular situation through Lexi's eyes has helped me be more patient and kind with her – even if events around us are not unfolding as I'd like them to.

My top 20 tips for travelling with babies or toddlers

Over the course of our travels, I've been lucky to have many travel tips shared with me, and we've figured out our own hacks as we've travelled too. Here they are for your adventuring pleasure:

1. Check in early so you have maximum chance of getting seats you want.

My preferences are the bulkhead seats for extra leg room and easy access to bathrooms, or anywhere that you can nab an extra couple of free seats so Baby can lie down. I've found that check-in staff at the airport can work miracles, especially if the flight isn't full.

2. Have one carry-on bag and a small suitcase.

The small suitcase is stored above your seat and has everything you need to replenish your carry-on bag with supplies. The carry-on bag lives at your feet and has the change grab-bag, some food, toys and whatever bits you need to hand. Refrain from buying cute bags/cases for the kids, as it'll just be another thing for you to carry through security and onto/off the planes.

3. Bring your baby carrier.

A baby carrier *is life* when travelling with an infant or toddler. They enable you to be hands-free with the baby so you can wrangle with other kids, suitcases, overhead storage on the plane, airport security and passport control. And you don't know what footpaths will be like overseas and if they will be pram friendly (as I discovered in Bali; they're not). Our Ergo is also our go-to to get Lexi to sleep on a plane. She has such FOMO that she won't fall asleep on us or a seat, so we strap her in the carrier, find a quiet corner of the plane and she drops off pretty quickly – then we can extricate her from the Ergo to sleep on us or lying flat if we've managed to score a couple of extra seats.

4. Practise peeing with the baby in the carrier.

Maybe a bit TMI here, but this newly acquired skill was a godsend when Lexi was smaller. Getting her out of the baby carrier in order to do a two-minute pee was a drag, and even more so if she was asleep at the time. The last thing I wanted to do was put her on the floor of a public toilet (and even worse, a plane toilet!) before she could walk, so being able to pee with her on me was a huge help. It goes without saying that playsuits/ jumpsuits are not exactly conducive to this practice, so I suggest planning your wardrobe with consideration as well ...

5. Have changes of clothes for everyone travelling.
Bring at least one change of clothes for each adult travelling, and allow for one change of clothes for every four hours for little ones – the full kit: so vests, socks, onesies, jumpers and so on. Every time I've travelled with Lexi I've ended up with either food, poo, wee or all three on me – and sitting in poo-soaked leggings for 14 hours is not high on my list of fun things to do. Also have a plastic bag to throw laundry into – you may need it.

6. Bring extra socks.
I need to kick my shoes off as soon as I'm on a long-haul flight, and I like Lexi to be able to run/walk around minus shoes too. Obviously planes are quite gross with the amount of people compacted into a small space, so I bring a few spare pairs of socks with us so she can change for each flight.

7. Have a grab-bag for changing.
You don't want to be assembling your nappy change items from the overhead compartment every time Baby needs a change, so have most of your supplies in a carry-on suitcase overhead, then have a smaller grab-bag to cover 3–4 changes under your seat. Disposable change mats are brilliant for travelling too – I bring one for each flight, then dump it at the end of that flight. The idea of the germs floating around in tiny, airless plane toilets makes me sick, so I like to leave them behind us wherever possible. We have a full pack of wipes in the overhead storage, then have 10–15 wipes in a smaller ziplock bag in the grab-bag. Oh, and have a small tub/tube of nappy cream. For some reason, Lexi's

bum is always sore on planes – probably from sitting in nappies for hours on end rather than running around like she normally does at home.

8. Pack the amount of nappies you think you need, then pack another 50 per cent on top of that.

Travelling from Abu Dhabi to Dublin, we were down to our very last nappy in our combined carry-on luggage as we landed – you don't need that kind of adrenalin hit, believe me. My rule of thumb is to pack one nappy per hour of travelling. This is generous, but I find Lexi needs to be changed a lot more regularly when she's flying, and there's those 'just in case' nappy changes. Also, bring double the number of wipes you think you'll need – they are invaluable for mopping up messes of any kind.

9. Wipe down plane surfaces with a wet wipe on boarding.

This was one of a few excellent tips from my Instagram follower Claire. When we board I wipe down any surfaces that Lexi will come into contact with so that we reduce somewhat on the germs she'll make friends with. I've no idea if it works or not, but it's an easy and quick one to do and every bit helps when travelling. Another quick one: wash Baby's hands every time you do a nappy change in the toilets, to stay on top of hand hygiene.

10. Prevent ear pain with a drink or feed on take-off and landing.

I hate the ear-popping stage of take-off and landing myself, and I can only imagine how scary it would be to a small person. When I was still breastfeeding Lexi, I would try to time her feeds so that she'd be hungry (and I'd have milk ready to go) when we were taking off, as the sucking action relieved the pressure on her ears. Ditto for landing. I was worried about how she'd cope once we'd weaned, but I've found that giving her coconut water in a bottle works just as well. For your child, it could be milk or juice – Lexi just loves coconut water and it's an easy thing to pick up in the airport as we walk to our gate (I buy two: one for take-off and one for landing). It also doesn't need to be refrigerated. We just need to hide the bottle until the right moment, otherwise she screams for it too early, the timing is off and she gets sore ears.

11. Don't let your child play with anything you don't want to lose.
Including lids of drink bottles and your phone ... I travel with a bottle of lavender essential oil and also an immune-defence essential oil, and Lexi was popping the bottles in and out of a little bag on one of our flights. They disappeared into the ether, resulting in time-wasting and expense to replace them.

12. Lean on the cabin crew.
They're not just there to serve meals and drinks, they can give you a dig-out with the kids as well – particularly if you're travelling solo. Obviously I'm not suggesting that they get full babysitting duties – however, they are very happy to hold/watch kids while you run to the bathroom, to bring you extra water/snacks if you need them as you're trapped under a sleeping baby, and even provide a morale boost (like one cabin crew member did for me when I burst into tears on our most recent flight as Lexi wouldn't settle and she needed to send me back to our seat as the seatbelt sign came on).

13. Pack shitloads of snacks.
Kids' appetites are unlikely to fall in with the aeroplane service schedule and your child may not eat the plane food, so you want to have lots of food on hand to keep them going. Foods that Lexi loves and that travel well are: nut butter sandwiches, cubes of cheese, berries, whole apples, bananas and rice cakes. Another great tip from Claire was to pack little cardboard tubs of instant oats, as hot water is usually available on a plane, at an airport or at a roadside service station. I've found that airport security are very understanding about what food they will let you bring onboard if it's for a child under two years old.

14. Pop a disposable change mat under the child if they have their own seat.

Another gold tip from Claire. Chances are a toddler, or even an older child, will tip juice or water all over themselves at some point in a plane journey, or their nappy may leak. Having a change mat underneath them means that you can return them to their former dry glory quickly by swapping a new mat and changing their clothes. I personally wouldn't be happy about sitting in a wet seat for several hours!

15. Bring kid-sized earphones.

When we were setting off on the recent Ireland trip, two friends loaned us little kiddie earphones – one set was even made of soft fleecy material and wrapped around the child's head. Lexi hasn't gotten into screens yet, but she did wear them for a short time, more for the novelty factor than to actually watch a cartoon. The plane-issue earphones are way too big for a small child's head and they just irritated Lexi and she flung them off.

16. Pack little toys they haven't seen before in bags within bags within bags.

I don't know what it is about bags for toddlers, but Lexi will happily play for 30 minutes taking things out of a bag, putting them back in, then taking them out again. We packed a mixture of bags – ziplock, drawstring, purses – and put random things in them (hint: the party favours aisle of the discount store is perfect for this!). This kept her occupied for ages on the flights, and nothing was precious so it was no big deal if it went AWOL.

17. Let your standards drop for food.

As I've shared in this book a bit, Wade and I are pretty specific on the kind of food we want to eat, and that we want Lexi to eat. Trying to minimise gluten, be sugar-free and preservative-free is a big ask when travelling, so I declare at the start of the trip that all bets are off. Lexi was very unsettled for two hours of our most recent flight – the cure was her passing lots of wind, and a croissant. She was happy, I was happy, and we kicked back into our usual eating when we got home.

18. Clear your schedule on return if you can, to allow for jet lag.

When Lexi was smaller, jet lag wasn't a thing and we only had to contend with our own disrupted sleep patterns. Returning to Australia is always harder than leaving, I find, and Lexi and I have had messed-up sleep for a week. For this recent trip, I actually moved our return flight a day earlier as with our original return date, I had a speaking commitment the day after we'd landed the night before. Having a day to reset, unpack, give Lexi some TLC and have a nap myself meant that I was in much better shape to actually add value to the corporate group I was training. If possible, I deliberately keep my schedule light for the first week back so that I'm not up with her during the night freaking out about how I'm going to be 'on' for work the next day. This is obviously a bonus that comes from running your own show. However, I would definitely err on the side of having one less holiday day in order to have that extra day when you get home to help little ones – and yourself – through the sometimes painful re-entry process.

19. Bring a blanket from home so new cots have something familiar in them.

Travelling – particularly if you're moving around a few times – can potentially get overwhelming for kids when they're faced with new sights, smells and sounds from a new bed every few nights. We always pop a blanket from home that Lexi is used to in whatever cot she finds herself in (aka 'Blankie').

20. Do a cost-benefit analysis of hiring vs bringing your own equipment.

Most airlines will allow you to check in a travel cot, car seat and pram for free. We check in our pram for long-haul trips, then we use the Ergo to navigate the airports. Going to Europe for the first time, I agonised over whether or not to take our pram as it all seemed very labour-intensive. I wondered if we should hire or borrow a pram on the other side, but Wade reasoned that we had spent so much on our pram and we knew/liked it so we should take it with us. We got a pram bag that packs it safely in case of rough handling by baggage handlers. We also pack our foam change mat in there, folding it around the wheels of the pram to give them extra cushioning (as apparently wheels are the most likely part to get damaged in transit).

The reason, not the excuse

So there you have it, my download on travelling with little humans. As much as travelling with Lexi requires intensive logistics and a *lot* of focus while in transit, it really is the best fun toting her around new places and creating special memories with her. Yes, travel is a different experience with kids in tow, but make them the reason – not the excuse – to get out and explore together.

CHAPTER 19

On love

You and I, remarkable reader, have spent a considerable amount of time together over the course of this book. We have covered *a lot*.

From the decision to start trying for a family, the process of stepping out of the business, the journey to get pregnant, birth, the heady, intense newborn days, returning to my business, deciding to sell that business, the Year of Challenges, starting up the new business and a reversed tree change, I've laid our story out for you, in all its imperfection and rawness.

We've spent a chunk of time exploring the hot-button issues that surround this Business/Baby Blend that I've now joined the ranks of. We've talked about the Mental Load, the impact having a child has on a romantic relationship, the beast of Mum Guilt and the importance of The Village. We've had checklists, spreadsheets, top tips, life hacks, roles and responsibilities. We've broken down the logistics of everything baby-related, from getting that kit sorted while they're growing inside us, to transporting them with minimum stress on a plane ...

But what I realised as I put the final touches to this book is that I hadn't talked about the most important thing: love.

People tell you about the love you'll have for your child. 'You just can't describe it', 'It's the best thing ever', 'You would quite literally do anything – and I mean anything – for that kid' and 'You'll understand when you have one'. Before I became a parent, it seemed to me that the world was divided into two camps – the private members' club of those who had personally experienced that love for a child (whether they had carried them or not) and those who had no idea what that love was like.

I wasn't clucky or broody to have a baby – even as we waited out those last few days of my (seemingly long) pregnancy. I never understood when women said they felt a twang in their ovaries on sighting a cute newborn; it's just not something I ever experienced. While I could appreciate the cuteness of tiny baby clothes, I didn't go to mush on seeing them. So I simply had no idea what feelings to expect when this little being emerged to join us in the outside world.

Although I was in labour for 3.5 days, it still didn't feel real that this person (all going well) would be joining us on the other side of that process. When we arrived at the hospital and were shown into our room, I spotted the baby trolley-bed thing in the corner – complete with fresh sheets and blankets. I realised that bed was for *our baby*. And yet it still didn't feel real.

Even after hours in the hospital, then the intense minutes of pushing her out, laying back panting against the bean bag, while the medical team cleaned her airways and Wade was calming her … Still, not real.

Our birth photographer Bel took a photo of her face and brought it to me on her camera, and it still felt totally alien that I had brought a human into the world. Then, a few minutes later, Wade carried a naked, chubby, BABY across the room and laid her on my chest. She turned to me with huge, wide-open, dark eyes and our gaze connected. She was beautiful. *This was real*.

We had already met physically and spiritually while she grew inside me, and we had been together for every single second, experience and emotion for the last 42.5 weeks – and finally we got to see each other. We gazed at each other with absolute recognition for quite a few minutes.

From that moment on, I loved her. In fact, I didn't even *consciously* feel like I loved her as she was just a part of me. It required no effort, it was easy. It was simple, organic, unfettered.

When Lexi and I flew back to Sydney after packing up our life on the Gold Coast, we stayed with our friend Jack Delosa for a few nights. It had been years since Jack and I had had a really good catch-up, so we were both excited that he happened to be home the night we got there (this is not a common occurrence). He ordered us Mexican on Uber Eats and popped open a bottle of wine. Over dinner, we marvelled at how different our lives were right now – he was living the consummate bachelor life, while my 15-month-old daughter was sleeping in her travel cot in the room next door to us and much of my life was geared towards keeping her fed, clean, comfortable and loved.

Jack had gotten rid of his washing machine so he could install a wine fridge in its place (yes, really) and his EA coordinated getting his laundry to the laundrette and back each week. He lived almost exclusively off Uber Eats. He would request a side of milk with his order – even though he hadn't ordered tea or coffee – as this saved him a trip to the supermarket. He could roll in and out whenever and however he pleased, and had no responsibilities to any other human – other than his team in his business.

As we compared our lives, Jack asked me a question: 'So what *is* that love that you feel for Lexi like?'

For a few minutes I didn't say anything at all. I realised that this was the first time someone had asked me that question. Friends and family who already had kids had never asked me, as they understood it themselves – at least their own experience of it. Those who hadn't had kids yet hadn't asked as, I guess, they hadn't given it any thought. But now Jack was asking and he was making me think.

Finally, I felt I could articulate it: 'The best way I could explain it is that it's the closest thing to God I've ever experienced. It's like there's no ego and no agenda in my love for her – it's just love in its purest sense.'

And that was it.

Even now I can't think of a better or more accurate way to describe how I feel about Lexi.

I don't take it lightly that we have her in our lives. Over the course of the year and a half it took us to get a positive result on the pregnancy test, I stopped thinking about becoming a mother as some automatic birthright and instead began to see it for what it is – an incredible fucking privilege. That was the gift our fertility challenges gave us.

To be in the front row as she makes little discoveries every day, to be the one she turns to when she's tired, hurt or has something exciting to share, to get to take her out into the world and see her connect with others in such a curious and fun way... It's the biggest privilege of my life.

Conclusion

One Monday night a few short weeks ago, I called my mum. I broke down in tears as soon as she answered the phone. As clearly as I could between sobs, I said: 'I'm not coping.'

I felt like my usual capacity to cope with uncertainty, pressure and curve balls had dissipated somewhere into the ether, to the extent that I couldn't fathom how I could possibly reconnect with that bounceback-ability I have prided myself on for years.

I recently learned that 'crisis' comes from the Greek word 'to sift', meaning that when we have a crisis it forces us to evaluate what's really necessary in our lives. As Glennon Doyle describes in her book *Carry On Warrior*: 'That's what crises do. They shake things up until we are forced to hold on to only what matters most. The rest falls away.'

What ensued was a painful period of evaluating where life was at, cutting back commitments, postponing key projects, questioning how much joy elements of my business were bringing me, and what was stressing me out about our house and home life.

Importantly, I got help. I committed to regular sessions with a psychologist, had sessions with my kinesiologist and consulted a naturopath to give my body as much physical support as I could. I dropped my 'everything's fiiiiiiine' veil with some close friends and shared the warts 'n' all story of what was going on. This was terrifying. I also devoted time to nurturing my relationship with Wade.

I pretty much kicked into Nana mode, creating a self-styled convalescence of sorts. High on the agenda were pots of tea, jigsaws, books for fun (and not for learning), hot showers, DIY facials, slow-cooked meals and retro comforting desserts (hello rice pudding and apple crumble). Rushing, striving, hustling, stressing gave way to a gentler place to land that I was crafting for myself.

As I write these words to you, I'm still feeling my way out of that not-coping space. But life is already feeling calmer, more focused and – well – more kind.

The reason I'm sharing this with you is not to end this book on a bum note, but to state very clearly that even with all our life systems organised and in place – the date nights, the Saturday morning yoga classes, the virtual assistants and the kickass email policy – this life can get overwhelming. At times, very overwhelming.

It's likely that many of us will have a period of reckoning (or if you're like me, several of these) over our lifetime. In those times we must hit the pause button and do ourselves the justice of checking in on what's really important.

A poem from Iain Thomas' *I Wrote This For You* describes how the world – every single day – will yell at us to make a priority of things that aren't, in actual fact, in our own best interest. He encourages us to pull our hand back, place it on our heart and say: 'No. This is what's important.' I want to gently encourage you to pull your hand back regularly. You'll know a pause is overdue when life begins to feel like it's spinning out of control and you cannot seem to catch your breath.

If this path many of us are treading – building a business while nurturing small humans – was easy, every woman we know would be running a booming business during school hours on a

Thursday while looking immaculate with 17 perfectly behaved children hanging off her.

It's not an easy path, but it is possible. Just remember you are not alone. There are thousands (probably millions) of women on this path with you. And we've got your back, as you have ours.

Seek us out, initiate connections with us, invest in these relationships. I can tell you that a recent evening spent with my business bestie Richenda walking, eating and talking (so much talking) did more for my mindset and my soul than any session with a professional did. We need to weave a silken thread between us and the next woman blending business with a family. When she does the same, we start to create a web of mutual understanding, encouragement and trust. If this web could talk, it would whisper over and over: 'I get it'. That web is what celebrates our successes with us, what eases the burden of the inevitable challenges in our path and what cushions us in instances of disappointment or despair.

I hope this book has furnished you with the ideas, the stories, the encouragement and the resources to create the family and business you dream of – and that, as a result of this book, you see possibilities for you and your life that you may never have considered before.

It has been a privilege to share my story, and the stories of so many women I adore with you. Thank you for coming on this journey with me.

To connect with me online, find me at my website:
lorrainemurphy.com.au
@lorraineremarks
/lorraineremarks

Recipes

As I mentioned in Chapter 4, bone broth is the perfect soul-soothing food to enjoy post-birth. Here are my favourite chicken and beef bone broth recipes.

Chicken bone broth

Note: We have a 5.5-litre slow cooker, so these quantities are what I use. If you have a smaller slow cooker then simply adjust the quantities. You can also make it on the stove top in a stockpot, I just like the set-and-forget benefit of the slow cooker.

And another note: Bone broth leeches all the mineral goodness out of the animal bones, so you want to use organic bones for broth making.

What you need:
- 2 x organic chicken frames (I freeze the carcass of a roast chicken, including leftover fat and skin, then when the second chicken rolls around a few weeks later, I pop both into the slow cooker together. You could also use a mix of drumsticks and wings)
- 1 x onion, quartered
- 1 x carrot, chopped into large chunks
- 6 x garlic cloves, skin on and flattened with the side of a large knife

2 x sticks of celery, chopped into large chunks

4 x bay leaves

1 x lemon, cut into quarters

1 x teaspoon whole black peppercorns

Handful of fresh herbs (I use up any sad parsley/thyme/rosemary I have languishing in the fridge)

1 x cup apple cider vinegar or white vinegar (to extract all the boney-minerally-goodness)

How to cook it:

1. If I'm using ready-roasted chicken frames/bits, then I put them straight into the slow cooker. If I'm starting with raw drumsticks and wings, then I'll put them in a roasting tray with the onion, carrot and garlic, and roast the lot at 200°C (fan forced) for 30 mins or so. I find that roasting intensifies the flavour a lot.
2. Pile all the other ingredients on top, then fill the slow cooker up to the top with boiling water.
3. Cook on high for two hours to get it cranking, then turn to low for 24 hours. If some water has evaporated by the halfway mark, top it up again with boiling water.
4. Once it's finished, allow to cool.
5. Strain the broth into a large bowl using a colander, then refrigerate.
6. After a few hours, there'll be a thin layer of fat/gunk on top, so scrape as much of that off as you can before using.

Beef bone broth

What you need:

1 x tablespoon of olive oil

Organic beef bones – enough to half fill your slow cooker or stockpot (Most butchers will have these in their freezer, or can toss some in a bag for you. I try to get ones with meat on them as it makes an extra-tasty broth)

1 x onion, quartered

1 x carrot, chopped into large chunks

6 x garlic cloves, skin on and flattened with the side of a large knife

2 x sticks of celery, chopped into large chunks

4 x bay leaves

1 x teaspoon whole black peppercorns

2 x star anise seeds

Handful of fresh herbs

1 x cup of white vinegar

How to cook it:
1. Preheat the oven to 200°C (fan forced).
2. Put the olive oil, bones, onion, carrot and garlic into a large pan and roast in the oven for 30 minutes.
3. Once roasted, add the contents of the pan to the slow cooker and pile all the other ingredients on top.
4. Fill the slow cooker up to the top with boiling water.
5. Cook on high for two hours to get it cranking, then turn to low for 24 hours. If some water has evaporated by the halfway mark, top it up again with boiling water.
6. Once it's finished, allow to cool.
7. Strain the broth into a large bowl with a colander, then refrigerate.
8. After a few hours, there'll be a thick yellow layer of fat on top, so scrape as much of that off as you can. (The broth will likely be quite jelly-like in consistency, that's a very good thing as it means the gelatin from the bones has been successfully sucked out!)

How to store it

I'll usually fill a large glass jar with broth to have in the fridge for the following days, and freeze the rest. The easiest way to store it is in ziplock bags that you can then lie flat in the freezer. You can also freeze some broth in ice cube trays, which makes it super easy for ad hoc cooking. It seems to last nicely for a week or so in the fridge, but you might want to check that yourself as I'm more on the free-and-easy end of the spectrum when it comes to use-by dates!

How to consume it

- Straight – I have it in a mug with a pinch of salt, and it's the most heart-warming, soothing drink.
- As the liquid in risotto – I'm borderline obsessed with my oven-baked risotto and we eat it at least every fortnight in our house. The chicken bone broth gives it the most amazing savoury flavour.
- In egg drop soup, or *stracciatella* as the Italians call it – super-simple and so tasty, especially with a slice of heavily buttered sourdough toast. Yummmmm ….
- To sauté vegetables – using a little broth instead of oil is delicious. I especially like to use it when pan-frying mushrooms, as I find they absorb so much oil otherwise. The broth makes them extra sweet and moreish.
- Add to soups and casseroles – I'll add a couple of cups to any soup or slow-cooked meals for extra flavoursome-ness (is that even a word?!).
- Make a broth bowl – using broth as your base, add some cooked vegetables, protein (so your choice of cooked meat, eggs or pulses) and some extra flavouring like chilli or herbs. One of my favourite broth bowls is made by cooking some zucchini, peas and celery in a little olive oil in a small saucepan, then adding shredded chicken, chicken bone broth and a teaspoon of miso paste. A super-fast, easy and healthy meal for one.

Acknowledgements

To the whole kickass team at Hachette – thank you for making our third adventure together as smooth, enjoyable and rewarding as the first two. I know there's a whole chorus of carefully orchestrated people behind the scenes, most of whom I don't get to meet. So I'll thank the people I *do* know ...

Robert, thank you for believing in and delivering my visions for my books. Susin, thank you for your diplomacy, thoroughness and tenacity in keeping me on point and limiting my waffle-ability. Rebecca, much gratitude to you for stepping me through the production process so deftly. Alana, thank you for being an extraordinary publicist (and moonlighting babysitter!). And many thanks to Grace West, for the third book cover you have created for me.

To all the women who were so generous in sharing their stories, ideas and advice throughout this book – you are heroes in my eyes, and now in the eyes of my readers! That's you Julie Masters, Richenda Vermeulen, Meredith Cranmer, Michelle Broadbent, Peta Kelly, Janine Wade, Pamela Jabbour, Kylie Camps, Nicola Swankie, Justine Flynn, Emma Isaacs and Melissa Ambrosini. Special shout-out to Jack Delosa too, who, sadly for him, doesn't qualify as a woman but who brings a whole lot of wisdom to my life regardless.

Special thanks and hat tip again to Michelle Broadbent, for being the much-loved grounding force in my business. Your smarts, kindness and fun – and little gifts of chocolate – are so appreciated.

My mentees and clients bring so much joy and curiosity to my life, and I want to thank all of you for believing in me to the point where I get to have the business I do.

Thanks you to my gorgeous Instagram and Love Letter communities – what a tribe you are!

To my past team at The Remarkables Group, thank you for being part of my first business adventure with me. Special love and thanks to Natalie Giddings and Ashleigh Bruton. You provided me with so much support during the pretty epic transition to becoming a mother and I will always hold a special place in my heart for you both.

Big love also to Sarah Chegwidden, for being by my side for many chapters of my life – from uni parties to growing The Remarkables Group with me and now as mothers together.

Thank you Jacqui Prydie and Nicole Bayliss, for your constant spiritual guidance throughout the roller-coaster ride that has been life in recent years. Your calming, reassuring and nurturing presence is something I can't imagine not having in my life.

To my Village Ladies: Annie, Leila, Jules and Gemma – thank you for having our little family's back, and for welcoming us into your homes. I cannot believe we have managed to create this together – one hurriedly dropped-off child, bath party and shared dinner at a time.

Our birth team was the reason we managed to have such a positive birth experience. To our midwife Jo, our doula Nadine and our Calm Birth educator Lauren Falconer – you ladies are like birth angels on earth.

To Lexi's beautiful daycare and her divine nanny Iva – thank you for being who you are so Wade and I get to do the work we do.

To Lexi's crew – Basil, Tali, Ethan, Saskia, Elvis, Leo, Shanti and Sol. Thank you for lighting up her world with your kindness, sparkle and ridiculous cuteness.

To Barry, Janet, Graeme, Jane, Kate, Jai, Maya, Sasha and Jamie – thank you for your constant love and for the adoration you shower on our little girl (and us, when you remember we still exist – ha!).

To my rents Susan and Richie. I don't think you'll ever know how much I value your love, encouragement and – when needed – practical support. Thank you for everything you did and do for me so I get to have the life I have.

To my sister Jenny. I must have done something really, really awesome in a past life to land you as my partner in life … maybe I treated an entire country to chocolate cake. To see you step into this new role as a mother has been magical – you are amazing at what you do, for everyone you do it for in your life.

To Blaine and Fiadh, thank you for making my sister so very happy.

To the divine force that has co-created this life I get to live – thank you thank you thank you. For helping me see goals into fruition, but also for the plot twists. I probably wasn't grateful *at all* at the time, but your genius becomes clear quite soon when I realise the path those twists put me on.

To my husband Wade. Thank you for being in my corner, for having my back and for riding the storms with me. I often don't know how to steer the ship (do you even steer a ship?! See – no idea), but your strong heart and strong arms mean that it doesn't matter. To see how much you love Lexi has shown me a whole new side to you as a man, and I hope that the men of the future take note.

To our shooting star – you are, and always will be, so loved.

To Lexi. My love, I couldn't possibly find the words to tell you how amazing you are and how grateful Dada and I are that you chose us. Instead I'll tell you what I tell you every night: 'I love you, I can't believe we get to have you in our lives, and thank you for today.'